W9-DAK-220

1837

William Lyon Mackenzie and the Canadian Revolution

1837

William Lyon Mackenzie and the Canadian Revolution

Rick Salutin and Theatre Passe Muraille

James Lorimer & Company, Publishers
Toronto 1976

Copyright © 1976: Part I by Rick Salutin; Part II by Rick Salutin and Theatre Passe Muraille. All rights reserved. No part of this book may be reproduced or transmitted in any form or by any means, electronic or mechanical, including photocopying, or by any information or retrieval system, without permission in writing from the publishers.

ISBN 0-88862-118-3 cloth   ISBN 0-88862-119-1 paper
Design by Don Fernley
Printed and bound in Canada

1837: The Farmers' Revolt was first published in the Spring 1976 issue of the *Canadian Theatre Review.*

1837: The Farmers' Revolt is fully protected by copyright. All inquiries concerning production of the play including scenes from it should be directed to Rick Salutin, Theatre Passe Muraille, 16 Ryerson Avenue, Toronto, Ontario.

Photo credits: Part I
Metropolitan Toronto Library Board: pp. 13, 37, 53, 71, 101, 125, 137, 141, 147, 151, 157, 161, 167.
Public Archives of Canada: pp. 47, 85, 87, 133.
J. Ross Robertson Collection, Metropolitan Toronto Central Library: pp. 123, 141 (top left).
Photo credits: Part II
Photographs of the original cast production by David Groskind.

Act I
(P. 211) *The Tavern*, (l. to r.) David Fox, Eric Peterson.
(P. 221) *The Lady in the Coach*, Eric Peterson as Lady Backwash.
(P. 237) *The Speech*, Eric Peterson.
Act II
(P. 245) *Drilling*, Janet Amos, Terry Tweed.
(P. 253) *Van Egmond's March*, (l. to r.) David Fox, Miles Potter, Eric Peterson.
(P. 261) *Knocks on the Door*, David Fox, Terry Tweed.

Canadian Cataloguing in Publication data

Salutin, Rick, 1942-
1837

Includes the text of the play 1837 : the farmers' revolt, by R. Salutin and Theatre Passe Muraille.

ISBN 0-88862-118-3 bd. ISBN 0-88862-119-1-pa.

1. Canada - History - Rebellion, 1837-1838. 2. Mackenzie, William Lyon, 1795-1861. I. Salutin, Rick, 1942-   1837 : the farmers' revolt. II. Theatre Passe Muraille. III. Title. IV. Title: William Lyon Mackenzie and the Canadian revolution.

FC454.S35   971.03'8   C77-001012-1
F1032.S35

For Kent Rowley and Madeleine Parent
speaking of Canadian fighters

Copies of the 60-page script of *1837: The Farmers' Revolt* are available in a separate low-cost paperback edition from the publishers.

*A Guide to 1837,*written with both history and literature teachers in mind is also available from the publishers. The author of the guide, Peter Flaherty, has taught literature and history at the high school level.

James Lorimer & Company, Publishers
35 Britain Street
Toronto

Contents

Part I 1837: Mackenzie and Revolution

Part II 1837: The Farmers' Revolt

PART I
1837:
Mackenzie and Revolution

Rick Salutin

Chapter 1

The stakes: Upper Canada in the 1830s*

The centre of the life of Upper Canada in 1837 was farming. But it had not always been so.

During the rule of the French the emphasis had been wholly on the fur trade. In those early days an anti-settlement policy had been pursued since very few people were necessary to carry on the trade, only those needed to establish a few trading centres and outposts.

When the British took control of the Canadas from the French in 1763, other staples like timber and foodstuffs were beginning to supplant furs as the chief attraction for the imperial power. These economic activities required settlement, immigration and land distribution policies. In addition, the British wanted to establish Upper Canada as a loyal British counterbalance to the refractory French province of Quebec. So, in the period prior to 1837, Upper Canada was becoming an English-speaking society of farmers.

But, although the farmers formed the bulk of the Upper Canadian population and did most of the productive work (not only in agriculture, but in logging as well), they were far from the most influential group politically.

Other groups in society were much more important because of the role Upper Canada was assigned in the British colonial system. The merchants, for example, were more influential. From the earliest days of colonization the main economic function of

* This chapter deals with what used to be called, in the history texts, The Causes of the Rebellion. But as a former Canadian history student laments, "I could never understand how the Causes of the Rebellion caused the rebellion." Another title could be The Political Economy of 1837.

Canada, from the imperial viewpoint, had been to export raw materials and staples to the mother country — France and then England. This required a class of merchants in the colony who would oversee the gathering and transshipment of whatever product the mother country wanted at the time. After the British conquest, an English mercantile group replaced the small group of French merchants who had played this role in New France.

In the early days of the colony, the Upper Canadian merchants were chiefly engaged in local trading or handling subsidiary assignments for Montreal merchant firms. Because of the small scale of the Upper Canadian economy at the time, the Montreal merchants were very powerful and dominated the trade with England. But Upper Canada's merchants were ambitious and eager to expand and, as Upper Canada became more settled, the merchants of Kingston, Queenston, Niagara-on-the-Lake and eventually York (which became Toronto in 1834) gained in importance.

This merchant class, which was very influential politically, offered little support to the farmers. The farmers were left to till as well as they could whatever land they were able to acquire. The merchants were only concerned with getting exorbitant prices for goods needed by the farmers and with high profits in their staple trade with England.

In addition to the merchantile group, there was also a sort of nascent industrial or manufacturing class. Because the main role of the colony was to supply raw materials, conditions in Upper Canada were not favourable to such enterprises. Nevertheless, starting with gristmills, sawmills and distilleries, industry of a sort developed. Tanneries, potash works,* cabinet and wagon makers and the like followed. Later came the beginnings of more developed industry: a steam mill near Niagara in 1824, machinery for the spinning of wool, foundries and even a steam engine factory. This class of manufacturers, though small, was a potential ally for the farmers, as both these groups were concerned with economic development within the colony itself, unlike the merchants who saw the colonial economy mainly as an appendage to the economy of the mother country.

* Potash was made from the ashes of trees burned after a plot had been cleared for farming. It was then sent to England for use in soapmaking.

Toronto in 1834, looking west from near Parliament Street.

Along with such beginnings of industry came an embryonic industrial working class — people who worked for the owners of the mills, factories and the like, as well as the blacksmith shops, taverns, stage lines, printers, logging companies, and those who worked on building the canals. The size of this class of "mechanics and labourers" was quite large for a colony as underdeveloped as Upper Canada. But often people who had come to Upper Canada hoping to farm for themselves had so much difficulty acquiring land at a reasonable price that they were forced to work for others. As well, merchants often took over farms in place of unpaid bills thereby pushing farmers into the work force.

There was also a large number of people who functioned solely or primarily within the government bureaucracy. Legislative appointees, surveyors, registrars, justices of the peace, postal officials, customs collectors, militia officers — Upper Canada was top-heavy with officialdom. Since the power of these appointments rested almost totally with the lieutenant-governor who was sent out to the colony from Britain, this group tended to be homogeneous. Though there were exceptions (among the revolutionary leaders, Lount was a surveyor, Matthews a militia officer, Duncombe a member of the Medical Board) there was a general tendency for officialdom to behave in a unified, self-protective and self-serving way.

Farmers, merchants, small-scale industrialists, workers, government officials — all operating in the shadow of the British imperial authorities. These different groups had different and often conflicting interests. They had wrestled in the economic and political arenas of Upper Canada for decades and, in 1837, the explosion took place.

Land

Because Canada was a British colony, all land belonged, first of all, to the king. There still exists, in Ontario today, what are called crown lands.

With this license to dispose of the land (the French, after all, had appropriated it from the Indians: in turn, the British acquired it from the French by conquest), the British proceeded to give away huge pieces of Upper Canada. (Not only Upper Canada, of course. All of Prince Edward Island had been granted free to a few absentee landlords on a single fine day in 1767.)

In Upper Canada land was granted — free — to a host of government favourites.

It went, often in place of pay or pensions, to retired military officers — soldiers of the Conquest, the American Revolutionary War and the War of 1812. Militiamen received 730,000 acres. Discharged soldiers and sailors got 450,000 acres. Officers and old warhorses of the Napoleonic wars did particularly well. One former officer, Colonel Thomas Talbot, received an initial 30,000 acres west of Lake Erie. He had an arrangement with the government by which he got another 200 acres for himself each time he sold 50 to farmers. In this way he eventually accumulated a fiefdom of 60,000 acres.

Land went in great chunks to United Empire Loyalists — refugees from the American Revolution. Those who arrived by 1798 got 200 acres each, and more — as much as 1,000 acres — went to each of their children when they came of age. By 1838, of the 5,750,000 acres that had been given away, some 3,200,000 acres had gone to Loyalists.

Favourites of the British and colonial administrations got land. Twelve thousand acres to the heirs of General Brock, another 12,000 to Bishop Mountain, the Anglican bishop of Quebec. To five legislative councillors and their families, 50,000 acres. To executive councillors and their families, 136,000. Enormous grants went to various people as payment for services rendered to the government — to surveyors and the like. As well, 255,000 acres went to magistrates and barristers.

The upshot was that much of the best land in Upper Canada accumulated in the hands of people who had neither the skills nor the intention of farming it. In 1824, of 8,000,000 acres that were owned privately, only 3,000,000 were occupied and only 500,000 acres were actually under cultivation. Many of those who acquired land in this way simply sat on it — or off it, in York or England — waiting for the price to rise when the land *around* theirs had been worked; or they sold outright to speculators, who, in turn, sat on the land. Everyone waited for everyone else to do some *work* on the land so that its value would rise—and the province languished. Many who wanted to farm simply left for the United States where different land policies were followed: others took the route of squatting.

Still more land — huge acreages — was kept out of productive use by being set aside as crown and clergy reserves. As land was surveyed and registered for sale by government agents, one seventh of everything was held back for use by the government. The intention was to lease these crown reserves, and with the rents received, pay government expenses thereby alleviating the drain on the British treasury itself. The main problem with this system was that it didn't work. By 1821, only ten percent of the crown reserves had been leased, and most of that land was usually used, not for farming, but for logging: move in, strip the lumber, and leave. More unused land accumulated.

Another seventh of all surveyed land was set aside for "the support of a Protestant clergy." The Constitutional Act of 1791, which set out this provision largely in the hope of combatting the Catholicism of French Canada, was vague enough in its wording to occasion incessant bickering among the various sects of Upper Canada as to *which* Protestant clergy was intended. It did not matter a great deal since the clergy reserves brought in as little revenue as the crown reserves; their main function seems to have been to retard development. Even in somewhat built-up areas, farms were cut off from each other and services impeded because of the presence of these unused reserves. They became one of the most celebrated Causes of the Rebellion: the Reformers early on urged their sale for the aid of public, non-sectarian education.

Through the mid-1820s, these land policies continually worked against the interests of the farmers. In response to a questionnaire on their grievances in 1817, farmers of Upper Canada replied:

> The reserve of two-sevenths of the lands for the crown and clergy, must for a long time keep the country a wilderness; a harbor for wolves; a hindrance to a compact and good neighborhood . . . . A defect in the system of colonization, and too great a quantity of the lands in the hands of individuals, who do not reside in the province, and are not assessed for those lands . . . . (Sandwich)
>
> Land held in fee by distant owners in large quantities, not responsible for defraying any charges for opening roads, while the whole burden falls on actual settlers, is a hindrance to the growth of settlement. (Norwich)
>
> In many places of this province, large tracts of land have been granted to certain individuals, and these being generally men of fortune, are under no necessity of selling their lands, but hold them at so high a price, that poor people are not able to buy them. (Trafalgar)
>
> What hinders the improvement of the township is bad roads, want of men and money. (Waterloo)
>
> . . . the immense tracts of land held by non-residents . . . we are certain that we do not exaggerate in stating the number of acres at from 12 to 15,000 exclusive of the crown and clergy reserves which are two-seventh parts of the whole land in the township. (Kingston)

By the way, the instigator of this survey, Robert Gourlay, whose only motivation was to *promote* immigration to Upper Canada, was imprisoned, tried, and exiled from the province.

A traveller in the 1830s gave a not untypical account of what farmers could expect to encounter in Upper Canada:

> The greater portion of British emigrants, arriving in Canada without funds and the most exalted ideas of the value and productiveness of land, purchase extensively on credit, and take up their abode in the midst of the forest, with the proudest feelings of independence, and in the confident hope of meeting their engagements, and becoming fine gentlemen at the end of a few years. Everything goes on well for a short time. A log-house is erected with the assistance of old settlers, and the clearing of forest is commenced. Credit is obtained at a neighbouring store, and at length it is found necessary to work a day or two in the week for hire to obtain food for the family. The few garden stuffs and field crops, grown the first year, produce little for want of a free circulation of air, and the imperfect manner in which they had been sown. Should fever and ague now visit the emigrant

> which is frequently the case, the situation of himself and family, enfeebled by disease, is truly wretched. Hope, is however, still bright, and he struggles through the second year, with better crops and prospects than the preceding one. The third year brings him good crops, which furnish a supply of food for his establishment. During this period he has led a life of toil and privation, being poorly fed and most uncomfortably lodged. But the thought of owning so many fair acres has been a never-failing source of joy and sweetener of life. On arrival of the fourth harvest, he is reminded by the storekeeper to pay his account with cash, or discharge part of it with his disposable produce, for which he gets a very small price. He is also informed that the purchase-money of the land has been accumulating with interest. The phantom of prosperity, conjured up by his imagination, is now dispelled, and, on calmly looking into his affairs, he finds himself poorer than when he commenced operations. Disappointment preys on his spirits, and the aid of whisky is perhaps sought to raise them. The hopelessness of his situation render him indolent and immoral. The land ultimately reverts to the former proprietor, or a new purchaser is found.

Despite these odds, farmers continued to work their land — whatever they managed to get hold of — and some prospered, relatively. In spite of, not because of, British land policies, agricultural wealth began to accumulate in Upper Canada. Land values began to rise. This attracted the attention of British investors and, in 1824, a new factor entered the scene — land companies. A number of British capitalists, on the lookout for profitable investments in the colonies, formed the Canada Company.

They proposed to the British government that they would buy all of the crown reserves and half of the clergy reserves, which they would then sell to prospective settlers for their own profit. This was to benefit the government by providing a new use for the unsuccessful reserves, and a source of funds for the payment of expenses in the colony.

The first hitch in this scheme was the irrepressible John Strachan, Anglican archdeacon of Upper Canada and leading light of the Family Compact. He did not want to yield the clergy reserves, which were only just then becoming profitable, and he was supported by the House of Lords in England. So instead of the clergy reserves the Canada Company was given a million-plus acres of land on Lake Huron — the Huron Tract.

A board of five commissioners consisting of both government and company figures went to Canada to decide the proper price to be paid for the land. Since the company was involved in actually setting this price, it is not surprising that they settled on a bargain figure. In addition the company was allowed to withhold a third of the purchase price for their own use in making "improvements" on the land. Again not surprisingly, the absence of such improvements was one of the great complaints of future settlers on Company lands.

The transaction was completed, and the Canada Company went into business. One of its first officials in Canada was William "Tiger" Dunlop. In 1830, the Company advertised in London:

> Have for sale in Upper Canada, about two millions, five hundred acres of Land, of the following description.
>
> First, Crown Reserves; being Lots of 200 Acres each; scattered throughout the older Townships of the Province.
>
> Second, Blocks of Land; of, from 1000 to 40,000 acres. — These are situated in the Townships of the Western District, and in the township of Wilmot in the Gore District.
>
> Third, A Town and Township called Guelph in the Gore District, in which there are already nearly 800 Settlers; with almost every kind of tradesmen and Mechanicks: Taverns, Stores, Schools, Saw Mills &c. and a Gristmill is in progress. This is a desirable location for settlers with small Capitals, as laborers and Servants are easily procurable; and lots, partly improved, can be purchased at a reasonable price.
>
> Fourth, The Huron Territory, containing one million, one hundred thousand acres. In the shape of a triangle, the base resting for upwards of sixty miles, on the bank of Lake Huron.
>
> The Town of Goderich has been commenced on the side of a harbor, formed by the confluence of the river Maitland and the Lake; and as a road is already cut to the Gore District; and another is in progress to the London District, it has already become the centre of Settlement. There are already about 500 inhabitants in the Huron tract — a Saw Mill is in operation — and a Gristmill building — several Taverns and Stores have been established; and a brewery and Distillery are in progress.
>
> The land is admitted on all hands to be equal to any in the province — it possesses lime, and building stone — brick earth, and potters clay, in abundance; and the produce of the country can be

> carried to market by water, through Lake Huron, by the river St. Clair, to the Lakes Erie, and Ontario, and the River St. Lawrence, to Montreal and Quebec.

By 1833, the Canada Company was considered the "most buoyant security in the London market." It continued to operate, and bring in a good profit, as late as the 1950s.

The Canada Company (what's in a name!) marked the arrival of large-scale capitalist operations in the still-primitive colonial economy. It was hailed as a solution to the underdevelopment of the time, just as American multi-nationals were received in Canada in the post-World War II period. True, the Company was an improvement on the total stagnation of the reserves, but how *much* better was it, and at what cost? The most trenchant criticism was Mackenzie's, who commented in 1824 when the project was still in its preliminary stages:

> I have abstained, hitherto, from giving any opinion of this proposed incorporation, and its effects, in order that I might first learn, from the contents of other journals, in as much as possible, the nature of its designs, and the mode in which it was proposed to carry them into execution.
>
> As well as I can judge, the company will prove of some immediate benefit to the Canadas; as causing money to be immediately expended in improvements of a general nature, and obvious utility.
>
> I am far, however, from having a friendly feeling to the principle on which it is proposed to be incorporated. It is true, a few shares are left for Canadians to take up; but those of the farmers who have cash, will have nothing to do with such an outlandish concern; and though three or four Montreal merchants may have taken a few shares, yet *almost* all the stockholders will reside in England.
>
> Say that the whole of the reserves are sold it at this time, at the average of wild lands in the province, that is, at about eight shillings and nine pence an acre: say that it pays over the full price to government, and that the sum so paid is laid out in that *economical* way in which the provincial administrators of the North American colonies have, hitherto, proceeded in their disbursements of public monies: say that not a whit more *favouritism* shall henceforth prevail than has hitherto been customary — there is still another question.
>
> It is premised that, by selling these lands to a company, at a fair price, and laying the whole of the proceeds out to the best advantage, within the colony, government intend to show that they wish its pros-

perity. Now let us examine these premises. Does government really dispose of the *Reserves* in the most advantageous way imaginable, or is the whole an organized system to drain the country of its specie, (be the same more or less,) to enrich England? I think I can make it appear that the latter is the fact. . . .

The company, the first year, clear on a tenth, from 100 to 150 per cent, and in after years, 200, 300, or even 500 per cent; and the whole, or almost the whole, of these gains, go to England to the stockholders who reside there. One million of dollars is advanced in England to improve the country now; and, in a few years hence, four, or even five millions is repaid to England in clear gains, as interest and principal. Yes, all this goes to these stockholders, though every penny of it might be retained in the province, if government would do as is done in the United States, that is, put up the reserves at a certain fixed price per acre, and sell all that went beyond that upset price, to approved buyers, reserving the rest to another more distant period: by so doing the full value would be paid, and the proceeds placed at the disposal of the colonial legislature, in the same way as other monies raised within the province.

It is true, this foreign company would lose their anticipated profits; but it is equally true, that these profits would go into the coffers of the province without abatement, and would, probably, be laid out in improving the roads and inland navigation as judiciously as it ever can be by commissioners appointed from England, and alone responsible there.

I may have taken a wrong view of the subject; but the general opinion here seems to be — we cannot do better — let the reserves be sold, go the profit to whom it may. And they will be sold — sold to monopolists — all must be monopoly with us. In our tea trade we suffer by a monopoly: in our foreign commerce, we are made a monopoly: even in our religion, the dominant sect makes the road to heaven, by law, a monopoly. Now a company starts up, and our reserves must become a profitable monopoly to England too . . . .

This article raises many of the issues which have continued to plague Canada because of foreign investment and control of our resources. Its arguments are familiar to readers of the Gordon Report, the Watkins Report, the Wahn Report, the Gray Report, and no doubt many official documents on the problems of the Canadian economy yet to come.

The situation for the majority of farmers did not appreciably improve; often it worsened. The cry "land to the tiller" has made more than one revolution in our own century, and its intention—though not the actual words—was at the centre of the Canadian Revolution of 1837.

Transportation

For farmers to survive at all, they need land, and some equipment. To *prosper,* they require markets, and the ability to move their surplus produce (above what they need for themselves) to the market, where they can exchange their own products for those of others. But transportation in Upper Canada was notoriously inadequate.

For the farmers the key need was roads. As a committee of the legislature (which Mackenzie chaired) reported in 1831:

> Two of the members of your Committee have during the last year examined the state of many of the bye roads through which the inhabitants of the back townships come to market with their produce, and find them in general in a wretched state. Were the revenue appropriated to pay the interest of a loan to Macadamize the great roads, and tolls afterwards established to keep them in repairs, it would enable the legislature to bestow a far greater sum, annually upon the bye roads, which would widen the circle in which produce is brought to this town, diminish the expense of carriage, induce new settlers to go back into the wilderness, enrich these settlers, stimulate the whole population to increased industry, and thus become a powerful means of adding to the wealth and prosperity of the country.

This passage refers to the back roads, which were the most important to the farmers for getting their goods to market. But the main roads, such as Dundas St., Yonge St., and Kingston Rd., running west, north and east from Toronto, were in very poor shape as well. The government spent more on them than on the back roads but the only time of year such roads were readily passable was winter when they were frozen over. They had, it seems, been built in the worst possible way. The Committee reported:

> Your Committee have seen large flat stones thrown upon and mixed up with the soil on Yonge Street and other roads in this district, a practice at variance with the true principles of road making, and the experience of other countries. — In the appendix to this report,

> marked A, your Committee have reported a synopsis of a few and simple principles of road making, in places where stone or gravel may be had. The common manner of road making here is to break up the foundation of the road to a great depth with a plough; and thus brought into the worst possible state for a foundation, the road is then made into a convex curve so flat in the middle that the water lodges, softens the road, renders it liable to form ruts, while it is so steep near the sides that a carriage approaching them is in danger of upsetting. Such a road, and more especially when large stones are put into it, and covered up with gravel, soon becomes worse than the natural soil for travel.

Though the farmers were in the majority and their interest was in roads, roads were either neglected or badly built, largely because smaller, but more powerful, groups in the colony had other interests, interests which determined the priorities for transportation systems.

The British themselves were, above all, interested in defence, especially against the United States. (Almost every governor appointed to Upper Canada had a military background.). They wanted canals, and especially the Rideau canal system along the Ottawa River and south from the present location of Ottawa to Kingston on Lake Ontario. In case of a war with the United States, that canal would enable them to transport troops and supplies to Upper Canada without passing under American guns on the other side of the St. Lawrence.

The British at this time were more interested in protecting Upper Canada than in developing it. They had their fingers in many colonial pies around the world and could choose which ones to exploit for the greatest and swiftest return. Development of a minor colony like Upper Canada was much less profitable than the exploitation of an India. Only when Upper Canada had developed on its own in spite of British policy did the British step in and reap the profits, as they did in the case of the Canada Company. So they built the Rideau Canal at enormous cost and effort, while transportation in the countryside of Upper Canada remained inadequate.

Another group was also interested in canals. The merchants of Upper Canada, because they were involved in buying and selling, acting as agents, forwarding raw materials to Europe and importing manufactured goods in return shared the era's "mania for canalling." Their pet project was the Welland canal. It would make passage from Lake Erie to Lake Ontario possible by canalling around the rapids of the Niagara River and the Falls.

The English merchants of Montreal wanted a passage straight through the St. Lawrence to the Atlantic and had pushed for years for a canal around the rapids above Montreal. But that scheme was perpetually bogged down in disputes between the (French) legislature and the ruling English clique.

The Upper Canadian backers of the Welland however had their eye on another trade route: the Erie Canal, recently completed, from Buffalo through New York state down to the mouth of the Hudson at New York city. Via the Welland, they expected to get in on the trade from the American west which could pass through the Welland, into Lake Ontario and then cut south into the Erie canal. In addition some of those American goods could find their way into Upper and Lower Canada, to be sold there, or passed on to England. And the merchants could also profit in the return trade, from New York State and from Europe through the port of New York.

The needs of Upper Canadian farmers figured to a relatively small degree in these calculations. Some of their produce might find its way into the United States but it was hampered there by duties the Americans imposed, while American produce coming into Upper Canada faced no such obstacles.

William Hamilton Merritt, a St. Catharines businessman, formed the Welland Canal Company in 1824 after years of trying. About one half of its initial funding came from American businessmen — not surprising in view of the obvious benefits of the project for Americans.

By the following year the newborn canal was in trouble. It had been poorly planned and managed and the initial financing was inadequate. The legislature, which had been promised that the canal would be a totally private venture, gave the company a large free land grant. It also increased the capitalization of the company from 25,000 to 200,000 pounds. In 1826, it loaned 25,000 pounds to the company. In 1827, another 50,000. Further loans came from the legislature of Lower Canada and the British Government. Things continued to worsen. By 1829 a ship had passed through the canal but the route was so poorly constructed it needed constant renovations. By 1837, the province had given more than 200,000 pounds in loans and shares and in that year promised another 245,000. Even that was not sufficient to bring the 28-mile canal up to scratch.

The loans were of course forgiveable, in the Canadian tradition. The Welland was the first in a long series of typical Canadian projects, undertaken by private businessmen and paid for by Canadian taxpayers, through government aid. The province finally took over the canal in 1841, but it was not really until the 1880s that it was functioning efficiently.

Mackenzie and the Reformers were not opposed to the Welland. On behalf of the farmers, Mackenzie supported not only the Welland, but also other canals and especially the St. Lawrence project. The increased trade would, he felt, bring a higher price to the farmer for his goods, since these would be in demand beyond the province. But he objected to the waste, and he was suspicious of the motives behind the project. "The Welland Canal may be a good thing. It is so. But is there no such thing as paying too dear for the whistle?"

Following the Reform victory in the election of 1834, Mackenzie was one of the new government appointees to the board of the Welland Canal Company. He used the opportunity to delve deeply into the Company's chequered history. Before long he had acquired so much damning material, from technical incompetence to Merritt's expenditures on theatres and cigars while courting English businessmen, that he began publishing a weekly journal of condemnation called *The Welland Canal.*

Trade

Canada was kept squarely within the framework of British mercantilism: the system whereby the trade, and in fact the whole economy of the colony, was regulated and confined in order to serve the needs of the mother country. The trade patterns and regulations which the British government imposed on Canadian economic life tended to benefit the small group of powerful merchants in the colony, but worked to the disadvantage of the majority — the farmers.

The leadership of the Thirteen Colonies had chafed under such restrictions, and had broken free of them in the American Revolution. The leading figures of Upper Canada — politicians and merchants — revelled in the same system. The British Corn Laws permitted Canadian grain to enter Britain with lighter duties than foreign crops. Accordingly Canadian produce was cheaper, and in greater demand in Britain, than American crops. The same held for Canadian timber. A similar arrangement in the opposite direction assured that British manufactures entered Canada more cheaply than American manufactures, and so were certain to dominate the Canadian market.

This system of preferences kept Canada well within the context of British designs. The colony was a base for raw material extraction, chiefly grain and timber, and a market for British manufactured goods. This seemed to serve both the farmer and merchant interests, but above all it served the British. As Mackenzie wrote, in the very first issue of his newspaper:

> Our foreign commerce, confined and shackled as it is, and it has been, is entirely in the hands of the British manufacturers . . . Our farmers are indebted to our country merchants, our country merchants are deeply bound down in the same manner and by the same causes, to the Montreal wholesale dealers. Few of these Montreal commission merchants are men of capital; they are generally merely the factors or agents of British houses, and thus a chain of debt, dependence and degradation is begun and kept up, the links of which are fast bound round the souls and bodies of our yeomanry; and that with few exceptions from the richest to the poorest, while the tether stake is fast in British factories.

The United States, meanwhile, was following its own interests. American businessmen wanted to penetrate the markets of the British empire with both their agricultural produce and their manufactures. They protected their own markets from Canadian imports by high tariffs and duties, but Canadian manufacturers had no such protection. American goods were permitted to enter Upper Canada duty free and either competed in the Canadian market with Canadian goods, or were shipped to Britain for sale there on the same terms granted to Canadian products.

This undercut any advantage Canadian producers, especially farmers, had under the mercantile system of preferences in the imperial market.

But it worked to the advantage of the merchants of Upper and Lower Canada because it gave them a higher volume of business. So Canadian farmers found themselves competing with American produce in Canada, while unable to do so in the United States. Mackenzie wrote:

> The markets of the Canadas are always open to the Citizens of the United States, duty free, to compete with the farmers, millers, and lumbermen of these colonies, in supplying our domestic consumption of Flour, Wheat, and Lumber, or for exportation by the St. Lawrence. Our Lumber, Flour, and Wheat, are, on the contrary, always subject to heavy taxation in the ports of the Union.

These arrangements were maintained both by the British Parliament, and by the government of Upper Canada, responsive as it was to the mercantile interests of the colony. Mackenzie wrote:

> If an additional quantity of wheat, flour, pork, beef, and other produce belonging to the people of the United States go down the Welland Canal from Ohio, via the St. Lawrence, upon equal or better terms than ours, and swell the exports at Quebec, what advantage is that to us? . . . The proprietors of a few frontier flouring establishments may profit by this law; Messrs. Chisholm, McMillan and a few more of our forwarding merchants and owners of schooners may gain temporary advantages; the government officers by their banks monopoly, and the lawyers and sheriffs by their exorbitant fees, may contrive to keep down the spirit of the people, by the present expensive system, but, unless some miraculous and unforeseen event should occur in their favour, the farmers must be deeply injured, and the progress of the colonists retarded.

One other group was left out in the cold by these trade policies: the industrialists. British policy worked to keep the Canadas in an industrially undeveloped state. Canada would send over raw materials; in return she would receive British manufactured goods. A little manufacturing had indeed begun in Upper Canada, but the only way it could grow was by a policy like that of the Americans: raise tariff walls against foreign manufactures to protect native industry until it became competitive in its own home market. Such industrialization was of little interest to the merchant group: they were for fast profits in trade and the circulation of goods and money, not the much slower returns of industrial investment.

In the 1830s the trade situation for Canada deteriorated. The United States and Britain struck agreements which reduced Canada's advantages in the British market. By 1835 the Reform assembly — representing the farming and industrial interests — complained of the mutual accommodation between Britain and the United States to the disadvantage of Canadians, who after all had no control over the basic directions of the system within which they had to operate.

Banks

Even in the underdeveloped economy of Upper Canada, a demand for banking institutions arose quite early. The demand was based, first of all, on the need for a medium of circulation, some widely-accepted form of money that would enable people to exchange goods and services according to a common standard. Without such a medium, internal trade was impeded, and along with it the growth of the colonial economy. A wide variety of money-tokens were in use — British, Portuguese, Spanish, French and American — all metallic currencies coined by their respective governments.

During the War of 1812, the British army issued paper bills that were widely honoured, and redeemed at the war's end. This paved the way for a paper currency that could be provided by notes issued by local banks. Some urgency stemmed from the fact that, since Upper Canada was merely a colony, it could not mint its own coinage, and thereby provide, through its government, a local medium of circulation. In the absence of an independent government, the burden was to fall on private banking institutions.

The other need was for credit. It was argued that economic development would not occur without institutions that issued loans. Individuals in Upper Canada simply could not accumulate enough capital to embark on large business projects. Foreign lending institutions were distant and generally uninterested in local development.

The banks that were formed in these circumstances were private companies of businessmen, usually merchants who had accumulated some wealth in trade. They subscribed a certain amount of money to the bank, which was then loaned out at varying rates of interest, and subject to government regulations that regulated both rates and the ratio between the total amount loaned and the total that was subscribed in stock.

This credit function of the banks was one more indication of the increasingly complex and capitalistic development of the Upper Canadian economy in the 1820s. The first bank in Upper Canada received its charter in 1821, three years before the formation of both the Canada Company and the Welland Canal Company.

The establishment of that first bank is a sordid story of infighting among different Upper Canadian merchant groups. The Bank of Montreal actually began operations before any Upper Canadian banks and started to move in on Upper Canada. A group of Kingston merchants then applied to begin a bank, but their application was stalled in England where it required final approval. In the meantime, a group of Toronto merchants along with Family Compact stalwart, John Strachan, connived to discredit the Kingston group and secure a banking monopoly in Upper Canada themselves. They succeeded.

In 1821, the Bank of Upper Canada received its charter. The government of Upper Canada agreed to provide one-quarter of the 200,000 pounds it needed to begin operations. When private subscribers failed to come through with their three-quarters, the government simply lowered the total demanded to allow the bank to get underway. This private banking operation was a side activity for important government figures. Of the 15 directors, who regularly issued themselves formidable dividends, nine were from the start powerful officials, and most of the rest soon became so. Strachan was the first director. Within ten years other banks were being chartered as well.

Mackenzie, on behalf of his farmer constituency, fought the banks bitterly. His argument was that the banks, as constituted, did not benefit the farmers. He also argued against the necessity of a bank-issued currency for the sake of trade, given the current state of development of the Upper Canadian economy:

> It is plain that the Flour can be ground, carted and shipped to a foreign place without the aid of Bank notes; and it is equally plain that if we of Upper Canada want less goods from that place than the price the Flour sells for, the difference will come back to us in gold and silver, or in a bill of exchange, which is a draught by the foreign merchant on some person here in whose hands he has goods, gold

> and silver, or endorsed acceptances to him, payable by our fellow citizens, or who has agreed to give him a credit. If the gold and silver come from abroad in one ship, it will be at hand to send by another, in a case where we want to buy salt or any other article or articles which will come to more money than the cargo exported by the ship which is to fetch the salt, &c. If we have not the gold and silver to send, we must take credit abroad on the faith of a future cargo of the fruits of our labour, or be content with a smaller return.

He argued further against the credit function of banks, at least as far as farmers were concerned:

> The cultivator of the soil in a country where very few pay rent ought to stand no small need of credit, and should of all things avoid banking credit. Bills to a bank at 90 days are a dangerous speculation to a farmer, who only reaps his harvest once a year, and may be tempted by the loan of money to purchase what he does not stand in need of, & unable to pay his debts from non-payments by those on whose punctuallity [sic] he perhaps placed too much reliance. The apparent ease with which a wealthy farmer can command money for himself or his friends by merely signing his name on the face or the back of a promissory note is real to too many of the agricultural community, and ruins the independence & breaks the peace of thousands, whose property is sacrificed and themselves transformed into humble and needy dependants upon others. If a farmer stands in need of credit, banking credit ought to be his last resource, he should borrow of a friend on interest, it would be the safest plan by far.

He was not opposed to banks in principle, but questioned their value to the people of Upper Canada in the current stage of the colony's development: "The advantages to be derived from Banking establishments in an agricultural country are perhaps more than counterbalanced by the numerous train of evils they engender."

He was particularly outraged by the limited liability of bank shareholders. Were the bank to fail and be unable to redeem its notes with hard currency such as gold and silver, the shareholders were not liable to pay to their full ability but merely as much as they had personally subscribed to the bank's capital fund. Their personal fortunes would not be touched:

> If a poor man cannot pay his debts, his bed is, in some of the States, taken from under him. If that will not satisfy his creditors, his body is

> imprisoned. The shareholders in a Bank are entitled to all the gain they can make by Banking operations, but if the undertaking chances to be unsuccessful, the loss falls on those who have trusted them. They are responsible only for the amount of stock they have subscribed.

Despite the rhetoric about public benefit, the banks didn't exist to aid anyone except those businessmen and financiers who ran them:

> Your heartless money-loving capitalist, therefore, while he will spurn from his door the worthy, honest, industrious farmer who offers to pledge his farm in mortgage as security for a loan for two or three years at 6 per cent declaring at the same time that he would not for the world take a farthing beyond the legal interest and that he has no cash to spare — this same person will invest his means in the Upper Canada Bank scourge, and instead of 6 per cent he will net 18 one year with another, as the result of the monopolizing policy and abominable judge-made law tariff system which have obtained in Upper Canada . . . .

Presumably Mackenzie would not have been opposed to a banking operation run in a different manner. Such a bank might indeed have served valuable purposes in the society of Upper Canada. But not the banks as they then existed:

> Presidents, Cashiers, Directors, and others, by the craft and mystery of banking, make themselves rich, without adding one dollar to the wealth of the country; and although banking may be necessary in a large commercial city, yet when conducted in the country, it ought to be managed in such a way as to give aid to trade, but never to encourage doubtful speculation. A province may be improved by encouraging agricultural and manufacturing inventions, but won't be saved by banking.

Poverty

Throughout the early part of the nineteenth century huge numbers of immigrants from the British Isles flocked to the Canadas to improve their lives, particularly after the end of the Napoleonic Wars (1815) when unemployment rose in the British Isles. Harvest failures during the following years and the failure of the potato crop in Ireland in 1821 brought tens of thousands. They arrived to find that almost all of the good land had already been given away and much of it was unavailable at reasonable prices because of land speculation. There was very little work in the towns; what little industry there was just managed to survive since the business world was geared to trade, not manufacturing. The result was widespread unemployment and poverty in Upper Canada.

Since there were no alms- or poorhouses, the poor were sent to jails. As early as 1792, the prisons were overcrowded. In 1810, a law ordered that jails be used to house "all and every idle and disorderly person, and rogues and vagabonds. . . ."

Private societies attempted to meet the needs of the poor. But they, too, were often very harsh on these early Canadian victims of unemployment in a country where there was no land and no jobs. In 1820, the Society for the Relief of Strangers in Distress resolved:

> 1st. That as a pecuniary relief, without some return of labor, is but too often productive of idleness, such relief should in future be withheld, except in cases where, from the positive sickness or absence of those of the family capable of manual labor, no means of earning a subsistence remain; provided, the measures proposed for furnishing employment when required should prove attainable.
>
> 2d. That the public walk about to be formed near this town, and the projected improvement of the Blue Hill in Yonge Street, appear to offer . . . most desirable opportunities for giving almost immediate employment to any applicants now in want of work. . . .
>
> 5th . . . That, as a further inducement to the projectors of such works to aid the measure proposed, as well as to prevent any but the really necessitous from burthening the Society with unnecessary applications for employ, it becomes highly desirable to fix a maximum of wages at a *lower* rate than what laborers are usually employed at, lest the well meant anxiety of the Society to assist the really distressed should unintentionally operate as an encouragement to the new settlers upon their arrival in the Province, to be dilatory and careless in seeking work from private individuals, or still more injuriously offer a sort of temptation to them to be diverted from their more important ultimate object, namely, that of proceeding to settle upon their new lands.

In 1830, a committee of the Assembly chaired by Mackenzie reported on the inhabitants of the Toronto jail:

> Your Committee found 25 persons in this prison, twelve criminals on

the ground floor, one criminal sick up stairs, one vagrant, the three lunatics above mentioned, and nine debtors. . . .

The debtors are with one exception, all on the upper floor, apart from the other prisoners. . . . These are allowed no support from their creditors, and some of them say they are entirely without means of subsistance. James Colquhoun is in jail for a debt of three pounds; the creditor has forgiven the debt, but the lawyer has not thought proper to forgive him fees. Colquhoun subsists altogether on the humanity of the jailor and other debtors. One Murphy told your Committee that he had nothing to eat and that both Colquhoun and himself had been for four days together, without tasting a morsel. There are six debtors confined on executions issued out of the Court of King's Bench.

One debtor is in jail, together with his wife, and a family of five children. Your Committee observed only one person at work. He was a shoemaker.

A natural accompaniment to this poverty and unemployment was the growth of social conditions appropriate to them — a kind of nineteenth century lowlife and slums. In 1828, Mackenzie described the state of the town of York:

Altho' the official return of the population of York is under 2000 souls, there are about sixty stores, houses of entertainment or taverns, in some of which strong beer or spirituous liquors are either sold or permitted to be drank at all hours of the day and night and on all days and nights of the week — many of these stores and taverns are creditably kept by respectable persons, but there are other houses, either of ill-fame, or the resort of the idle, the dissipated, the worthless, and the profligate, which are known to the magistrates, and in some cases owned by them, but which they permit to exist and to multiply, as hotbeds of vice and infamy, and allurements to draw youth (along) the swift road that leadeth to destruction.

There is no ordinary town-watch or night police, to see the streets cleared of strumpets, drunkards, thieves, and vagabonds. If a man calls out MURDER in the night, as it appears French did when assaulted by Nowlan, he can only be aided, if in real danger, by individuals unarmed, and that at the risque of their own lives. No watchmen being near, the man of rank and the labourer may alike chance to bite the dust, the victims of brutality, passion, or inebriety.

In front or in rear of the houses of many of the inhabitants of this town, and even on the public streets, individuals are permitted to collect, or to throw out and exhibit all sorts of filth and nastiness —

> puddles of stinking water and offals, noisome and pestiferous, are allowed to exist without complaint — and even at the old jail, on the glebe lands of the church, in view of the principal street of the town is a pestilent stenchhole permitted to set, in aid of the marsh, spreading the elements of disease among our citizens.
>
> Ponds of stagnant water, in which decayed vegetable substances are rotting, may be seen under the houses of many of the townspeople. But although this occasions disease to pass up through the boards of the floor to the ignorant or careless inmates, nothing has been done to compel the owners or occupiers of such houses to clear away the contagious puddles — which are to be found outside of houses as well as below them.

Drunkenness was often the social accompaniment of un- and underemployment. It was far more serious and widespread than hard drug use in our own time. Distilleries and breweries were *the* most common industrial establishments. One historian says they were as common as gas stations are today. A traveller in the mid-1830s says that two thirds of the people he passed on the road were drunk. He found steamboats and hotels full of drunks, "part of them in rags and swearing in a disgusting manner." Temperance societies existed to combat the problem. Such a demoralized population did not merely represent a social and economic failure; they were a political liability as well. Mackenzie wrote in 1834:

> The vice of drunkenness, both in man and woman, obtains in this province to an almost incredible degree — a careful observation enables us to say that it appears to be on the increase. In this disgusting practice, we recognize another formidable obstacle to political reform.

Religion and Education

The conflicts that set groups against each other over such economic issues as land, trade and banking were also present in the less concrete areas of religion and education. These, too, were arenas of political and class struggle.

From the beginning, it was the policy of the British government to establish the Church of England as the leading religious force in Upper Canada. Lord Simcoe, before he became the first governor of the province, stated: "In regard to the colony of

Upper Canada which is peculiarly situated among a variety of republics, every establishment of church and state which upholds a distinction of ranks and lessens the undue weight of the democratic influence must be indispensably introduced."

Not only would the Anglican Church militate against "American" tendencies; it would also counterbalance the sinister forces of Roman Catholicism in Lower Canada. Religion, in other words, was clearly seen by all sides to be an active political force. It was central in the lives of the people of the time. Mackenzie regularly reviewed sermons in his paper, much as a modern newspaper might deal with movies.

Though Anglicanism was never formally established in Upper Canada as the official state religion — as it was in England itself; nevertheless it aspired to such a role in the colony. Upper Canada, however, was not England. From the beginning the Church of England was in the minority. It was the religion of the upper classes in the towns. Many people who came to the colony, both from the United States and Britain, brought other faiths. Methodism was the religion of the Upper Canadian countryside, drawing its congregation from the farmers and working people of the colony.

Methodism came to Upper Canada chiefly from the United States along with the earliest flow of American settlers. There was also a branch of British Methodism (the British Wesleyans) which the British had encouraged to enter Quebec to combat Catholicism and which spilled over into Upper Canada after the War of 1812. In 1821 a compromise was reached between the two branches whereby the American-based Methodists were left alone to operate in Upper Canada and the British Methodists were assigned to Quebec. In 1824 the Upper Canadian Methodists gained virtual autonomy from the American Methodist organization, and in 1828, they became formally independent.

In addition to the Methodists, there were Baptists, Presbyterians, Quakers, Roman Catholics and numerous other religious groups. None of which prevented the minority Church of England from attempting to dominate the religious life of the province. Until 1831, for example, only Anglican clergy were empowered to perform legal marriages.

Speaking of marriages, the connection between the Church of

England and the ruling political group, the Family Compact, was almost complete. John Strachan personified this relationship. He had come out to Upper Canada as a young Scottish schoolmaster for the children of the rich. He converted from Presbyterianism to Anglicanism, became rector and archdeacon of York, and, eventually, the first Anglican bishop of Upper Canada. He was the dominant figure on the Executive Council, the Legislative Council, the Bank of Upper Canada, the University and on and on, as Mackenzie lamented.

Strachan was indefatigable in pursuing his church's domination. In 1826, he went to England to lobby for Church of England interests. While there he produced a "Chart" of religious affiliations in the province so false that the outcry against him from Upper Canada was almost universal. A young Methodist preacher, Egerton Ryerson, responded to Strachan in the pages of Mackenzie's newspaper. Three years later, the Methodists established their own newspaper, *The Christian Guardian*, with Ryerson as editor. During its early years, the *Guardian*, was a staunch and influential advocate of political reform; it, and the Methodism it represented, were to the Reform camp what the Church of England and its organs were to the Tory side.

The most contentious issue was the clergy reserves. The Constitutional Act of 1791 had set them aside "for the support of a Protestant clergy." This was widely assumed to mean the Church of England, but the assumption was contested by other denominations who felt equally entitled to a piece of that particular pie. In 1819 Strachan assured passage of a bill which would attach the reserves exclusively to his beloved church. For a long time the reserves had produced little revenue and, for the most part, merely retarded development. But later in the decade they began to produce revenue and, at this point, the Church of England, having secured the right to sell, not merely lease, the reserves, reaped financial benefits which helped in its struggle to supercede the other denominations.

In 1826, the Assembly demanded that the reserves be used to support all denominations equally or, if that was impossible, to sell them and use the funds for universal, non-denominational education in the province.

This was a new attitude: secular and anti-sectarian. The British and European precedents for education had involved church control of one sort or another, but the Americans were experimenting with a universal, secular system of education, and this was widely approved in Upper Canada.

This debate about religion went beyond the issue of church-controlled education. In 1828, 8,000 people in Upper Canada signed a petition to the British Parliament asking that body:

> . . . to leave the ministers of all denominations of Christians to be supported by the people among whom they labour . . . to do away with all political distinctions on account of religious faith . . . to remove all ministers of religion from seats and places of power in the Provincial Government — to grant to the Clergy of all denominations of Christians the enjoyment of equal rights and privileges in everything that appertains to them as subjects . . . and as ministers of the Gospel, particularly the right of solemnizing Matrimony . . . to modify the Charter of King's College established at York in Upper Canada, so as to exclude all sectarian tests and preferences — and to appropriate the proceeds of the sale of lands heretofore set apart for the support of a Protestant Clergy, to the purposes of general education and various internal improvements.

In 1830, an Assembly with a majority of Tories and a minority of Reformers eliminated the post of Chaplain to the Assembly as an indication of opposition to any form of official religion. Here was one area in which the Reformers (representing the farmers and industrialists) seemed able to gather support even from the midst of the Tory (merchant, Family Compact) camp.

To offset the potentially liberalizing effect of the "religion" issue, the Compact and the British authorities undertook to neutralize the most powerful religious voice for reform — Upper Canadian Methodism, and particularly, Egerton Ryerson. Their strategy was to attempt to detach Methodism from political reform, not to suppress it altogether. Both the British and the local government led by Strachan pressed for the re-entry of the British Methodists into Upper Canada. This group could be expected to have a conservative political effect on Upper Canada's Methodists. In fact Ryerson's own brother and coworker wrote him from England about the political conservatism of the British branch and urged: "Better to bear the temporary censure of enemies in Canada, than the permanent evil & annoyance

Egerton Ryerson: the "Benedict Arnold" of Upper Canada.

of having a Church & State Tory Superintendent from this country."

Nevertheless, in 1832, the leadership of Upper Canadian Methodism, under Egerton Ryerson, agreed to the union. Exactly what persuaded Ryerson is not clear. Ryerson had gone to England during the course of the negotiations for union and his politics seemed to have altered completely. Immediately after union, Upper Canadian Methodism began receiving government assistance along with the Church of England, a complete turnabout from Ryerson's original position on the relation between church and state. From the time of the union on *The Christian Guardian* left the Reform cause and practically ceased to deal with political issues at all.

Mackenzie saw this as a political move designed to split the

Reform ranks and he wrote:

> ANOTHER DESERTER!
>
> The Christian Guardian, under the management of our rev. neighbour Egerton Ryerson, has gone over to the enemy, press, types, & all, & hoisted the colours of a cruel, vindictive tory priesthood. His brother George when sent to London became an easy convert to the same cause, and it appears that the parent stock were of those who fought to uphold unjust taxation, stamp acts, and toryism in the United States. The contents of the Guardian of tonight tells us in language too plain, too intelligible to be misunderstood that a deadly blow has been struck in England at the liberties of the people of Upper Canada, by as subtile and as ungrateful an adversary, in the guise of an old and familiar friend, as ever crossed the Atlantic. The Americans had their Arnold and the Canadians have their Ryerson.

Upper Canadian Methodism itself split over this political aspect of the union with the British Methodists. The farmers, who made up the bulk of Methodism, resented their leadership trying to draw them away from their natural allies, and aligning them with the imperial authorities. A separate Methodist church for Upper Canada was set up, circuit riders reported "a torrent of opposition" to the union, and numerous subscriptions to *The Christian Guardian* were cancelled.

The essentially political character of religious life in Upper Canada was clear to all sides.

As for education, here too Strachan strove mightily to dominate on behalf of the Church of England. He was particularly determined to combat the American influence on education in the province. Many of the teachers and teaching materials came from the United States. Here again the underlying motivations were political. A report of the Executive Council, on which Strachan was the leading member, stated:

> The Council are convinced . . . that the Youth now growing up in the Province . . . [should] have an opportunity of receiving their education under Tutors, not merely eminent for their learning, but for their attachment to the British Monarchy, and to the Established Church . . . It is quite evident that such an Institution in alliance with the Church, would tend to establish a most affectionate connexion, between the Colony and the Parent State . . . would gradually infuse into the whole population, a tone and feeling entirely English, and

> . . . render it certain that the first feelings, sentiments and opinions of Youth should be British.

These predilections were opposed by the Reformers who desperately wanted education for their children, but a secular education of the sort being instituted in the U.S.

The farmer-Reform constituency also stressed elementary and secondary education, while Strachan pressed incessantly for a university which could train and indoctrinate an elite. The battle over the university seesawed between Upper Canada and London. A university charter was first granted, then it was withdrawn. In 1829 the Lieutenant Governor, Sir John Colborne, set up Upper Canada College instead, insisting that Upper Canada would at least have a good preparatory school. The institution was soon known among the opposition as a good Prepare-a-Tory school.

Immigration

Upper Canada was a British invention, post-Conquest and post-American Revolution. Largely uninhabited it had to be filled in by people. So immigration policy, which like all policies was an imperial prerogative, was a prime concern from the start. Though it went by fits and starts, and priorities shifted somewhat, by 1826, the basic position was well enunciated by Lieutenant Governor Maitland: "The speedy settlement of the colony, however desirable, is a secondary objective compared to its settlement in such a manner as shall best secure its attachment to British Laws and Government."

The first settlers were safe enough: they were the Loyalists. (Not that the Loyalists were unwaveringly loyal: Peter Matthews, hanged along with Samuel Lount following the loss at Montgomery's Tavern, came from U.E.L. stock.) Yet almost simultaneously with them, in the aftermath of the American Revolution, came other Americans looking not for a return to the British womb, but simply for land and opportunity, no matter under whose political aegis. These people brought with them more democratic attitudes and the seed of a conflict was sown.

By 1815, there were perhaps 90,000 people in Upper Canada. But the War of 1812 was a watershed in immigration policy. The population had, by and large, been unenthusiastic about helping the British fight off the U.S. In fact the majority seemed either pro-American or deeply uninterested. This lack of "patriotism," *i.e.,* willingness to die in a British cause, was blamed on the American origins of so much of the population. The War marked the beginning of a thereafter ceaseless anti-Americanism among the local governing elite (soon to become known as the Family Compact); efforts were made to keep careful watch on the Americans already there, and to discourage others from coming. All of this was no easy task since Americans were so prominent in the colony and held much of the land. (Loyalists, of course, were *not* considered Americans.)

The tack taken by the authorities was to attack the political, but not the property, rights of those who had come to Upper Canada from the United States. A bitter debate over the issue — which became known as the Alien Question — raged during the 1820s.

Previously, citizens of the United States who emigrated had simply taken an oath of allegiance and assumed all the rights of British citizenship. (Naturally, there was no such thing as Canadian citizenship.) Now their right to vote and hold office was challenged if they had not undergone a naturalization process of seven years residence along with other requirements. Many technicalities were involved, but the thrust was a challenge to the political legitimacy of American immigrants in Upper Canada. The issue went round and round. The Assembly favoured no restrictions at all on Americans; the Legislative Council (i.e. the Compact) wanted to grant them only property rights. The Colonial Office leaned this way, then that, and finally resolved the situation favourably for the Americans already resident in Upper Canada. The Compact had lost on the specific issue, but they had injected a new force — anti-Americanism — into the colony's politics, and they went ahead to do all they could to discourage further immigration from the U.S.

Such immigration was never actually banned (though discussions about a ban took place) but the strife over the Alien Question had itself a negative effect on potential immigrants. And anyway, prospective settlers were already bypassing Upper Canada in droves for the more attractive circumstances of the newly opened Western states.

At the same time as Americans were being *dis*couraged, immigration from the British Isles was *en*couraged. The depressed British economy following the Napoleonic wars, crop failures, economic depression and the desire of the British ruling class to find a safety valve for dangerous revolutionary sentiments among a disaffected, unemployed mass of people — all these played their part. People wanted to leave, and the government wanted them to leave. A spate of books on immigration to the New World appeared. Though the majority of British immigrants went to the United States, large numbers did go to British North America as well, and the bulk of these wound up in Upper Canada. During the early 1820s, various government programs assisted people in emigrating. Peter Robinson, brother of John Beverley Robinson of Family Compact eminence, was in charge of such a program for poor Irish settlers and helped establish several communities, including Peter(!)borough.

Most of these immigrants through the mid-1820s were Scottish and Irish, not English. They were relatively, or absolutely poor, could not afford the jacked-up prices for what little land was available in Upper Canada, and found themselves as unemployed as they had been at home. Many continued on to settle in the States. From the local government viewpoint this was only partly regrettable since such immigrants belonged to the wrong churches, and were liable to be politically disaffected. In addition, the programs of assistance to them were costing a great deal.

In the latter half of the decade, more English began to arrive, and some of these were relatively well-to-do. By occupying many important government positions, these people contributed to a more conservative political tenor in the colony, and represented a force of reaction that could be counted on by the authorities when the revolt eventually broke out.

This shift in the profile of the immigrants also meshed with the then-voguish theories of E. G. Wakefield who held that land in the colonies should be sold at *high* prices, ensuring that the buyers would have the incentive and the means to farm it profitably. In the process, argued Wakefield, a hungry industrial work force would be created, consisting of those who could not afford to buy farms. It was a theory which squared well with the practice of land speculation in Upper Canada. Wakefield himself accompanied Durham to Canada on the mission which followed the uprisings. At any rate, the migrations continued, and reached a high point in 1831 and 1832.

For those immigrants who did not find what they had come for—land, opportunity, a *new* world—the solution was obvious. Move on to the United States. Durham estimated that of all the immigrants to British North America fully sixty percent continued on to settle in the States. Another estimate: that of the half million British emigrants to British North America between 1830 and 1840, three quarters went on to the U.S. There was also a flow of immigrant arrivals in the United States who came on to Canada, but this was well outweighed by the drain into the States.

The Upshot

Disgruntled immigrant arrivals were not the only people who left Upper Canada for the States. If you couldn't get land, or couldn't keep it, and couldn't transport your goods to market, or your family to church, or couldn't find a church to take your family to, or a school for your children, and you found your produce undercut by American grain entering Canada duty-free while yours couldn't go the reverse route, and the bank wasn't interested in doing anything but foreclosing on exorbitant mortgages, and there was no work in the towns if you did lose your land, and you *didn't* want to just leave for the States like so many others, there was an alternative — change things.

Amiably, electorally, at first. And when that means proved insufficient, then by whatever means necessary.

The only thing that saved Upper Canada from an earlier, bigger and *successful* revolution was the safety-valve of the United States. Had it not been so close by, there is no possibility that those farmers would have put up with those land and other policies. As it was, the Canadian Revolution did come and it was primarily a revolution about land.

Chapter 2

Politics: Who rules, who resists

Like every society, Upper Canada had a system of government. Though a fairly simple society at the time, it was still too complex to exist without a political order. Its relations with other societies required regulation, diplomatically and militarily. Projects such as roads, canals and schools concerned the entire population and required organization of the society. Internal conflicts between, for example, haves and have-nots or native peoples and Europeans, had to be regulated, usually in the interests of one side or the other. The wealth of the colony, its land, timber, furs, produce, was up for grabs, and different groups were in contention over that wealth. Government presumably could regulate these conflicts.

Government regulates the entire society, though not necessarily in the interest of the entire society. The most interesting questions about governments and systems of government are: Which individuals and groups of individuals control the government and how do they run it? (Whose interests does the government serve?).

In contemporary Canada, where "government" seems almost equivalent to "elected representatives," such questions might seem out of place. Then again they might not; but that is another matter. In the society of Upper Canada, however, the leaders of government and its major figures were not elected at all. Only one small section of the government was elected and even that section was not elected by a universal vote of the population, and had almost no power in the major areas of decision-making and policy.

The Government

The anchor of the government of Upper Canada was the Colonial Office in London, England. The policies were made there, and from there the people to implement those policies were sent out to the colony. The internal structure of government for the colony was established under the guidance of the Colonial Office and this form of government was then set up within the colony itself. Some of its outlines were established in the Constitutional Act of 1791; others were drawn up in accordance with instructions given by the Colonial Office to the various governors sent here.

The government of Upper Canada was subject not only to the Colonial Office but to the government of Lower Canada as well. Lower Canada was the older colony and before the mid-nineteenth century was much larger and more developed than Upper Canada. While the British were building Upper Canada into a rival to the predominantly French colony, they maintained the main channels of overall governing in the latter.

The Governor in chief of both the Canadas resided in Quebec City and the lieutenant governor of Upper Canada was subordinate to him. Still, the lieutenant governor of Upper Canada did correspond directly with the Colonial Office in London for his instructions on policy matters, and did not have to go through Quebec on most questions. The governor in chief at Quebec was also the military commander-in-chief of Upper Canada. The Postmaster General at Quebec operated the postal service of Upper Canada. The trade of Upper Canada was dominated by Lower Canada, since most of it passed through the port of Quebec, and customs duties on goods bound for Upper Canada were levied by the government in Quebec. This gave rise to endless wrangling over Upper Canada's proper share of the total duties collected. Even in religion, the Anglican bishop of Quebec stood as the head of the Anglican church in Upper Canada. Upper Canada did not even receive its first archdeacon, a position subordinate to the bishop, until 1828 when John Strachan was appointed. He later became Upper Canada's first bishop.

The structure of government of Upper Canada was set within this framework of direct subordination to the Colonial Office, and intermediate subordination to the government at Quebec.

At the top was the lieutenant governor. He was appointed by the Colonial Office, received his instructions from them, and corresponded directly with them on most matters of concern in the colony. In spite of the distance and amount of time consumed by travel (a one-way voyage was a matter of weeks at the least and could easily take two months) the Colonial Office communicated with the lieutenant governor in considerable detail on most local matters. In addition, the government in England retained what was called "the right of Imperial disallowance" (a veto) of any bills or measures undertaken in the colony.

To help him run the affairs of the colony, the lieutenant governor had an Executive Council. This was a kind of cabinet, but its members were advisors, not ministers in charge of specific administrative departments. This small body held ultimate control over all land dealings in the colony, and in Upper Canada, land was wealth. It also heard appeals. Its members were appointed by the lieutenant governor, either at the direction of the Colonial Office, or with their concurrence. It was controlled by the lieutenant governor who did not have to act on its advice except in connection with minor matters such as the erection of parsonages and ports of entry.

The actual running of government functions was done by various officials. The most important of these were the attorney general, solicitor general, chief justice and other high judges, receiver general, surveyor general, secretary, registrar, auditor general of land patents, and commissioner of crown lands. In others words, these were the lucrative posts with control over land, justice, tax and customs collection, and other such areas of wealth and power. These posts were all filled by direct appointment of the lieutenant governor and/or the Colonial Office, with more or less participation by the Executive Council.

The lieutenant governor appointed local judges, militia officers, sheriffs (who in turn chose juries), and the most important local officials, justices of the peace. The justices of the peace were responsible for roads, jails, tax collections, establishment of markets, and the granting of liquor licences.

As one historian, summarizing the power of the lieutenant governor in the government of Upper Canada, says:

> The question of the extent of the patronage of the governor is impor-

> tant. He virtually appointed the executive and legislative councillors, the judges of the King's Bench, and the heads of executive departments. He appointed all the officers of the legislative council and assembly, except the speaker of the assembly. He appointed a sheriff in each district, justices of the peace, coroners, judges of the district courts and of the surrogate courts, registrars of counties, clerks of the peace, and commissioners of customs. Immigration officers in the various districts were his nominees. After 1828, the whole of the Indian establishment was at his command. As head of the provincial militia he appointed one thousand five hundred officers. In the days of free grants of land an unexampled source of patronage had been provided, the effect of which was still apparent in 1815. Even after 1815 grants to militia officers could be withheld at the governor's pleasure. The crown revenues were at his command for pensions, aid to churches, etc. After the foundation of King's College and Upper Canada College the governor selected their staffs. He also appointed district boards of education.

With all this power in the hands of the lieutenant governor and his Executive Council, and through them in the Colonial Office — one might wonder what point there could be in having legislative bodies at all in the colonies. Nevertheless the British had established such bodies.

They set them up partly to prevent the development of the kind of dissatisfaction that had led to revolution in the Thirteen Colonies. The expenses of running and defending the colonies were high, and the British did not intend to pay those costs themselves. On the contrary, the people of the colonies were meant to pay. But the British government did not want to impose taxes directly, not with the battle cry of the American Revolution, "no taxation without representation," still fresh in their ears. So they set up local legislatures to levy and collect the taxes. (The British also hoped for a fringe benefit by way of "anglicization" of the French population in Lower Canada through British parliamentary practices.) Yet the British did not really trust the local population politically, so they established two legislative houses: one elected; the other, appointed.

This latter, non-elected body was called the Legislative Council. It was intended as an equivalent to the British House of Lords, a laughable thought at best in Upper Canada. There was even a plan to provide its members with hereditary titles, though

The election of 1836. "The People's William" is Mackenzie, as opposed to *King* William, hero of the Orangemen.

this was never done. Members were appointed for life by the lieutenant governor. By 1829 this body had eighteen members.

Paired with it was the Legislative Assembly. This was the only elected body in the whole governmental structure of Upper Canada. By 1836, it had 69 members, elected by counties. They were voted in every four years, or at the dissolution of the legislature by the lieutenant governor. There was a property qualification for voting, and a higher property qualification for holding seats in the Assembly. Even so, this was a more democratic arrangement than prevailed in the British House of Commons itself at the time.

With the structuring of power in the colony, there was very little the Assembly could legislate. Its main function, from the British viewpoint was to raise tax money to pay the costs of administering the colony. In addition, the Assembly could concern itself with the construction of roads, schools and other public works. And they were free to criticize, attack and condemn where the policies of the governor, his council and his officials were concerned. In this context, it became the main role of the Legislative Council to disallow bills passed by the Assembly. (Joint passage by both houses was required before they were sent on to the governor for acceptance or rejection.) In this way the Legislative Council saved the governor the political embarrassment of rejecting most of the bills passed by the only elected body in the colony during those sessions when the majority of the Assembly were opposed to the government.

The only effective tactic for the Assembly in confronting the lieutenant governor was to withhold the tax monies it had raised. It was entitled to do so. But even this device did not serve to hamstring the lieutenant governor because he could call on other sources of revenue to cover government expenses if pressed. One such source was customs duties collected at Quebec. These were sent directly to the lieutenant governor. Then there were the revenues called Kings Rights: income from rent on crown lands, rents from mills and ferries and certain licences. The lieutenant governor could use such sources to pay the salaries of officials, expenses of government departments, costs for canals, *etc*. In fact, especially after the Canada Company deal of 1826, the governor found it unnecessary to request *any* tax money from the legislature for government expenses during 1828, 1829 and 1830. These were precisely the years in which a political opposition first held majority control of the Legislative Assembly.

In fact, such "outside" revenues did amount to taxation without representation. They came *from* the people of the country and went *to* the government, without any elected representatives getting in between. In truth, the actual taxation powers of the Legislature were meagre: licences, fines, duties on the small amount of imports coming into Upper Canada directly from the United States. Such powers amounted more to a token of democratic control of public expenses than a reality.

There were also some direct expenditures by the British government — mostly military. These rose steeply from 1836 (164,000 pounds) to 1841 (900,000 pounds), in direct response to the Revolution of 1837 and the subsequent threats from the American border states. The British were not prepared to sustain this kind of expenditure in Canada for long; nor did they want to put up with the internal political unrest that made it necessary. These were two of the main reasons for the eventual introduction of the system which became known as responsible government.

In structure, then, the government of Upper Canada consisted of 1) the lieutenant governor 2) his Executive Council 3) a host of officials, big and small, who ran the business of the government 4) a legislature consisting of the appointed Legislative Council and the elected Legislative Assembly. But who were the *people* who filled in these various government positions?

Men, not women, to begin. Not necessarily Englishmen, though many had recently arrived from England. The lieutenant governor, always a military man, and his secretary, a very influential figure, were themselves always Englishmen on posting to the colonies. As for other positions, in the early years of the colony many of the top officials were sent out from England as well. But as time passed, most government figures were Upper Canadians, however recently arrived. Not surprisingly, a small group of allied individuals held most of the government positions. What *is* surprising though is how many positions were often filled by one and the same individual. Seldom have so many jobs been filled by so few people.

In 1829, for example, the five senior executive councillors were also in the Legislative Council: four of them held important official positions; almost all the other members of the Legislative Council held official positions, and many held more than one. Writing from England in 1833, Mackenzie put the case in one of the first examples of the long tradition of Canadian political satire.

The following curious but accurate statement will convey to the minds of liberal Englishmen a tolerably fair picture of colonial rule. When I left Upper Canada last year, some of the offices, sinecures, and pensions of the government were divided as follows:—

No. 1. *D'Arcy Boulton,* senior, a retired pensioner, £500 sterling.

2. *Henry,* son to No. 1, Attorney-General and Bank Solicitor, £2400.

3. *D'Arcy,* son to No. 1, Auditor-General, Master in Chancery, Police Justice, etc. Income unknown.

4. *William,* son to No. 1, Church Missionary, King's College Professor, etc., £650.

5. *George,* son to No. 1, Registrar of Northumberland, Member of Assembly for Durham, etc. Income unknown.

6. *John Beverley Robinson,* brother-in-law to No. 3, Chief Justice of Upper Canada, Member for life of the Legislative Council, Speaker, £2,000.

7. *Peter,* brother to No. 6, Member of the Executive Council, Member for life of the Legislative Council, Crown Land Commissioner, Surveyor-General of Woods, Clergy Reserve Commissioner, etc. Income £1300.

8. *William,* brother to Nos. 6 and 7, Postmaster of Newmarket, Member of Assembly for Simcoe, Government Contractor, Colonel of Militia, Justice of the Peace, etc. Income unknown.

9. *Jonas Jones,* brother-in-law to No. 2, Judge of the District Court in three districts containing eight counties, and filling a number of other offices. Income about £1000.

10. *Charles,* brother-in-law to No. 9, Member for life of Legislative Council, Justice of the Peace in twenty-seven counties, etc.

11. *Alpheus,* brother to Nos. 9 and 10, Collector of Customs, Prescott, Postmaster at ditto, Agent for Government Bank at ditto, etc. Income £900.

12. *Levius P. Sherwood,* brother-in-law to Nos. 9, 10, 11, one of the Justices of the Court of King's Bench. Income £1000.

13. *Henry,* son to No. 12, Clerk of Assize, etc.

14. *John Elmsley,* son-in-law to No. 12, Member of the Legislative Council for life, Bank Director, Justice of the Peace, etc.

15. *Charles Heward,* nephew to No. 6, Clerk of the District Court, etc. Income £100.

16. *James B. Macaulay,* brother-in-law to Nos. 17 and 19, one of the Justices of the Court of King's Bench. Income £1000.

17. *Christopher Alexander Hagerman,* brother-in-law to No. 16, Solicitor-General. £800.

18. *John M'Gill,* a relation of Nos. 16 and 17, Legislative Councillor for life. Pensioner, £500.

19. and 20. *W. Allan* and *George Crookshanks,* connexions by marriage of 16 and 17, Legislative Councillors for life, the latter President of the Bank. £500.

21. *Henry Jones,* cousin to Nos. 9, 10, etc., Postmaster at Brockville, Justice of the Peace, Member of the Assembly for Brockville. Income unknown.

22. *William Dummer Powell,* father of No. 24, Legislative Councillor for life, Justice of the Peace, Pensioner. Pension £1000.

23. *Samuel Peters Jarvis,* son-in-law to No. 22, Clerk of the Crown in Chancery, Deputy-Secretary of the Province, Bank Director, etc. Income unknown.

24. *Grant,* son to No. 22, Clerk of the Legislative Council, Police Justice, Judge Home District Court, Official Principal of Probate Court, Commissioner of Customs, etc. Income £675.

25. *William M.,* brother to No. 23, High Sheriff Gore District, Income from £500 to £800.

26. *William B.,* cousin to Nos. 23 and 25, High Sheriff, Home District, Member of Assembly. Income £900.

27. *Adiel Sherwood,* cousin to No. 12, High Sheriff of Johnstown, and Treasurer of that district. Income from £500 to £800.

28. *George Sherwood,* son to No. 12, Clerk of Assize.

29. *John Strachan,* their family tutor and political schoolmaster, archdeacon and rector of York, Member of the Executive and Legislative Councils, President of the University, President of the Board of Education, and twenty other situations. Income, on an average of years, upwards of £1800.

30. *Thomas Mercer Jones,* son-in-law to No. 29, associated with No. 19 as the Canada Company's Agents and Managers in Canada.

This family connexion rules Upper Canada according to its own good pleasure, and has no efficient check from this country to guard the people against its acts of tyranny and oppression. It includes the whole of the judges of the supreme, civil and criminal tribunal (Nos. 6, 12, and 16)—active Tory politicians. Judge Macaulay was a clerk in the office of No. 2, not long since. It includes the President and Solicitor of the Bank, and about half the Bank Directors; together with shareholders holding, to the best of my recollection, about 1800 shares. And it included the crown lawyers until last March, when they carried their opposition to Viscount Goderich's measures to reform to such a height as personally to insult the government, and to declare their belief that he had not the royal authority for his despatches. They were then removed; but with this exception the chain remains unbroken. This family compact surround the Lieutenant-Governor, and mould him like wax to their will; they fill every

> office with their relatives; dependants, and partisans; by them justices of the peace and officers of the militia are made and unmade; they have increased the number of the Legislative Council by recommending, through the Governor, half a dozen of nobodies and a few placemen, pensioners, and individuals of well-known narrow and bigoted principles; the whole of the revenues of Upper Canada are in reality at their mercy;—they are Paymasters, Receivers, Auditors, King, Lords, and Commons! . . .

This was the group which came to be known, in a fine political phrase, as the Family Compact. They were chiefly notable for their control of government positions in all areas of the political structure. But, as can be seen from Mackenzie's diatribe, they were also in key positions in the economic structure (banks, canals, land companies) and the cultural establishment (church, education). Who were these men, and how had they arrived where they were?

The Family Compact

It was British colonial policy to encourage the formation of an elite. In the earliest years of Upper Canadian settlement, the Colonial Secretary had written to his appointee in the colonies concerning his plans for a Legislative Council parallel to the House of Lords:

> The object of these regulations is both to give the Upper branch of the Legislature a greater degree of weight and consequence than was possessed by the councils of the old [i.e. American] Colonial governments, and to establish in the Provinces a Body of Men having that motive of attachment to the existing form of Government, which arises from the possession of personal or hereditary distinction.

They chose men either from the families of United Empire Loyalists who had migrated following the American Revolution or from the families of arrivals to Upper Canada from England during the first generation after that Revolution. Compact membership was divided more or less equally between these two groups. Christopher Hagerman, G. H. Markland, James B. Macaulay — all from Kingston — are examples of second generation Loyalists. William Allan D'Arcy Boulton, and John Strachan were among those who had come out from the British Isles.

They were wealthy by the lights of the Upper Canada of those

Bishop John Strachan of the Family Compact.

days. Upper Canada, after all, was a fairly primitive piece of work in its first decades until about 1820. There was not a great deal of wealth to be acquired in such a relatively simple society. But those who acquired a disproportionate share of what there was, could be counted on to uphold the established order against any subversive, and particularly American, influences. The wealthy of any society have the greatest stake in maintaining things as they are. The British therefore looked to those with wealth, and then in many cases provided them with more wealth, which only increased their desire to maintain the status quo. The Compact members had come by their wealth through several different routes. One route was through being a merchant — buying and selling grain from, and supplies to, the farmers. Some of the early Compact members like the Kingston group for example, and James Baby, William Allan, and John McGill, built their wealth on such activities. However business was still small-scale in the early days of Upper Canada because the province was undeveloped, and because the truly powerful merchant interests resided in Montreal where they controlled the much more well-established mercantile empires that had existed since the days of the French. The merchants of Upper Canada, by and large, were subservient to Montreal merchants for their own buying and selling, just as these Montreal figures were vassals of London interests .

A more potent road to wealth was land. Not farming — a backbreaking and breakeven task at best in those times — but land ownership. Many of the Compact families had received huge plots because they were Loyalists. Others — those who came out from England as military men, for example — received land in place of pensions. D'Arcy Boulton and his family were granted 16,000 acres. John Strachan had received 3,202 acres by 1816, John McGill had 5,560, and W. D. Powell and his family got 10,903 acres. This land could be sold at excessive prices to land-hungry settlers, or held for speculation, or both.

Such were the men whom the British chose for government appointments. And government appointment was perhaps the surest road to wealth of all in early Upper Canada. To become one of the governor's key advisors meant control over land. Land could be granted to friends, relatives or oneself for that matter. Customs collection, tax collection, post office appointment — they were all potential bonanzas.

As such men grew richer, they became even more zealous, conservative upholders of the established order — Tories as they were called — than they had been before. They were acting in their own interests: they considered the established order to be theirs as well as Britain's. They were no mere tools of the Colonial Office: in fact, as their own vested interests grew, it became increasingly possible for them to come into conflict themselves with the Colonial Office over specific issues of policy and they were not above explicit threats of disloyalty if they felt threatened by any particular policy.

John Strachan was a special case among the Compact members. He was perhaps most powerful of all of them. Yet he was neither merchant nor landowner — not at first. He came out to Upper Canada as a young Scottish (Presbyterian) schoolmaster engaged to tutor the children of the rich. He soon converted to the Church of England and became its most fervent spokesman. His contribution to the ruling elite was not economic clout, but a sort of spiritual or cultural force, expressed through the dominant cultural institution of the time — religion. The British recognized, as do all ruling powers, that control of what people think and believe can be as important as control of what they do and own. Strachan was involved in politics (Executive Council, Legislative Council) and economics (Canada Company, Bank of Upper Canada); indeed he became one of the richest and most powerful citizens of Upper Canada and extended his cultural hegemony to include institutions of education. But the centre of his strength remained his role as churchman, from which he acted as, in Mackenzie's phrase, "tutor and political schoolmaster" to the colonial elite.

So, in its beginnings and up until the 1820s, the members of the Family Compact surrounded the lieutenant governor as his advisors, monopolized government positions, were busily involved in land ownership and speculation and had mercantile interests. It was not a terribly impressive game, but for this "shopkeeper aristocracy," as one dissident labelled them, it was the best in town. Their ambitions did not carry them much farther. At the beginning, there were no entrepreneurs or large-scale businessmen in the Compact. The small scale of the Upper Canadian economy in its early decades did not make private business undertakings a very enticing road to advancement. Anna Jameson, a shrewd English observer, lamented this lack of business acumen among Compact members:

> I allude to the disinclination evinced by far too large a portion of the Canadian youth of the class indicated, to engage in those pursuits which the primitive condition of the country they inhabit, no less than their own well-being, imperatively requires that they should follow. In lieu of devoting themselves to agricultural and commercial occupations, they blindly seek, in an undue ration to qualify them-

> selves for those of a professional nature: Because, from the fallacious notions in which they have been reared, they conceive, or affect to consider, the two first to be beneath them.

But times changed. And as they changed, so did the Compact.

By the 1820s the increase in population and economic activity had raised the possibility of significant private enterprises for the first time in the colony. The War of 1812 brought a rush of business from the British army; paper bills issued by the army were widely used and stimulated trade in the colony; some people got (slightly) rich quick, though the bottom fell out of the new prosperity for most people at the war's end, leaving the farmers in particular with little more than neglected farmland. But fortunes had been made and ambitions kindled.

The Canada Company, the Welland Canal Company and the Bank of Upper Canada were the outstanding examples of large-scale private business enterprises that arose in the 1820s. And with them, the Family Compact emerged from their cocoon into the business arena. They did not usually spawn such operations, but they made sure to get in on them and, where possible, take them over. The Compact's role in the Canada Company operation is an example.

The concept of the Canada Company, a company to buy the entire crown and clergy reserves and then sell them for private profit was devised by the Englishman John Galt. He organized a group of English capitalists into the Company; they negotiated with the British government, and prepared to send a commission of five to Upper Canada to settle on the price to be paid. An all-English capitalist operation. But here the Compact stepped in. On the eve of Galt's departure with the commission, Strachan wrote to him from Upper Canada, "Now I wish to lay it down as a principle never to be departed from, that it is in the interest of the Canada Co., to support the Colonial authorites [meaning the Compact] and never to take a side against them." Strachan in fact got his way; his beloved clergy reserves were excluded from the final bargain (one million acres of Huron county were thrown in instead) and when Galt proved intractable, the Compact conspired to have him recalled by the Company directors in London. The new appointee to Galt's post — Thomas Mercer Jones —

came out from England and proceeded to marry Strachan's daughter, eventually earning himself a number of his own in Mackenzie's listing of the Compact. The other agent of the Company in Canada was also a Compact figure, and a number of Compact members were directors of the Company.

The Welland Canal Company is another instance of the Compact's new economic thrust. William Hamilton Merritt, a St. Catharines businessman, had been attempting to promote the project unsuccessfully for seven years before he united with Compact members in 1825. As John Beverley Robinson reminded him in a letter years later:

> ... a very little communication with you convinced me that your motives were pure and disinterested and highly patriotic ... what confirmed my confidence was the observing that ... it seemed your earnest wish to have the direction of the Company committed to gentlemen whom you could not hope to bend to anything unworthy.

These "gentlemen" to whom Merritt had finally decided to "commit" the direction of the Company were Robinson, George and D'Arcy Boulton, William Allan — all Compact stalwarts — J. H. Dunn, receiver general of the province, and Joseph Wells, a Compact supporter. By entering into alliance with the Compact, Merritt himself was soon a firm member. For their part, the Compact figures used their positions in government to acquire an endless pipeline of government loans and concessions to the Welland Canal Company: 25,000 pounds in 1826; 50,000 in 1827; 25,000 in 1830; 50,000 in 1831; and a promise of 245,000 in 1837, of which a mere 68,144 pounds were actually received; plus land grants, special trade regulations, intercessions with the Colonial Office, and so forth.

Here the Compact, which had originally specialized in profiteering through government office, used those offices to get into and profiteer in the new area of high-powered capitalist enterprise. Similarly the Compact members used their land holdings of old for new profit in connection with the new businesses. Henry Boulton, for example, brother to one and son to another of the Canal Company directors, owned land on the Niagara peninsula, and pressed for a route that would enhance the value of his holdings.

The case of the Bank of Upper Canada is similar. Compact members used their political influence to outmanoeuver non-Compact Kingston interests who also wanted a bank charter from the British parliament. Then they assured a large government stock subscription to this private bank of theirs, and even had the temerity to reduce the original amounts of stock required so that the government source became the main one. The president and solicitor of the Bank of Upper Canada and about half its board of directors were Compact figures.

In short, by 1837, the Family Compact were on their way to becoming a full-fledged ruling class (within the limitations of overall imperial control) rather than a penny-ante shopkeeper aristocracy. In the expanding economy of Upper Canada, they were learning to change with the times. They had started as merchants or landholders. By virtue of the leverage these roles gave them, they had received government appointments. They had used these appointments to amass further wealth. Now they were taking the wealth acquired in government service as the base on which to expand their personal economic activity into the area of large-scale capitalist enterprise.

Take the career of William Allan, a Compact mainstay. From a merchant background in England, he came to Upper Canada in the 1790s and set up shop — literally. Then he became postmaster and collector of customs at York — both lucrative government jobs. He was an officer during the War of 1812. In 1821 he became the first president of the Bank of Upper Canada. He was a director of the Welland Canal Company, and a commissioner of the Canada Company land operation. He sat on the Legislative Council from 1825 until his death in 1833. In 1833 he also became the first president of the British American Assurance Company, one of the early instances of the insurance business which was to grow and flourish among the Canadian business class in the years to come.

Yet at the same time that the Compact members expanded their economic range, they stayed close to their shopkeeping and landholding roots. They did not enter into industry or manufacturing in any significant way. The capitalist enterprises they engaged in concerned the buying and selling of land (Canada Company), or the transportation of products to and from markets

(Welland Canal Company), or the ultimate in commercial activities — banking — the trade in money. These activities indicate a certain lack of entrepreneurial imagination so necessary to the building of factories and industries. This lack of a creative capitalist impulse — this "mercantile" cast of mind — in the business community has continued to characterize Canadian businessmen into our own period when the largest all-Canadian capitalist enterprises continue to revolve around transportation (CPR), trade (Eaton's), or banking.

The Compact was not a formal organization. It was connected by political, familial and business relationships. But it acted in a highly unified way. There were members more and less central to it. York was the core. But figures elsewhere formed in effect "little" Family Compacts around the colony. In Kingston, Hagerman was the dominant figure. In Hamilton there was Alan Macnab. West of Lake Erie, Colonel Thomas Talbot ruled a huge area. Though the Compact were suspicious of Talbot's independent British connections, they made common cause with him when it came to suppressing movements for reform. Of his virtual fiefdom, a local newspaper wrote:

> The county of Middlesex, from its first settlement up to this moment, has been controlled . . . as absolutely and despotically as is the petty sovereignty of a German despot. This they have been enabled to do through the immense influence their high official stations give them. Magistrates, officers of the excise, surveyors, militia officers, commissioners to carry the appropriations of public money into effect, all are appointed through the recommendations and influence of these sages of the District, thus forming a host of worthies who are ever at the beck of their Patrons. We assert without fear of contradiction that the Hon. Colonel Talbot rules with a more absolute sway, and his power is infinitely more to be dreaded than that of the King of Great Britain.

The Family Compact is simply the name applied to that group of men who, by their positions in the economy and the government, dominated the life of Upper Canada. There is nothing very remarkable about this in itself. Such a group exists in most societies. As Sir Francis Bond Head, lieutenant governor in 1837, wrote in defence of the Compact:

> "The bench," "the magistrates," "the clergy," "the law," "the landed proprietors," "the bankers," "the native-born inhabitants," and "the supporters of the established Church" form just as much of a "family compact" in England as they do in Upper Canada, and just as much in Germany as they do in England.

What distinguished the Compact was not their role as an elite, but rather two particular aspects of that role.

- They were never a true ruling class such as one would find in an independent nation like Britain or the U.S. They were dependent; the British ruled. They held sway by aligning themselves with the imperial power, in the person of the lieutenant governor, carrying out imperial policies, and reaping various powers and benefits within the colony for playing that role. This made them vulnerable to external forces. When it eventually suited British interests to support groups other than the Compact, the old stalwarts were left in the lurch. And Britain did indeed abandon the Compact with the event of Durham's mission in 1838, and the changes in policy that followed it.
- They were a very small and exclusive group. This made them vulnerable to forces within the colony. The society of Upper Canada was expanding in size and complexity. There were many ambitious souls in the growing population. Room had to be made at the top; the coziness of the old days in business and government was increasingly unviable. Either the newcomers would be allowed in, something which the Compact rarely permitted; or those newcomers would form an opposition that would increasingly disrupt the smooth functioning of the established order.

It is to the formation of this opposition, its political formation, that we turn next.

The Opposition

Political opposition in Upper Canada did not emerge in open, organized, parliamentary form until 1828. Then it sprang up suddenly, almost fullblown. Previously there had been opposition to the government and to the Compact, but of a spasmodic and fragmented sort.

In 1807 a judge appointed from England, Robert Thorpe, became the centre of popular and political opposition. He criticized the government, stood for and won a seat in the Assembly, gathered the dissidents there around him, and even when recalled to England, continued his agitation. Ten years later, in 1817, a Scottish landowner, Robert Gourlay, arrived in Upper Canada with a grand scheme for emigration from the British Isles. As a prelude to this work, he circulated a questionnaire among Upper Canadians which elicited in response a great many complaints and accusations about the prevailing system. Gourlay used those responses to mount a campaign for reform and eventually was imprisoned and then exiled for his activities. Almost twenty years later, during the revolution of 1837, he was still trying to win readmission to Upper Canada and refused support to Mackenzie for fear it would prejudice his appeal.

Political opposition also surfaced in the form of dissenting newspapers. The earliest such paper was the *Upper Canadian Guardian or Freeman's Journal*, founded in 1807. Mackenzie published his first newspaper, *The Colonial Advocate*, starting in 1824. It became the most widely-read paper in the colony at a time when journalism was the chief form of popular education and culture. A number of other opposition or "reform" newspapers appeared during the 1830s. For decades there had been individual voices and groupings of opposition in and out of the Assembly, the only political body to which they had any access at all. But political opposition in the form of an opposition *party* occurred with the election of 1828.

A majority of what were called Reformers were elected to the Assembly in that year. Their leaders were Dr. John Rolph, an English doctor and lawyer, Marshall Spring Bidwell, an emigrant from Massachusetts who had been active in American politics, and William Baldwin and his son Robert. The elder Baldwin was a lawyer from Ireland; his son was to become the chief propagandist for what became known as responsible government. The rise of what turned into the Reform party (party politics were only coming into existence at this time) reflected and paralleled the agitation for reform in England during this period. The English Reform movement, which culminated in the Reform Bill of 1832, was closely and enthusiastically followed by the Reformers of Upper Canada.

Following their victory of 1828, they elected one of their own members to be speaker of the Assembly, practically the only official position in the colony over which they had control. The government — the lieutenant governor, the Family Compact, the horde of officials — mobilized against them. For the next eight years Upper Canadian parliamentary politics seesawed with Reform victories in the elections of 1828 and 1834 and defeats in 1830 and 1836. What did the Reformers stand for?

They came together earliest over issues concerning religion: the obstructive and sectarian role of the clergy reserves, and Strachan's bid for Church of England control of the proposed university. The Reformers also made general and specific attacks on corruption and privilege. They demanded a far greater control over the colony's finances than the Assembly had. They pressed for certain humanitarian measures, such as the abolition of imprisonment for debt, and the abolition of primogeniture, the legal principle whereby the entire estate of a deceased passed to the eldest son alone. These somewhat unsystematic campaigns led them toward demands for various constitutional and legislative reforms: an elected Legislative Council, the independence of judges (who were appointed by the government and could be dismissed without cause), the introduction of the ballot instead of voice voting, and early formulations of the principle of responsible government. At this stage, responsible government amounted to a call for more participation by elected representatives in the appointment of government officials and advisors. Since the Assembly had practically no power and its bills could be disallowed by either the government-appointed Legislative Council, or the lieutenant governor himself, frustration mounted and led naturally to further cries for legislative reform.

For their part the Family Compact and their supporters, the Tories as they came to be called in the new party alignment of Reform versus Tory, spurned the opposition. Strachan called them "Levellers and Democrats." Talbot, referring to Temperance, another humanitarian concern of the Reformers, labelled the opposition "rebels" who "commenced their work of darkness under the cover of organizing Damned Cold Water Drinking Societies, where they met at night to communicate their poisonous and seditious schemes."

So, in its early phase, the Reform movement was characterized by a rather slapdash approach which led to an emphasis on legislative (or constitutional, or parliamentary) reform. But even more it was characterized by whom it attacked, and whom it did not attack. It attacked the Compact: it did not, for the most part, attack the lieutenant governor. This was natural since the officials at hand were the most visible cause of grievances in the colony. But there was also a fear of being associated with anything that smacked even vaguely of the attitudes that had led to the American Revolution. A kind of sacrosanctity attached to the lieutenant governor and to the imperial link which he represented; attention focussed instead on the local powers "surrounding" him and "bending" him to their purposes. This hands-off attitude toward the governor and the government *he* represented extended to all the Reformers, including Mackenzie, though perhaps least to him. Over the coming nine years, it was the willingness to rethink this attitude toward the imperial connection which split the ranks of the opposition in two.

This split within the opposition — within Reform itself — developed gradually between 1830 and 1837.

The Tories defeated the Reformers and achieved a majority themselves in the Assembly after the election of 1830. During this session, which lasted until 1834, Mackenzie was expelled five times, and each time re-elected by his constituents. Such treatment at the hands of a Tory majority along with increasing frustration at the impotence of the Assembly even when it had a Reform majority led the more radical members of the Reform group to search for a different political forum than the parliamentary one. They addressed popular meetings and rallies in the countryside. They organized political unions, local organizations modelled after similar organizations in England at the time. These bodies met regularly to discuss politics, pass motions, take positions rather than leaving it all to the representatives elected every few years. Such increasing reliance on popular rather than parliamentary forums drove the radicals' analysis farther than it had been. They began to see that tinkering with the legislature would not suffice to change the lives of working farmers. A more thorough-going program would be required.

Events in England at the time also created division among the Reformers. The Reform Bill of 1832 was the height of achievement for the English Reform movement. Mackenzie, who had been in England at the time of passage and had observed the aftermath, concluded that little in reality had been accomplished. His hopes and those of others for reform in Canada through reform in England were greatly diminished. Actions by the Colonial Office during the same period also reduced his expectations. Mackenzie had carried a massive petition of grievances to England; at first it was attentively received by the Colonial Office which even seemed to accept the Reformers' recommendations; but then the Colonial Office reversed itself in favour of the Tories in Upper Canada. The result was a loss of confidence in the imperial connection as a source of any kind of improvement.

The moderate Reformers kept plugging along, refining their notion of responsible government. But the more radical figures drew the conclusion that, if England could not be relied on, the people of Upper Canada would have to rely on themselves. They were moving toward a conviction of the necessity for self-government and independence.

The moderate Reformers found the views of Mackenzie and his colleagues becoming too radical for them, but to some extent the expulsions helped to paper over the developing rifts. It was difficult for the moderates to criticize Mackenzie severely without seeming to ally themselves with the Tory elements which kept expelling him from the Assembly. In fact, owing to the obvious justness of his cause and the popular support he continued to receive, they had no choice but to support him. Peter Perry, a staunch and respectable Reformer said that "no two persons disapproved more at times of Mr. Mackenzie's occasional violence than Mr. Bidwell and himself, but they both supported him on principle, seeing that the people had been insulted in his person." This proved to be a tenuous basis for unity.

February of 1834 saw the formation of what amounted to a radical political party in York county. Rolph, Bidwell and Baldwin did not join it. Parallel organizations were established in other counties. Basically, they stood for constitutional reform that amounted to self-government. The underlying issue between Radicals and Reformers had become that of independence versus (mere) reform. It was not, however, stated this way and any such imputations were denied by the Radicals. The constituency of the Radicals increasingly diverged from that of the Reformers. The

Reformers appealed to professionals, commercial figures and wealthier farmers. The Radicals appealed to the smaller farmers, labourers, artisans and some manufacturers.

The election of 1834 saw the defeat of the Tories and a victory for the combined forces of opposition, but the split between Reformers and Radicals persisted. The organization of Radicals continued at a general meeting in Toronto in December, 1834, which founded the Canadian Alliance. This was a popular political organization which intended to support candidates for election, but was more than another party. Mackenzie was its corresponding secretary. The demands for constitutional reform again came near to a call for independence, but again the issue itself was skirted. The meeting simply opposed "all undue interference by the Home government" in the "domestic affairs of the Colonists." Egerton Ryerson, whom Mackenzie had already labelled the Benedict Arnold of Reform, said in *The Christian Guardian* that the Alliance had abolished "Colonial connexion and monarchy" in favour of "Republican independence and democracy."

The emerging issue was being stated more clearly by the reactionaries than by the Radicals. For the Radicals, the independence issue was both too obvious and not obvious enough. It was too obvious because fifty years after the American Revolution, questions of self-government and opposition to imperial oppressiveness inevitably raised the spectre of another war of independence. It was not necessary to be very explicit on the topic of independence in a British North American colony in 1837. People speedily caught the drift.

On the other hand, it was extremely difficult to make the issue of independence simple and clear, far more difficult than had been the case half a century earlier. The situation in Upper Canada differed from that in the Thirteen Colonies. There independence had meant revolution against an oppressive mother country; no third parties were involved. But ever since that time, the British authorities in Canada had sought effectively to tie any disaffection from Britain to affection for the United States. Anti-British meant pro-American. Independence therefore meant "treason," "disloyalty" and "American" — three words treated as virtual synonyms: treason against the mother country in the favour and possibly the pay of another, hostile nation — the United States. It was a subtle, treacherous slope for political discussion. The Radicals attempted to activate the terminology of "patriotism": loyalty to Canada, not disloyalty to England. But, though independence from England had clearly become their cause, they had not yet clearly resolved their attitude toward the United States. Consequently they tended to skirt the issue, leaving room for the Tories to raise it in the most venomous way possible.

For the government side had no such reluctance about using the issue. They brought it to a head in the election of 1836. Under the active leadership of the new lieutenant governor, Sir Francis Bond Head, the Tories insisted that the election was a choice between loyalty or independence, and that independence meant nothing less than joining the United States. In the process they lumped Reformers and Radical reformers together indistinguishably. Bond Head announced that *he* was the Reformer as opposed to the revolutionaries of the opposition. The Tories in this way managed to recruit and unite on their side Orangemen, Roman Catholics, and Methodists all together.

The tactic worked. The moderate Reformers were not able to escape the taint of the Radicals. The Radicals were not able to successfully deny revolutionary intentions; nor were they willing to foursquare proclaim such goals. Many Radicals had not yet moved quite that far; others feared popular reaction. The Tories swept to victory. Mackenzie was defeated in an election for the only time in his life. The strife-filled election of 1836 represented the polarization of political life in Upper Canada over the issue of independence versus colonial status. For the Radical Reformers or at least for many of them it became clear that they could not carry their struggle farther in the context of colonial elections and colonial parliaments. They were too susceptible to distortion, manipulation and oversimplification by the government forces. They would have to refine their position and find other means of pursuing and achieving their goals. To raise the issue of independence in a colonial election had merely proven the impossibility of debating, much less resolving, that issue in such a context.

By the summer of 1837 Mackenzie was organizing for revolutionary war. For allies he turned away from the Reformers and concentrated on members of the Radical Reform group; Samuel Lount, a blacksmith from Holland Landing; Peter Matthews, a farmer from a Loyalist family; Dr. Charles Duncombe from the London district; Anthony van Egmond, the 67-year old Dutch cavalry colonel and landowner in Huron county, grandson of the liberator of the Dutch Netherlands, who had himself commanded cavalry under Napoleon in the heyday of the export of the French Revolution, and then fought against Napoleon at Waterloo.

Of the Reformers, only Dr. T. D. Morrison and Rolph came with Mackenzie, and both were very uncertain allies in the developments to come. Rolph, in particular, played a role full of ambiguity. Baldwin and Bidwell both ceased their political activities following the election, though Baldwin was to return. The great uprising of 1837 was a kind of continuation of the election of 1836; it pitted the Tories, led by Bond Head and the Compact stalwarts, against the Radicals, led by Mackenzie. The issue of 1837 was again independence, but with two differences: the battleground was a literal one, not merely an election; and this time the issue itself was not skirted by the Radicals.

Independence

That the issue of the Revolution of 1837 was independence is attested by a remarkable series of documents from the summer, fall and winter of that year.

On July 31, a "Declaration" was adopted by the Radical Reformers of Toronto. It was addressed to their fellows throughout the province. Two days later Mackenzie published it. Subsequently it was referred to by the Radicals themselves as the "Declaration of Independence." It began:

> The time has arrived, after nearly half a century's forbearance under increasing and aggravated misrule, when the duty we owe our country and posterity requires from us the assertion of our rights and the redress of our wrongs.
>
> Government is founded on the authority, and is instituted for the benefit, of a people; when, therefore, any Government long and systematically ceases to answer the great ends of its foundation, the people have a natural right given them by their Creator to seek after and establish such institutions as will yield the greatest quantity of

happiness to the greatest number.

Our forbearance heretofore has only been rewarded with an aggravation of our grievances; and our past inattention to our rights has been ungenerously and unjustly urged as evidence of the surrender of them. We have now to choose on the one hand between submission to the same blighting policy as has desolated Ireland, and, on the other hand, the patriotic achievement of cheap, honest, and responsible government.

The right was conceded to the present United States, at the close of a successful revolution, to form a constitution for themselves; and the loyalists with their descendants and others, now peopling this portion of America, are entitled to the same liberty without the shedding of blood—more they do not ask; less they ought not to have. But, while the revolution of the former has been rewarded with a consecutive prosperity unexampled in the history of the world, the loyal valor of the latter alone remains amidst the blight of misgovernment to tell them what they might have been as the not less valiant sons of American independence.

After an enumeration of the history of injustice in Upper Canada, the Declaration concluded:

> We earnestly recommend to our fellow citizens that they exert themselves to organize political associations; that public meetings be held throughout the Province; and that a convention of delegates be elected, and assembled at Toronto, to take into consideration the political condition of Upper Canada, with authority to its members to appoint commissioners to meet others to be named on behalf of Lower Canada and any of the other colonies, armed with suitable powers as a Congress, to seek an effectual remedy for the grievances of the colonists.

This call echoed that for the Continental Congress held a half century previously and which had produced the American Declaration of Independence.

The same mood was expressed in other literary forms. In August, the *St. Thomas Liberal* rhymed:

"Up then! for Liberty—for Right,
  Strike home! the tyrants falter;
Be firm — be brave, let all unite,
  And despots' schemes must alter.
Our King — our Government and laws,
  While just, we aye shall love them,

> But Freedom's Heaven-born, holier cause
> We hold supreme above them."

That same month the words "Liberty or Death" appeared on a flag at a rally at Lloydtown.

Mackenzie prepared a draft constitution for the soon-to-be independent "State of Upper Canada." It was to be presented to the "congress" called for in the Declaration. He modelled it, of course, on the American constitution, and published it in his newspaper, now called *The Constitution*, on November 15. It began:

> Whereas the solemn covenant made with the people of Upper and Lower Canada, and recorded in the statute book of the United Kingdom of Great Britain and Ireland, as the thirty-first chapter of the Acts passed in the thirty-first year of the reign of King George III., hath been continually violated by the British Government, and our rights usurped; *And Whereas* our humble petitions, addresses, protests, and remonstrances against this injurious interference have been made in vain — We, the people of the State of Upper Canada, acknowledging with gratitude the grace and beneficence of God, in permitting us to make choice of our form of Government, and in order to establish justice, ensure domestic tranquillity, provide for the common defence, promote the general welfare, and secure the blessings of civil and religious liberty to ourselves and our posterity, do establish this Constitution.

The first article established the separation of religion and state. ("The legislature shall make no law respecting the establishment of religion . . . .") It continued for 81 articles.

The most eloquent statement to come out of the Revolution of 1837, though, is an unsigned handbill that was distributed in the countryside outside Toronto during the ten days before the attack on the city. It was written by Mackenzie and stands as perhaps the most passionate appeal for national independence in Canadian history:

> INDEPENDENCE!
> *There have been Nineteen Strikes for Independence from European Tyranny, on the Continent of America. They were all successful! The Tories, therefore, by helping us will help themselves.*
> The nations are fallen, and thou still art young,
> The sun is but rising when others have set;

And though Slavery's cloud o'er thy morning hath hung,
The full tide of Freedom shall beam round thee yet.

Brave Canadians! God has put into the bold and honest hearts of our brethren in Lower Canada to revolt — not against "lawful" but against "unlawful authority." The law says we shall not be taxed without our consent by the voices of the men of our choice; but a wicked and tyrannical government has trampled upon that law, robbed the exchequer, divided the plunder, and declared, that, regardless of justice, they will continue to roll their splendid carriages, and riot in their palaces, at our expense; that we are poor, spiritless, ignorant peasants, who were born to toil for our betters. But the peasants are beginning to open their eyes and to feel their strength; too long have they been hoodwinked by Baal's priests — by hired and tampered-with preachers, wolves in sheep's clothing, who take the wages of sin, and do the work of iniquity, "each one looking to his gain in his quarter."

Canadians! Do you love freedom? I know you do. Do you hate oppression? Who dare deny it? Do you wish perpetual peace, and a government founded upon the eternal heaven-born principle of the Lord Jesus Christ — a government bound to enforce the law to do to each other as you wish to be done by? Then buckle on your armor, and put down the villains who oppress and enslave our country — put them down in the name of that God who goes forth with the armies of his people, and whose Bible shows that it is by the same human means whereby you put to death thieves and murderers, and imprison and banish wicked individuals, that you must put down, in the strength of the Almighty, those governments which, like these bad individuals, trample on the law, and destroy its usefulness. You give a bounty for wolves' scalps. Why? Because wolves harass you. The bounty you must pay for freedom (blessed word!) is to give the strength of your arms to put down tyranny at Toronto. One short hour will deliver our country from the oppressor; and freedom in religion, peace, and tranquillity, equal laws, and an improved country will be the prize. We contend, that in all laws made, or to be made, every person shall be bound alike — neither should any tenure, estate, charter, degree, birth, or place, confer any exemption from the ordinary course of legal proceedings and responsibilities whereunto others are subjected.

Canadians! God has shown that he is with our brethren, for he has given them the encouragement of success. Captains, Colonels, Volunteers, Artillerymen, Privates, the base, the vile hirelings of our unlawful oppressors, have already bit the dust in hundreds in Lower Canada; and although the Roman Catholic and Episcopal Bishops

INDEPENDENCE!

There have been Nineteen Strikes for Independence from European Tyranny, on the Continent of America. They were all successful! The Tories, therefore, by helping us will help themselves.

The nations are fallen, and thou still art young,
Thy sun is but rising when others have set;
And tho' Slavery's cloud o'er thy morning hath hung,
The full tide of Freedom shall beam round thee yet.

BRAVE CANADIANS! God has put into the bold and honest hearts of our brethren in Lower Canada to revolt—not against "lawful" but against "unlawful authority." The law says we shall not be taxed without our consent by the voices of the men of our choice, but a wicked and tyrannical government has trampled upon that law—robbed the exchequer—divided the plunder—and declared that, regardless of justice they will continue to roll their splendid carriages, and riot in their palaces, at our expense—that we are poor spiritless ignorant peasants, who were born to toil for our betters. But the peasants are beginning to open their eyes and to feel their strength—too long have they been hoodwinked by Baal's priests—by hired and tampered with preachers, wolves in sheep's clothing, who take the wages of sin, and do the work of iniquity, "each one looking to his gain in his quarter."

Canadians! Do you love freedom? I know you do. Do you hate oppression? Who dare deny it? Do you wish perpetual peace, and a government founded upon the eternal heaven-born principle of the Lord Jesus Christ—a government bound to enforce the law to do to each other as you would be done by? Then buckle on your armour, and put down the villains who oppress and enslave our country—put them down in the name of that God who goes forth with the armies of his people, and whose bible shows us that it is by the same human means whereby you put to death thieves and murderers, and imprison and banish wicked individuals, that you must put down, in the strength of the Almighty, those governments which, like these bad individuals, trample on the law, and destroy its usefulness. You give a bounty for wolves' scalps. Why? because wolves harrass you. The bounty you must pay for freedom (blessed word) is to give the strength of your arms to put down tyranny at Toronto. One short hour will deliver our country from the oppressor; and freedom in religion, peace and tranquillity, equal laws and an improved country will be the prize. We contend, that in all laws made, or to be made, every person shall be bound alike—neither should any tenure, estate, charter, degree, birth or place, confer any exemption from the ordinary course of legal proceedings and responsibilities whereunto others are subjected.

Canadians! God has shown that he is with our brethren, for he has given them the encouragement of success. Captains, Colonels, Volunteers, Artillerymen, Privates, the base, the vile hirelings of our unlawful oppressors have already bit the dust in hundreds in Lower Canada; and altho' the Roman Catholic and Episcopal Bishops and Archdeacons, are bribed by large sums of money to instruct their flocks that they should be obedient to a government which defies the law, and is therefore unlawful, and ought to be put down, yet God has opened the eyes of the people to the wickedness of these reverend sinners, so that they hold them in derision, just as God's prophet Elijah did the priests of Baal of old and their sacrifices. Is there any one afraid to go to fight for freedom, let him remember, that

God sees with equal eye, as Lord of all,
A Hero perish, or a Sparrow fall:

That the power that protected ourselves and our forefathers in the deserts of Canada—that preserved from the Cholera those whom He would—that brought us safely to this continent through the dangers of the Atlantic waves—aye, and who has watched over us from infancy to manhood, will be in the midst of us in the day of our struggle for our liberties, and for Governors of our free choice, who would not dare to trample on the laws they had sworn to maintain. In the present struggle, we may be sure, that if we do not rise and put down Head and his lawless myrmidons, they will gather all the rogues and villains in the Country together—arm them—and then deliver our farms, our families, and our country to their brutality—to that it has come, we must put them down, or they will utterly destroy this country. If we move now, as one man, to crush the tyrant's power, to establish free institutions founded on God's law, we will prosper, for He who commands the winds and waves will be with us—but if we are cowardly and mean-spirited, a woeful and a dark day is surely before us.

Canadians! The struggle will be of short duration in Lower Canada, for the people are united as one man. Out of Montreal and Quebec, they are as 100 to 1—here we reformers are as 10 to 1—and if we rise with one consent to overthrow despotism, we will make quick work of it.

Mark all those who join our enemies—act as spies for them—fight for them—or aid them—these men's properties shall pay the expense of the struggle—they are traitors to Canadian Freedom, and as such we will deal with them.

Canadians! It is the design of the Friends of Liberty to give several hundred acres to every Volunteer—to root up the unlawful Canada Company, and give FREE DEEDS to all settlers who live on their lands—to give free gifts of the Clergy Reserve lots, to good citizens who have settled on them—and the like to settlers on Church of England Glebe Lots, so that the yeomanry may feel independent, and be able to improve the country, instead of sending the fruit of their labour to foreign lands. The 57 Rectories will be at once given to the people, and all public lands used for Education, Internal Improvements, and the public good. £100,000 drawn from us in payment of the salaries of bad men in office, will be reduced to one quarter, or much less, and the remainder will go to improve bad roads and to "make crooked paths straight;" law will be ten times more cheap and easy—the bickerings of priests will cease with the funds that keeps them up—and men of wealth and property from other lands will soon raise our farms to four times their present value. We have given Head and his employers a trial of 45 years—five years longer than the Israelites were detained in the wilderness. The promised land is now before us—up then and take it—but set not the torch to one house in Toronto, unless we are fired at from the houses, in which case self-preservation will teach us to put down those who would murder us when up in the defence of the laws. There are some rich men now, as there were in Christ's time, who would go with us in prosperity, but who will skulk in the rear, because of their large possessions—mark them! They are those who in after years will seek to corrupt our people, and change free institutions into an aristocracy of wealth, to grind the poor, and make laws to fetter their energies.

Mark my words Canadians!

The struggle is begun—it might end in freedom—but timidity, cowardice, or tampering on our part, will only delay its close. We cannot be reconciled to Britain—we have humbled ourselves to the Pharoah of England, to the Ministers, and great people, and they will neither rule us justly nor let us go—we are determined never to rest until independence is ours—the prize is a splended one A country larger than France or England natural resources equal to our most boundless wishes—a government of equal laws—religion pure and undefiled—perpetual peace—education to all—millions of acres of lands for revenue—freedom from British tribute—free trade with all the world—but stop—I never could enumerate all the blessings attendant on independence!

Up then, brave Canadians! Get ready your rifles, and make short work of it; a connection with England would involve us in all her wars, undertaken for her own advantage, never for ours; with governors from England, we will have bribery at elections, corruption, villainy and perpetual discord in every township, but Independence would give us the means of enjoying many blessings. Our enemies in Toronto are in terror and dismay—they know their wickedness and dread our vengeance. Fourteen armed men were sent out at the dead hour of night, by the traitor Gurnett, to drag to a felon's cell, the sons of our worthy and noble minded brother departed, Joseph Sheppard, on a simple and frivolous charge of trespass, brought by a tory fool; and though it ended in smoke, it shewed too evidently Head's feelings. Is there to be an end of these things? Aye, and now's the day and the hour! Woe be to those who oppose us, for "In God is our trust."

and Archdeacons are bribed by large sums of money to instruct their flocks that they should be obedient to a government which defies the law, and is therefore unlawful, and ought to be put down; yet God has opened the eyes of the people to the wickedness of these reverend sinners, so that they hold them in derision, just as God's prophet Elijah did the priests of Baal of old and their sacrifices. Is there any one afraid to go to fight for freedom, let him remember, that

God sees with equal eye, as Lord of all,
A hero perish, or a sparrow fall:

That the power that protected ourselves and our forefathers in the deserts of Canada—that preserved from the cholera those whom he would — that brought us safely to this continent through the dangers of the Atlantic waves — aye, and who has watched over us from infancy to manhood, will be in the midst of us in the day of our struggle for our liberties, and for governors of our free choice, who would not dare to trample on the laws they had sworn to maintain. In the present struggle, we may be sure, that if we do not rise and put down Head and his lawless myrmidons, they will gather all the rogues and villains in the country together — arm them — and then deliver our farms, our families, and our country to their brutality. To that it has come, we must put them down, or they will utterly destroy this country. If we move now, as one man, to crush the tyrant's power, to establish free institutions founded on God's law, we will prosper, for He who commands the winds and waves will be with us; but if we are cowardly and mean-spirited, a woeful and a dark day is surely before us.

Canadians! The struggle will be of short duration in Lower Canada, for the people are united as one man. Out of Montreal and Quebec, they are as one hundred to one — here we Reformers are as ten to one; and if we rise with one consent to overthrow despotism, we will make quick work of it.

Mark all those who join our enemies, act as spies for them, fight for them, or aid them; these men's properties shall pay the expense of the struggle; they are traitors to Canadian freedom, and as such we will deal with them.

Canadians! It is the design of the friends of liberty to give several hundred acres to every volunteer — to root up the unlawful Canada Company, and give *free deeds* to all settlers who live on their lands; to give free gifts of the Clergy Reserve lots, to good citizens who have settled on them; and the like to settlers on Church of England Glebe lots, so that the yeomanry may feel independent, and be able to improve the country, instead of sending the fruit of their labor to foreign lands. The fifty-seven Rectories will be at once given to the people, and all public lands used for education, internal improvements, and the public good. £100,000, drawn from us in payment of the salaries of bad men in office, will be reduced to one quarter, or much less, and the remainder will go to improve bad roads and to "make crooked paths straight;" law will be ten times more cheap and easy — the bickerings of priests will cease with the funds that keep them up — and men of wealth and property from other lands will soon raise our farms to four times their present value. We have given Head and his employers a trial of forty-five years — five years longer than the Israelites were detained in the wilderness. The promised land is now before us — up then and take it — but set not the torch to one house in Toronto, unless we are fired at from the houses, in which case self-preservation will teach us to put down those who would murder us when up in the defence of the laws. There are some rich men now, as there were in Christ's time, who would go with us in prosperity, but who will skulk in the rear, because of their large possessions — mark them! They are those who in after years will seek to corrupt our people, and change free institutions into an aristocracy of wealth, to grind the poor, and make laws to fetter their energies.

Mark my words, Canadians! The struggle is begun — it might end in freedom; but timidity, cowardice, or tampering on our part, will only delay its close. We cannot be reconciled to Britain — we have humbled ourselves to the Pharaoh of England, to the Ministers and great people, and they will neither rule us justly nor let us go; we are determined never to rest until independence is ours — the prize is a splendid one. A country larger than France or England, natural resources equal to our most boundless wishes; a government of equal laws; religion pure and undefiled; perpetual peace; education to all; millions of acres of lands for revenue; freedom from British tribute; free trade with all the world — but stop — I never could enumerate all the blessings attendant on independence!

Up then, brave Canadians! Get ready your rifles, and make short work of it; a connection with England would involve us in all her wars, undertaken for her own advantage, never for ours; with governors from England, we will have bribery at elections, corruption, villainy, and perpetual discord in every township, but independence would give us the means of enjoying many blessings. Our enemies in Toronto are in terror and dismay; they know their wickedness and dread our vengeance. Fourteen armed men were sent out at the dead hour of night, by the traitor Gurnett, to drag to a felon's cell the sons of our worthy and noble-minded brother departed, Joseph Sheppard, on a simple and frivolous charge of trespass, brought by a Tory fool; and though it ended in smoke, it showed too evidently Head's feelings. Is there to be an end of these things? Aye, and now's the day and the hour! Woe be to those who oppose us, for "In God is our trust."

One further independence proclamation was issued: from Navy Island in the Niagara River, where Mackenzie and others took refuge following the defeat at Montgomery's Tavern. Mackenzie signed the statement as "Chairman pro. tem. of the Provisional Government of the State of Upper Canada." It attempted to rally his followers within the country, and included an explanation for the loss in Toronto. But, of course, it profoundly lacks the optimism and confidence of the declarations, proclamations and appeals issued before the fighting began.

Responsible Government: The "Epilogue" to 1837?

The Radical Reformer independence forces waged revolutionary war for over a year, first from within Upper Canada, then from points along the American border. They were decimated; they were defeated militarily and their leadership was executed, imprisoned, or exiled. At the end, the British were in firm command of their possession and the Tories in total control locally.

Yet less than three years later, in the election of 1841, the old Reform forces mounted an election campaign so vigorous it made even the election of 1836 pale. With the cries of "rebellion" and "treason" so recent, the Reformers must have felt very confident to take on the loyal Tory reactionaries so soon. It was, in fact, possible only because they had managed to keep their hands very clean during the period of the uprising. They sat it out, and made certain they were seen sitting it out.

During and after the revolt, the Tories and the Compact attempted to tar the Reformers with a revolutionary brush, as they had during the election of 1836, but the Reformers mounted a counter-campaign emphasizing their loyalty and respectability. In May 1838, Egerton Ryerson wrote a letter to a Kingston newspaper in which he criticized the forced exile of Reform mainstay, Marshall Bidwell, by the government as unjust; then he went on to defend the Reform group against charges of complicity in the uprising. By the beginning of July the Reformers had founded a new newspaper in Toronto, *The Examiner*, to defend their conduct and press their cause. Its editor was Francis Hincks, a recent arrival and very close associate of the Baldwins. The Baldwins themselves met with Lord Durham in the summer of 1838. Durham had been sent out by the British government to deal with the aftermath of the rebellions in Upper and Lower Canada and recommend changes in the government of the colonies. In that meeting and in a subsequent letter, the Baldwins proposed responsible government as the solution to the problems of Upper Canada and the one sure means of eliminating colonial dissatisfaction with the British connection.

From the beginning, the notion of responsible government had been part of the Reform position. As early as 1828, the elder Baldwin had written to the Duke of Wellington, then British Prime Minister, about the desirability of "a provincial Ministry (if I may be allowed to use the term) responsible to the Provincial Parliament, and removable from office by His Majesty's representative at his pleasure and especially when they lose the confidence of the people as expressed by the voice of their representatives in the Assembly." Eight years later a committee of the (Reform) House of Assembly spoke of "the necessity of having a responsible Government."

This continuing call for responsible government was more than anything an attack on the privileged role of the Family Compact in the government of the colony. The Reformers maintained that the lieutenant governor should be obliged to select his Executive Council, in effect his cabinet, from the party elected to a majority in the Assembly, the only place where the voters had made their will known. This would make the highest positions in government accessible to members of the Reform group, such as the Baldwins, and not merely to the Compact. To buttress their case the Reformers never failed to claim that such a system would merely install in Canada a method which already operated in the government of England itself, where the King was required to call on the majority leader to be his Prime Minister.

But the contradiction between the two political situations is almost too obvious to be pointed out. England was a sovereign nation, independent in the conduct of all its affairs. Since the monarch was a politically neutral figure, his "selection" of a ministry was a formality. But Upper Canada was not a sovereign nation; it was a colony. The lieutenant governor, the "King's representative", was the political appointee of the (extremely potent) *government* of England, not of its figurehead king. In such a colony, dependent on a foreign government, what sense other than outright contradiction could be made of a government "responsible" to the local electorate?

This absurdity was not lost on anyone except the proponents of responsible government themselves. The British saw it. A commission appointed by the British government in 1836 reported that the concept of responsible government meant the functions of the governor:

> would in reality be divided among such Gentlemen as from time to time might be carried into the Council by the pleasure of the Assembly. The course of Affairs would depend exclusively on the revolutions of party within the Province. All union with the Empire, through the Head of the Executive, would be at an end, the Country in short would be virtually independent; and if this be the object aimed at, it ought to be put in its proper light, and argued on its proper Grounds, and not disguised under the plausible demand of assimilating the Constitution of these Provinces to that of the Mother Country.

Mackenzie put the matter more tersely but made exactly the same point from exile in 1841, when he wrote, "RESPONSIBLE GOVERNMENT!! — A fine thing to talk about, but it means independence of foreign control, so far as it has meaning."

But the British, having ridiculed the theory in principle, were more than willing to have a go at it in practice, so long as the practice bent the whole thing their way. Durham, who recommended a form of responsible government, introduced an extremely significant distinction. He allowed that he would indeed "place the internal government of the colony in the hands of the colonists themselves." That is, the government, or Ministry selected from the majority party in the legislature, would have control of "local matters." But he reserved for imperial control, "the constitution of the form of government — the regulation of foreign relations, and of trade with the mother country, the other British colonies, and foreign nations — and the disposal of public lands."

Durham's successor as governor in chief, Poulett Thomson, proceeded to carry this shilly-shallying into some form of practice. He had explicit instructions from his colonial secretary that the implementation of responsible government in a colony was an impossibility because the governor cannot serve two masters — a government at home in England, and one in the colony. Almost simultaneously, however, the Secretary advised him to feel free to shift his ministers, advisors, or whatever in and out of office in the interest of harmony with the elected representatives. Thomson went on to play these two conflicting tunes. On the one hand, he rejected any suggestion that would make the "power of the

Governor subordinate to that of a Council." On the other hand, he wanted "to govern the Colony in accordance with the wishes and feelings of the People," to appoint as his advisors and officials "men whose principles and feelings were in accordance with the majority" and "in all merely local matters . . . to administer the affairs of the colony in accordance with the wishes of the Legislature."

What it all meant was that access to the highest positions of government within the colonial context was to become available to those outside the Family Compact, as well as those within. The privileged position of the Compact was to be annulled. The ruling elite of the colony was to be expanded, mainly through the inclusion of the Reform forces. Within the parameters of "local matters" power would no longer be wielded only by the Compact. At the same time, those areas of policy which Durham had enumerated as imperial concerns would remain outside the realm of Canadian control. These were what most concerned the British anyway: trade, land disposal, overall political control. In fact, not much had changed in the division of power between imperial and Canadian forces; but the definition of who held those powers on the Canadian side had been expanded.

Yet even this division between internal and external was evidently false, and could not really survive the tests of reality. Each area inevitably impinges on the other. Potential conflicts were inevitable. The real assumption at the base of the British acceptance of responsible government in its modified form was that no Canadian government would act, even in its own "local" realm, in ways that were inimical to British interests. And this was a safe assumption at the time, since the forces that *were* hostile to British interests in Upper Canada — the independence forces — had been so thoroughly smashed during 1837-8. The "opposition" that remained — the Reform group — were totally in harmony with and subservient to imperial interests in the colony. They could be allowed to do what they wanted on the assumption that nothing they wanted would conflict with what the imperial government wanted. The independence movement had been obliterated; the Reform movement had stepped aside while that issue was being decided, then stepped back in to press its own, quite different, goals under the banner of responsible government.

By the summer of 1839 the Reformers were mounting a grand campaign for responsible government behind the cover of Durham's recommendations. They established "Durham Clubs" and held "Durham Meetings" throughout the colony. Egerton Ryerson joined the Reform party, as did former Compact figure, W. H. Merritt. Longtime Tory, Tiger Dunlop, was saying by 1841 of the Compact, "I will use every endeavour to crush it, as I would to destroy a wolf, or a noxious reptile." By the time of the election of 1841, the Reformers were rolling in full tilt in the name of responsible government, and ready to roll over the old Family Compact. It was as if 1837 had never happened.

As for the Compact, they were, in effect, disbanded by being expanded. They were too small and exclusive for the growing political economy of Upper Canada. The British lost nothing by such an expansion, though for the Compact it amounted to virtual extinction as a social and political entity. Robinson and Hagerman were pensioned off as judges. Strachan was put out to ecclesiastical pasture and spent most of his time on religious matters. Merritt, as mentioned, went right over to the Reformers. It was a dignified burial for the Family Compact.

It has become a myth of Canadian history that the uprisings of 1837-8 paved the way for, and made possible responsible government — that the goal that was not achieved by force was then achieved peacefully. But such was not the case. There were two conflicting movements within the political opposition in Upper Canada: one was an independence movement; the other was a movement for responsible government. These were represented by the Radical Reformers, and the Reformers. The independence forces made their move in 1837 and were decimated so totally that such a movement never appeared again in Canadian history with the strength and self-confidence shown at that time. The responsible government movement, a sort of "home rule" faction, sat out the independence wars and then continued, into the 1840s, to press for and gain many of their objectives. It is possible that the proponents of responsible government were greatly aided by the fight of those who rose up for independence: it made the British move very quickly to improve their position in the colony. But the reverse does not apply: the accomplishment of responsible government in no way represented the achievement of the goals of the fighters of 1837. The upshot of this argument must be, of course, that Canada has never yet gained independence.*

* The strength of the myth about 1837 and responsible government has been reflected in many of the reviews of the play. Again and again reviewers comment that the uprising in the play was prelude to the achievement of responsible government. Yet nowhere in the play is this implied. Independence is the goal in the play, and overthrow of imperial control. The play ends tragically, with a hanging, and the implication that the goal of the revolt — independence — has still to be won, in our own time. Responsible government is in fact not a bad definition of the political situation in Canada even now, *vis-a-vis* the current imperial power, the U.S.A. It certainly seems more appropriate than the image of two independent nations. President Nixon of the U.S. actually told Prime Minister Trudeau, during Trudeau's visit to Washington in 1971, that he — Nixon — was in favour of Canada *becoming* independent.

Chapter 3

Mackenzie: The people's politician

Writing to a friend from exile in the United States, years after the defeat of his cause in 1837, Mackenzie spoke of his fateful entry into Upper Canadian politics in 1824. He was referring to the Family Compact and said "At nine-and-twenty I might have united with them, but chose rather to join the oppressed, nor have I ever regretted that choice, or wavered from this object of my early pursuit."

This is an accurate statement of the essence of Mackenzie's public career. He was a popular leader. His constituency was "the people" in the sense that that term had been used since the French Revolution: the mass of the population who did the bulk of the work on the land and in the urban centres, and who had almost no direct role in the making of political and economic decisions. This meant above all those who worked the land, the "yeomen" as they were often called. What marks Mackenzie's historical role is his responsibility to this constituency, and their loyalty to him from the beginning until the end.

Before his first appearance on Upper Canada's public stage, Mackenzie's career had been a typical one. He left Scotland for Canada in 1820, at the age of 25. He came from the family of a destitute weaver. He had an education, though little money. In Canada he worked first as an accountant on the Lachine Canal. Then he entered a business partnership as a shopkeeper selling books and drugs in York and in the town of Dundas. Next he moved to Queenstown and opened a general store of his own. It was a characteristic Scots-Canadian tale: emigration from Scotland, hard work, saving, beginning in business on one's own, gaining economically and perhaps eventually moving into politics. But when Mackenzie entered politics, the pattern changed.

It was predictable that he would become a Reformer. Access to the ruling group was not available to him and those like him. But he differed from most of the other Reformers whose political stance reflected their own self-interest. As merchants, moderately wealthy landowners, professionals, nascent industrialists, they found themselves hampered in their own advancement by government policies. So they became the political opposition, and pressed for reform. They enlisted the mass of the people in support of their cause because they needed that support politically and because, as well, the people would indeed have benefitted from many of the changes they advocated. (Self-interest was the motive of the Radical Reformers as well as moderates. Van Egmond, who took command at the battle of Toronto, held thousands of acres in the Huron Tract which was failing to develop under current policies. Montgomery the innkeeper, Doel the brewer, Fletcher the farmer all stood to gain from new, more self-centred economic policies. Their often genuine concern for others contained a healthy mix of self-interest.)

Mackenzie however virtually abandoned his own economic interests on the day he entered the public forum with his newspaper. He left a promising if modest career in business to do so, and never again pursued a commercial career of any consequence. In this respect it is interesting to compare him with Papineau, the leader of the movement of 1837-8 in French Canada. Papineau came from the land-owning upper class of French Canadian society. He took up the leadership of the Reform cause in Quebec but at the same time always remained committed to his own class interests. "I am a great reformer as regards political change," he said, "but a great conservative as regards the preservation of the sacred right of property." Consequently he was never as totally identified with the mass of the working people as was Mackenzie. He provided leadership in the struggle against the British and the Chateau Clique in Quebec, but always from his own class position outside that of the mass of the Quebec farming population. This adherence to his social roots inevitably made his views less radical and himself less a popular spokesman than was Mackenzie in Upper Canada. It fell to others in Quebec to take up more radical positions and lead the struggle in its advanced stages.

Papineau opposed armed uprising even as it was taking place, and subsequently withdrew from the struggle entirely, though he was nevertheless exiled to the U.S. under sentence of death if he returned.

The revolutionary movement of 1837-8 in Lower Canada was more widespread and more effective in its political and military expression than that in Upper Canada. Indeed in considerable degree the actions of the French Canadians inspired and propelled the Upper Canadians. Yet of the two leaders, Mackenzie was more totally committed to service of the people. He was always in the forefront of political struggle, and when the context shifted from debate to battle, Mackenzie, unlike Papineau, was in the thick of the fighting. Lower Canada had the greater revolutionary movement, but Upper Canada had perhaps the greater leader.

The people he served repaid Mackenzie's constancy. He was elected and re-elected by the voters of York County from the first time he offered himself in 1828. When the Tory majority expelled him in 1832 he was re-elected by 119 to 1, and a grand parade and celebration took place. After each of his four subsequent expulsions by the Assembly he was returned by the voters. Eventually, to show their disgust with the government and their support of Mackenzie, they stormed and invaded the legislative chamber itself. The only election Mackenzie lost came in the Bond Head deluge of 1836 when he publicly admitted his campaign had been lethargic as he had already lost faith in the effectiveness of electoral politics. After the defeat at Montgomery's Tavern a price of 5,000 pounds was put on Mackenzie. During his escape to the American border he was seen by many people, yet not a single one of them reported him or tried to claim the reward. When he returned to Upper Canada in 1850, following thirteen years of political exile and disgrace, he stood for the first vacant seat in the legislature and won it against the redoubtable George Brown of *The Globe*. He held that seat until he retired from it. He also took up the publication of another newspaper, continuing to serve his constituency, "the oppressed", through the two main roles he had played for so long: journalist and politician.

Journalist

In the aftermath of the Revolution of 1837, an observer unsympathetic to Mackenzie's cause wrote, "The misguided individuals in the late disturbances, on being questioned upon the subject, unreservedly admitted, that until reading Mackenzie's flagitious and slanderous newspaper, they were happy, contented, and loyal subjects." The statement is certainly false, but it pays tribute to the vast influence of Mackenzie's political journalism.

Journalism was the popular culture and popular education of the time. Upper Canadians read newspapers far more than they read books. Anna Jameson, the British traveller, called newspapers "the principle medium of knowledge and communication" in Upper Canada. Beyond that, she found the newspaper offices in Toronto to be "absolutely the only place of assembly or amusement, except the taverns and low drinking-houses". Newspapers were thick with print. People passed them around, or gathered in groups to hear them read. In his own paper Mackenzie carried, in addition to local and provincial news, summaries of world events, reviews of the previous Sunday's sermons in various churches (Mackenzie was favourable to all religions but frowned on theatre), accounts of scientific developments and inventions, descriptions of journeys around the colony and abroad and much more.

In 1824, in the first issue of his *Colonial Advocate,* Mackenzie declared, "it is the system we condemn, and few numbers shall go forth until we make ourselves distinctly understood on this head." At the time he was the only journalistic voice for reform in the colony. The other papers spoke for the rulers of Upper Canada and served to reinforce their hegemony by assuring people that those in power were uniquely qualified to be there; that it would be a disaster if the less educated, less pedigreed members of the population tried to rule themselves. As Mackenzie explained, "it is the wisdom of the aristocracy to try and make the people fearful of themselves." The Tories harped on their own breeding and education; they wrote of the horrifying effects of "republicanism" in the United States where any greedy uneducated fool or criminal could gain political power — and did.

Through his own newspaper, Mackenzie put himself at the service of those farmers whom the Tory press denigrated as the "herd of the swine of Yonge St." "We have made our election" he wrote in that first issue, "it is to have only one patron and that patron is the People." To the Tory derogration of working farmers, derogation intended to make people doubt their own abilities and rely on the Upper Canadian "aristocracy," Mackenzie wrote:

> On you alone, farmers, does Canada rely. You are the sole depositories of civil and religious liberty. If you look to the provincial executives, they are foreigners, having an interest differing widely from yours, and are hardly able, even if we grant that they have the will, to reconcile jarring interests arising from a crooked colonial policy; but possessing patronage and power, having in their gifts, offices and emoluments, honours and dignities, lands and heritages; influence immense, if we consider the size of the country.
>
> To yourselves, therefore, Farmers, in the hour of trial, must you look for aid. The eyes of the whole Colonies, and of America, are fixed on you. You are the only true nobility that this country can boast of.

To claims that "the people" were incapable of the complexities of government, he charged: "It is roads and bridges, and schools, and salaries, and militia laws, and justice court laws, and such like that are to be considered, and is not a plain man fit to judge of such matters better than a person paid to mystify truth?" In answer to the pretensions of the Compact — the "aristocracy of the new world" — that their superiority gave them the right to rule, he asked:

> Have the Robinsons any thing to boast of in their Virginian descent? Is their boasted loyalty of a purer and more exalted rank than that of those who pursue in this colony a less odious line of conduct? — What was their origin and ancestry? — Where is the table of their line of descent? — Is it a secret in these parts that many, very many such Virginian nobles as the Robinsons assume themselves, were descended from mothers who came there to try their luck and were purchased by their sires with tobacco at prices according to the quality and soundness of the article? And is it from such a source that we are to expect the germ of liberty? Say rather is it not from such a source that we may look for the tyranny engendered, nursed and practised by those whose blood has been vitiated and syphilized by the accursed slavery of centuries . . . .

PROCLAMATION

BY WILLIAM LYON MACKENZIE,

Chairman pro. tem. of the Provincial Government of the State of Upper Canada.

INHABITANTS OF UPPER CANADA!

For nearly fifty years has our country languished under the blighting influence of military despots, strangers from Europe, ruling us, not according to laws of our choice, but by the capricious dictates of their arbitrary power.

They have taxed us at their pleasure, robbed our exchequer, and carried off the proceeds to other lands—they have bribed and corrupted ministers of the Gospel, with the wealth raised by our industry—they have, in place of religious liberty, given rectories and clergy reserves to a foreign priesthood, with spiritual power dangerous to our peace as a people—they have bestowed millions of our lands on a company of Europeans for a nominal consideration, and left them to fleece and impoverish our country—they have spurned our petitions, involved us in their wars, excited feelings of national and sectional animosity in counties, townships and neighbourhoods, and ruled us, as Ireland has been ruled, to the advantage of persons in other lands, and to the prostration of our energies as a people.

We are wearied of these oppressions, and resolved to throw off the yoke. Rise, Canadians, rise as one man, and the glorious object of our wishes is accomplished.

Our intentions have been clearly stated to the world in the Declaration of Independence, adopted at Toronto on the 31st of July last, printed in the Constitution, Correspondent and Advocate, and the Liberal, which important paper was drawn by Dr. John Rolph and myself, signed by the Central Committee, received the sanction of a large majority of the people of the Province, west of Port Hope and Cobourg, and is well known to be in accordance with the feelings and sentiments of nine tenths of the people of this state.

We have planted the Standard of Liberty in Canada, for the attainment of the following objects:

Perpetual Peace, founded on a government of equal rights to all, secured by a written constitution, sanctioned by yourselves in a convention to be called as early as circumstances will permit.

Civil and Religious Liberty, in its fullest extent, that in all laws made, or to be made, every person be bound alike—neither shall any tenure, estate, charter, birth, or place, confer any exemption from the ordinary course of legal proceedings and responsibilities whereunto others are subjected.

The abolition of hereditary honours, of the laws of entail and primogeniture, and of hosts of pensioners who devour our substance.

A Legislature composed of a Senate and Assembly chosen by the people.

An Executive to be composed of a Governor and other officers elected by the public voice.

A Judiciary to be chosen by the Governor and Senate, and composed of the most learned, honourable, and trustworthy of our citizens. The laws to be rendered cheap and expeditious.

A free trial by Jury—Sheriffs chosen by you, and not to hold office, as now, at the pleasure of our tyrants. The freedom of the Press. Alas for it, now! The free presses in the Canadas are trampled down by the hand of arditrary power.

The vote by ballot—free and peaceful township elections.

The people to elect their court of request commissioners and justices of the peace—and also their militia officers, in all cases whatsoever.

Freedom of Trade—every man to be allowed to buy at the cheapest market, and sell at the dearest.

No man to be compelled to give military service, unless it be his choice.

Ample funds to be reserved from the vast natural resources of our country to secure the blessings of Education to every citizen.

A frugal and economical government, in order that the people may be prosperous and free from difficulty.

An end forever to the wearisome prayers, supplications and mockeries attendant upon our connexion with the *Lordlings* of the Colonial Office, Downing St. London.

The opening of the St. Lawrence to the trade of the world, so that the largest ships might pass up to Lake Superior, and the distribution of the wild lands of the country to the industry, capital, skill, and enterprise of worthy men of all nations.

For the attainment of these important objects, the patriots now in arms under the standard of Liberty, on NAVY ISLAND, U. C. have established a Provisional Government of which the members are as follows, (with two other distingnished gentlemen, whose names there are powful reasons for withholding from public view,) viz:

WILLIAM L. MACKENZIE, Chairman, Pro Tem.

NELSON GORHAM, ADAM GRAHAM,
SAMUEL LOUNT, JOHN HAWK,
SILAS FLETCHER, JACOB RYMALL,
JESSE LLOYD, WILLIAM H. DOYLE,
THOMAS DARLING, A. G. W. G. VAN EGMOND.

CHARLES DUNCOMBE.

We have procured the important aid of Gen. Van Rensselaer of Albany, of Colonel Sutherland, Colonel Van Egmond, and other military men of experience; and the citizens of Buffalo, to their eternal honour be it ever remembered, have proved to us the enduring principles of the revolution of 1776, by supplying us with provisions, money, arms ammunition, artillery and volunteers; and vast numbers are floating to the standard under which, heaven willing, emancipation will be speedily won for a new and gallant nation, hitherto held in Egyptian thraldom by the aristocracy of England.

BRAVE CANADIANS! Hasten to join that standard, and to make common cause with your fellow citizens now in arms in the Home, London and Western Districts. The opportunity of the absence of the hired red coats of Europe is favourable to our emancipation. And short sighted is that man who does not now see that although his apathy may protract the contest, it must end in INDEPENDENCE, freedom from European thraldom for ever!

Until Independence is won, trade and industry will be dormant, houses and lands will be unsaleable, merchants will be embarrassed, and farmers and mechanicks harrassed and troubled; that point once gained, the prospect is fair and cheering, a long day of prosperity may be ours.

The reverses in the Home District were owing, 1st, to accident, which revealed our design to our tyrants, and prevented a surprise, and 2dly, to the want of artillery. 3500 men came and went, but we had not arms for one in twelve of them, nor could we procure them in the country.

Three hundred acres of the best of the publick lands will be freely bestowed upon any volunteer, who shall assist personally in bringing to a conclusion the glorious struggle in which our youthful country is now engaged against the enemies of freedom all the world over.

Ten millions of these lands, fair and fertile, will, I trust, be speedily at our disposal, with the other vast resources of a country more extensive and rich in natural treasures than the United Kingdom or Old France.

Citizens! Soldiers of Liberty! Friends of Equal Rights, let no man suffer in his property, person or estate—let us pass through Canada, not to retaliate on others for our estates ravaged, our friends in dungeons, our homes burnt, our wheat and barns burnt, and our horses and cattle carried off; but let us show the praiseworthy example of protecting the houses, the homes, and the families of those who are in arms against their country and against the liberties of this continent. We will disclaim and severely punish all aggressions upon private property, and consider those as our enemies who may burn or destroy the smallest hut in Canada, unless necessity compel any one to do so in any cause for self defence.

Whereas, at a time when the King and Parliament of Great Britain had solemnly agreed to redress the grievances of the people, Sir Francis Bond Head was sent out to this country with promises of conciliation and justice—and whereas, the said Head hath violated his oath of office as a governor, trampled upon every vestige of our rights and privileges, bribed and corrupted the local legislature, interfered with the freedom of elections, intimidated the freeholders, declared our country not entitled to the blessings of British freedom, prostrated openly the right of trial by jury, placed in office the most obsequious, treacherous and unworthy, of our population—and sought to rule Upper Canada by the mere force of his arbitrary power, imprisoned Dr. Morrison, Mr. Parker, and many others of our most respected citizens, banishing in the most cruel manner the highly respected speaker of our late House of Assembly, the Honorable Mr. Bidwell, and causing the expatriation of that universally beloved and well tried eminent patriot, Dr. John Rolph, because they had made common cause with our injured people, and setting a vast price on the heads of several, as if they were guilty persons—for which crimes and misdemeanors he is deserving of being put upon his trial before the country—I do therefore hereby offer a reward of FIVE HUNDRED POUNDS for his apprehension, so that he may be dealt with as may appertain to justice.

In Lower Canada, divine providence has blessed the arms of the Sons of Liberty—a whole people are there manfully struggling for that freedom without which property is but a phantom, and life scarce worth having a gift of. General Girard is at the head of 15,000 determined democrats.

The friends of freedom in Upper Canada, have continued to act in strong and regular concert with Mr. Papineau and the Lower Canada Patriots—and it is a pleasing reflection that between us and the ocean a population of 600,000 souls are now in arms, resolved to be free!

The tidings that worthy patriots are in arms is spreading through the Union, and the men who were oppressed in England, Ireland, Scotland and the continent are flocking to our standard.

We must be successful!

I had the honor to address nearly 3,000 of the citizens of Buffalo, two days ago, in the Theatre. The friendship and sympathy they expressed is honorable to the great and flourishing republic.

I am personally authorised to make known to you that from the moment that Sir Francis Head declined to state in writing the objects he had in view, in sending a flag of truce to our camp in Toronto, the message once declined, our esteemed fellow citizen Dr. John Rolph openly announced his concurrence in our measures, and now decidedly approves of the stand we are taking in behalf of our beloved country, which will never more be his until it be free and independent.

CANADIANS! my confidence in you is as strong and powerful, in this our day of trial and difficulty, as when, many years ago, in the zeal and ardour of youth, I appeared among you the humble advocate of your rights and liberties. I need not remind you of the sufferings and persecutions I have endured for your sakes—the losses I have sustained—the risks I have run. Had I ten lives I would cheerfully give them up to procure freedom to the country of my children, of my early and disinterested choice. Let us act together; and warmed by the hope of success in a patriotic course, be able to repeat in the language so often happily quoted by Ireland's champions,

The nations are fallen and thou still art young,
Thy sun is but rising when others have set;
And tho' Slavery's cloud o'er thy morning hath hung,
The full tide of Freedom shall beam round thee yet.

Militia-men of 1812! Will ye again rally round the standard of our tyrants! I can scarce believe it possible. Upper Canada Loyalists, what has been the recompense of your long tried and devoted attachment to England's Aristocracy? Obloquy, and contempt.

Verily we have learnt in the school of experience, and are prepared to profit by the lessons of the past. Compare the great and flourishing nation of the United States with our divided and distracted land, and think what we also might have been, as brave, independent lords of the soil. Leave then, Sir Francis Head's defence to the miserable serfs dependent on his bounty, and to the last hour of your lives the proud remembrance will be yours—"we also were among the deliverers of our country."

Navy Island, December, 13, 1837.

Mackenzie's proclamation from Navy Island, December, 1837.

In response to this passage, and the article in which it appeared, some of the sons of Family Compact members invaded Mackenzie's office while he was not present and threw his type into Toronto Bay.* There is no doubt they took his threat very seriously. By challenging the myths they propagated in their newspa-

* One of the myths of generations of Canadian history students is that they threw in his *press* — a Herculean task, even for the scions of the ruling class.

pers, he challenged the control they exerted over people. Like most ruling groups, they attempted to dominate the organs of information and education in order to present versions of reality favourable to themselves.

Mackenzie took the skills involved — journalistic skills, communications skills — and put them at the service of the ruled instead of the rulers. He became the ideologue of the oppressed. When the Tories expelled him from the assembly in 1831, it was on charges of libelling the Assembly in his newspaper. Mackenzie replied this was mere pretext: he was being harassed for the side he took, not for the way in which he took it. In fact, though such passages as the above may seem like strong stuff, their passion and intensity were absolutely typical, perhaps even a bit restrained, in comparison with the political journalism of the time. To prove his point, Mackenzie referred to passages in the Tory press, such as a poem in the *Gore Mercury* (owned by Alan Macnab, later commander of government forces against the revolutionaries) on the subject of a previous, but Reform, house of assembly:

Each post of profit in the House
  To greedy sharks assigned,
And public records of the state
  Clandestinely purloined.

The Attorney from the Senate House
  Endeavored to expel,
Whose Hall they made look like a room
  Where raving drunkards dwell.

For months this ribald conclave
  Retailed their vulgar prate,
And charged two dollars each per day
  For spouting billingsgate.

Two years their saintships governed us
  With lawless, despot rule,
At length the sudden change broke up
  The league of knave and fool.

The Mercury had also referred to reformers as "juggling, illiterate boobies;" it had called Methodist spokesman Egerton Ryerson "a man of profound hypocrisy and unblushing effrontery, who sits

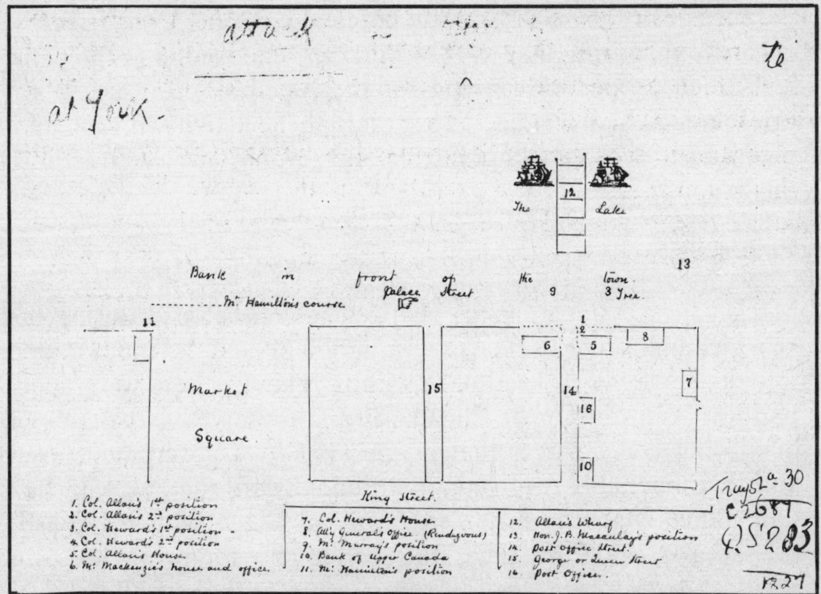

Diagram published by Mackenzie in the Colonial Advocate in the account of the attack on his own newspaper.

blinking on his perch, like Satan when he perched on the tree of life. . . ." It said that Mackenzie himself was guilty of "dark calumnies and falsehoods — false oaths, false acts — with many other sins of blackest hue." Nevertheless only Mackenzie was expelled from the House for journalistic misconduct.

Through the 1820s Mackenzie's press stood virtually alone against the propaganda generated by the Tory and government-controlled newspapers. More opposition papers were gradually founded, however, and by the 1830s the press in Upper Canada had divided, like the House of Assembly, along Reform and Tory lines. In Kingston, *The Spectator* spoke for Reform, and the *Chronicle* for the Tories. In Cobourg it was *The Reformer* against *The Star*. In Hamilton the *Free Press* against *The Mercury*. In Toronto *The Colonial Advocate* confronted *The Courier* and *The Patriot*. Egerton Ryerson's *Christian Guardian* started on the Reform side, moved toward a conservative stance in late 1833, and after the insurrection rejoined the ranks of Reform, purged as they were of Radicals. These newspapers vied fiercely for public attention and support.

Journalism was so ferociously political in Upper Canada that it is hardly surprising that in 1828 Mackenzie moved in to the political arena proper by running for the Assembly. But except for brief periods he never ceased his journalistic activity. It accompanied his other careers as politician and revolutionary activist until the end of his life.

Politician

Mackenzie's political stance changed and developed during the years leading up to 1837. As the situation altered, he endeavoured to alter his views to keep pace with it. Though there were many political issues in Upper Canada during those years, the issue of overriding concern was that of the system of government itself and that inevitably involved an attitude toward the link with Britain. Since Mackenzie was so firmly in touch with his constituency and with the times themselves, by following his own political development we can gain a sense of the overall political development that led to the outbreak of revolution.*

Mackenzie's political development began before his stint in the Assembly while he was an editor, just as it continued after that career when he became a revolutionary. He described his politics in the beginning as "Whig". This meant a commitment to the ideas of the constitutional monarchy and the aristocratic elements of the British class system, combined with a certain evolution of electoral and democratic forms not in conflict with the former. In England Whig politics espoused a wider franchise and greater role for the House of Commons, along with continued importance for the House of Lords. Transferred to the colony, the Whig attitude translated into a commitment to develop democratic institutions within the overall imperial framework. In the

* Mackenzie has often been accused of a lack of clarity and consistency in his thought. One historian writes, for example, "The tortuous character of Mackenzie's political ideas was given a further twist by his woolly economic policies." But, as another scholar has remarked, historians have a fondness for very simple thought and generally prefer a character such as Robert Baldwin, who had one idea in his life and repeated it endlessly. Unfortunately historical reality itself tends to be tortuous and a political leader must be willing to move with it or be left behind. Mackenzie did move intellectually but always remained at the same time committed to one underlying goal: to serve the people of Upper Canada.

first number of *The Colonial Advocate,* Mackenzie had written:

> Sincerely attached to freedom, we yet think it not incompatible with a limited monarchy. We would never wish to see British America an appendage of the American presidency; yet would we wish to see British America thrive and prosper full as well as does that Presidency. We trust to see this accomplished, if Britain does not fall into the error of considering her colonists her slaves as much as Virginia does her negroes.
>
> We dislike much to hear Mr. Daniel Webster, of Massachusetts, gibe us as the distant dependency of a distant monarchy, &c. &c. and hope the time will come when Canada will be pointed out as a model for other countries — not pointed at with scorn, as the King's printer has it.
>
> We like American liberty well, but greatly prefer British liberty. British subjects, born in Britain, we have sworn allegiance to a constitutional monarchy, and we will die before we will violate that oath.

However Mackenzie's attempt to deal with the political problems of Upper Canada during the following years, including the experience of the attack on his office, led him to alter some of his assumptions:

> After wearing the dress of a Whig for some years, I conscientiously adopted that of a radical reformer, ceased to put confidence in the inherent wisdom of hereditary peers, or to express admiration of the constitutional balance, and began my legislative labours in the House of Assembly by a notice for the abolition of the law of primogeniture.

Mackenzie had changed his view to the extent that he considered the ruling elite of Upper Canada did not and could not constitute an "aristocracy;" they were merely a self-interested gang. It was therefore not the system of government, but those who held power within it, that constituted the problem in Upper Canada. He firmly believed this "problem" could be attacked and solved within existing political structures. He wrote:

> It is not a change in the form of Government which will remove any difficulties or grievances under which you labour; nor will railing at the United States perpetuate the dominion of your rulers. The grand panacea is self reformation . . . . You have far less reason to complain of the defects of the established constitution than of the corruption, ignorance, carelessness and subservience of successive assemblies.

But the Reform Assembly elected along with Mackenzie in 1828 accomplished little. Most of their measures failed to pass the other legislative body, the Legislative Council, or were disallowed by the lieutenant governor. Then came the election of a Tory majority in 1830. Mackenzie, who had been re-elected, continued to attack the government and increased his criticism in his newspaper and in public speeches. In particular he railed against the banking bills introduced and passed by the Tories. They in turn carried the first of the five motions of expulsion against him in December 1831. This and subsequent expulsions pushed Mackenzie further toward his natural constituency, the mass of the people, who kept re-electing him, and led him to seek different, more popular political forums than the legislature. He went about the countryside speaking at rallies and organizing political unions. He grew more and more skeptical of the possibilities of political change available through the legislative structures of Upper Canada. In March 1831 he wrote:

> I do not at this moment see our remedy. The people would petition [i.e. to the government through their members in the assembly] but what does it avail? Yet the more I see into the system the more I dislike it, and feel disposed to do all I can (and that is but little) to bring about a better state of things.

Mackenzie continued to regard the Family Compact as the chief obstacle to progress. In fact he saw them to be the *only* obstacle and considered their interests in conflict not only with those of the people, but with those of the British government itself.

> The only enemy you have to contend with is the faction in power here, and its fellow-workers the faction of disappointed state priests, pensioners, charlatans and tax consumers which now forms the opposition to the royal government in England. The executive government in this province, from its highest officer to its lowest and most ignoble minion, can ill conceal the hatred they bear to his Majesty's Ministers in England. The host of court locusts and servile parasites who swarm in this colony are in terror lest a moderate reform in England and union of sentiment among the colonists should be the means of putting a stop to their cruel rapacity.

Accordingly he formulated a new strategy — circumvent the political institutions controlled by the local oligarchy:

> The next question I would propose for your consideration is — *What is to be done?* My answer would be — *Petition the King:* approach the throne of your venerated monarch with dutiful loyal and affectionate addresses, from every town, township, village and hamlet in the colony; humbly yet firmly recapitulate your grievances, and patiently but perseveringly seek redress.

By "the King" Mackenzie meant the British government whose interests he did not consider inimical to those of the colonists. He organized a petition of grievances directed not to the Upper Canadian government, but to the imperial government in England. On it he assembled more than 24,500 signatures. This was a massive number. The total population was under 300,000 and transportation was notoriously bad in the colony. Mackenzie set out himself with the petition in order to argue its cause before the government in England. Just before he left, in April 1832, he described his attitude to the political situation:

> The older I get the more clearly do I perceive that the constitutions of these colonial regions were made by the few governing to be administered for their own benefit; and what I am at a loss in is as to the means whereby they can be altered so as to preserve our connexion and friendship with the land of our forefathers and of our birth and yet give to men of talent, enterprise and genuine patriotism that fair field which is now engrossed by ambition and sycophancy.

He arrived in England, full of hope of resolving colonial grievances by imperial means.

He remained a little over a year. At first he was received with great respect by the Colonial Office. The Tories of Upper Canada, in fact, were scandalized by the courtesy of his reception in Britain. To further inflame matters, Mackenzie influenced the Colonial Secretary, Lord Goderich, to dismiss Boulton and Hagerman, the Compact officials most instrumental in Mackenzie's expulsions. The victory was short-lived however. Hagerman and Boulton journeyed to England; a new Colonial Secretary was appointed; and the two Compact stalwarts were restored to official positions. Mackenzie left the experience convinced that the Colonial Office could not be relied on to effect the change in the colonial ruling class he thought so necessary.

During his visit, political agitation in England itself was reaching its height. Mackenzie watched the final reading of the Reform Bill of 1832 in the House of Commons. But he was more impressed with the activity in the streets, and concluded that the Bill had accomplished little for most of the people of England. It functioned mainly as a means of warding off the radical democratic demands being voiced by the Chartist movement. All the less could Reform in England be counted on to bring about change in faroff Upper Canada.

He was particularly vexed by the situation of Ireland. If that nation, so near to England for so long a time, had achieved so little toward its economic and political improvement, what hope was there for a distant colony in the context of the same empire:

> If I could think, even for a moment, that the yeomanry of Upper Canada, would require to drink from the same bitter cup of adversity which Ireland has quaffed to the very dregs, before they would unite for their common advantage, and the general happiness, I would not continue to toil and labour as I have done for these last 9 years, often with many great personal privations contending . . . .

When he returned from England in the summer of 1833, he no longer held the hope that political improvement in Upper Canada could come about through the agency of the British home government. The people of Upper Canada would have to rely on themselves. He seemed driven toward two conclusions: self-government for the colony; and extra-parliamentary political action as the means of achieving it.

Toward the end of 1833, Mackenzie removed the word "Colonial" from the masthead of *The Colonial Advocate.* In February of 1834 he was instrumental in the formation of the association of Radicals in York county. It called effectively, though not explicitly, for self-government. After the election of 1834, which saw the return of Mackenzie along with a Reform and Radical Reform majority, he continued the extra-parliamentary organization of the self-government movement through the founding of the Canadian Alliance. At this point he was operating both within and outside of the formal political structures of the colony.

In the Assembly, he assumed the chairmanship of a special Committee on Grievances. He used this committee as an opportunity for a sort of summing-up of all the objections to the situation in Upper Canada as it then was. He concluded that the "chief source of Colonial discontent" could be traced to "the almost unlimited extent of the patronage of the Crown, or rather of the Colonial Minister for the time being and his advisers here, together with the abuse of that patronage." The Family Compact were the chief benefactors of this system; but he no longer considered them alone to be the source of the problem. The source was also the imperial government itself, and the system by which the colony was subjected to it — in short, Upper Canada's colonial position.

Around the time of the release of the report, Mackenzie wrote to a friend in Quebec more personally and more explicitly:

> I have read your letter with much pleasure, but will candidly acknowledge that the compliment you pay my loyalty sits less easy on my shoulders than it would have done three years ago, when I first met you at Quebec.
>
> Until my return from England in the fall of 1833, I used what little influence I possessed with the yeomanry to persuade them that by petitioning England, a remedy would be found to every wrong of which they had just reason to complain.
>
> But I have been in England—I have seen the usage Ireland met with—the treatment other colonies received—the promises made today to be broken tomorrow—
>
> In short, I have seen enough to convince me that we shall continue to have the very worst possible government in Upper Canada until we get rid of the system which binds us to the earth. I therefore am less loyal than I was, and would be wanting in candour if I did not admit the fact — I like sincerity in others and try to practice the virtue myself although it is attended sometimes with a temporary inconvenience.

In January of 1836 the new lieutenant governor, Sir Francis Bond Head, arrived. Confrontations with the Reform Assembly followed, then dissolution, and the disastrous election of the summer of 1836 in which the Reformers were routed and the Tories returned. It was the only election Mackenzie ever lost, but even before the voting he had addressed the people about the limitation of the current electoral system. In June, before the election, he told them:

> I have taken less pains to be elected by you this time than I ever did before, and the reason is, I do not feel that lively hope to be able to

> be useful to you which I once felt.
>
> We are, of course, to wait for the answer to our petitions to England. If it be favorable, it will be our duty to uphold the system of monarchical government, modified, of course, by the removal of that wretched playhouse, the Legislative Council, together with the mountebanks who exhibit on its boards. If the reply be unfavorable, as I am apprehensive it will, for the Whigs and Tories are alike dishonest, contending factions of men who wish to live in idleness upon the labors of honest industry then the Crown will have forfeited one claim upon British freemen in Upper Canada, and the result it is not difficult to foresee.

The nature of that election and its results confirmed him in the conclusions he had been coming to. In October 1836 he wrote:

> We are personally of opinion, that the conduct of the executive towards the people of Upper and Lower Canada has been such as in effect to absolve them from an allegiance, the principle of which is reciprocal obligations not deadly injuries. But this extreme view is perhaps not taken by the majority of the people, nor do we, for the present, see the utility of further considering it.

Mackenzie phrased this as his "personal" point of view and allowed, "for the sake of argument," that loyalty to the British crown was still incumbent on the citizens of Upper Canada. But the way ahead was clear. The British would not alleviate the grievances of Upper Canada, therefore self-government was necessary. Self-government was impossible without independence. The means to that end could not be electoral. The electoral process was too dominated, and too easily manipulated by, the colonial authorities. Bond Head's conduct during the 1836 election had merely made that fact apparent; it had been so all along. The "personal" opinion became the basis for political action. The political unions were transformed into quasi-military organizations. Support was gathered, and by the summer of 1837 there began that remarkable series of documents on Independence.

Mackenzie had passed through a train of political stances between his entry into public life as editor of *The Colonial Advocate* in 1824, and the events of 1837. Beginning with a commitment to the people of Upper Canada, he had tried various solutions. He tested each against reality and, where he found it wanting, altered it and tried again. What never altered was the basic commitment to his constituency. Eventually he concluded that their material prosperity and their political advancement were tied to the same cause: a revolution for national independence. As he put it in September of 1837:

> The Whitchurch union has advanced in knowledge so far as to conclude that it would be better for the country if our fellow citizens could manufacture carriages for our governors. Perhaps they will take one step more, and open their eyes to the important truth that Upper Canada will never prosper till the people can manufacture their governors, without having to borrow them from the other end of the world, and send them off again as well loaded with wealth as Sinbad the Sailor was when the bird mistook him for a piece of meat and flew off with him out of the valley of diamonds.

That the Canadian Revolution of 1837 failed does not necessarily mean that Mackenzie was mistaken about the solution to his nation's problems; he may merely have failed to implement it.*

* Mackenzie is one, and perhaps the only, figure in Canadian history who has continued till this day to inspire the most vehemently partisan assessments. He generally receives not merely dismissal but great rancour from Canadian historians, and they are a guild not generally known for their qualities of passion. To take just one example, a biographer who claims he *likes* Mackenzie, characterizes him, within three pages, as nervous, wild, inquisitorial, mad, delirious, acid, compulsive, irrelevant, capering, a nuisance, cranky, distracted, and schizotic. The adjectives "little", "tiny", "diminutive," and the like appear — to borrow a term — almost compulsively in most accounts of Mackenzie by historians; he was in reality five feet six inches tall. When the first stage production of *1837* played in Toronto, a letter to the Toronto Star castigated the memory of Mackenzie and the play that had approved of him. It was signed by a descendant of the Sheriff Jarvis whose house Mackenzie had ordered burned during the siege of Toronto. That Mackenzie — dead lo these many years and a defeated revolutionary even longer — continues to provoke such passion among Canadians is due I think to one fact: the issues he raised and the challenges he posed continue to be unresolved and of great moment to Canadians today.

Chapter 4

Rivals for loyalty: England and the States

England

Everything that happened in Upper Canada in 1837 was determined by the situation in England. This was due to more than the normal interdependence of nations. Upper Canada was a British colony. A colony does not contain its own centre where power and decisions are concerned. To understand what is happening in the colony, it is necessary to go outside it, to the imperial centre. In its final form the climax of 1837 was over the attempt to shift the centre of Upper Canadian society from England to Upper Canada itself, and the resistance of the Empire to that shift.

England in the 1830s was passing through a period of severe crisis in its own history. The country seemed to have reached a kind of economic dead end. The Industrial Revolution, which had begun in England during the eighteenth century, well before the rest of Europe, seemed to have run its course. Early industrialization took place mostly in the cotton goods sector of the textile industry and, to a lesser extent, in iron and coal. Elsewhere in the British economy industrialization had not made significant inroads. The process of industrializing seemed complete: there was no reason to assume it would occur in other sectors of the economy; perhaps this was all there was to it. In addition a prolonged slump had set in following the Napoleonic wars. An economic malaise settled over English society.

This was accompanied by unrest in the political realm. During the upheavals in Europe following the French Revolution, those in power in England had held the lid on very firmly at home.

Revolutionary social tensions were channeled toward the patriotic struggles of the wars against Napoleon and France. But with the end of those wars domestic opposition got a fresh start. The stagnation of economic growth merely added to this. As one historian writes:

> At no other period in modern British history have the common people been persistently, profoundly, and often desperately dissatisfied. At no other period since the seventeenth century can we speak of large masses of them as revolutionary, or discern at least one moment of political crisis (between 1830 and the Reform Act of 1832) when something like a revolutionary situation might actually have developed.

The Duke of Wellington was both the symbol and the reality of conservatism in this situation. He had subdued Napoleon, that representative of the spirit of the French Revolution, and in the years following played a central role in domestic English politics. A popular rhyme ran

> The Levellution has begun,
> So I'll go home and get my gun
> And shoot the Duke of Wellington.

It is not surprising that in this uncertain situation the value of the colonies also seemed less than certain. The role of the British colonies prior to the American Revolution had been understood in terms of the policy of mercantilism. The successful breakaway by the Americans had brought this policy into question, but the struggle against revolution in Europe had left the reassessment of colonial policy in abeyance. The empire clearly had value. Colonies were a source of wealth, of markets for British goods, and of relief for excess population, the unemployed, the discontented and the like. Yet there was also a severe money drain involved in maintaining the colonies, and in this respect the American Revolution had prompted a dilemma. The colonies could not be asked to pay the costs of their own maintenance without raising the cry of "taxation without representation"; but granting representation, that is, some form of self-government, meant the likelihood of the colonists following policies in their own interests rather than those of the mother country. Further, the economic malaise in England necessarily affected the colonies and, by rebound, their usefulness to the mother country. At the same time growing social unrest in England spawned sympathy for the grievances of the colonists. The suggestion was even seriously made that England divest herself of the empire. This came not only from the parliamentary radicals, who spoke largely out of agreement with the democratic aspiration of the colonists; it also came from such conservatives as the young Disraeli, who felt the financial burden of empire could not be counterbalanced by any economic advantage Britain could pursue in her current state. The debate about abandoning the colonies became quite sharp, fuelled as it was by arguments from both self-interest and altruism. Yet in reality it was probably less about *whether* to maintain the colonies, than about precisely what to do with them in the circumstances of post-Napoleonic, post-revolutionary, and perhaps even post-industrial Britain.

The solution to all these problems appeared suddenly in the 1840s: railroads. It was the railroad boom which unlocked the industrialization of the rest of the British economy; it spurred growth, output and profit. At the same time it tipped the British as to what to do with the colonies: build railroads in them. However this solution was not manifest in the pre-1840s period, and a certain irresolution in the Colonial Office fed into growing discontent abroad.

In 1836 a report to the British cabinet summarized imperial objectives in North America:

> The ultimate objects of the Policy of the British Government in relation to the North American Provinces, are few and simple. Every end which is really desirable would be fully accomplished, if adequate security could be taken for maintaining the connexion between the two Countries as Members of the same Monarchy — if the outlet for poor emigrants could be kept open — and if those Commercial interests which may be supposed to depend upon the Colonial character of the Canadas, of New Brunswick, and of Nova Scotia, could be protected.

The use of the North American colonies as an outlet for the unemployed of the British Isles remained a primary objective until very late. In 1837, in fact, a parliamentary report stated, "at present the North American colonies are more valuable to England as receptacles for her surplus population than any other way." Yet this safety-valve aspect of the colonies had a double edge. The colonies were stagnating economically because of their attachment to a weak British economy as well as their own unproductive land policies. This worked against their usefulness in absorbing population. As early as 1820 a cabinet minister had reported that recent emigrants to Canada "so far from finding increased means of subsistence, had experienced a want of employment fully equal to that which existed in the most distressed districts of this country."

"Commercial interests" had always been a part of the British stake in the Canadas, ever since British merchants had displaced the French merchants of Montreal in the fur trade. By the mid-1820s these interests were becoming more than just a stake in trade. The investment of British financiers in land companies (The Canada Company in Upper Canada, the British-American Land Company in Lower Canada), the rise of banks, investment in canals, all indicated that the economies of British North America were reaching a point where there were now profits to be reaped by British capital. These early indications of a larger treasure increased the eagerness of the British to hang on to the colonies at the same time as they whetted the appetites of ambitious souls in the colonies themselves for a bigger, if not controlling, share in the developing wealth.

Within the framework of overall colonial policy, policy toward British North America, and policy toward the Canadas, little Upper Canada had its particular place. In the 1820s and 1830s, it was the least populous and least developed of the North American colonies. Yet it occupied a very strategic position because it was located, geographically and politically, between two entities of enormous significance in the calculations of imperial policy — between Lower Canada and the United States.

Lower Canada was an old, populous, valuable possession for the British. After the loss of the Thirteen Colonies it became their major asset in the New World. It had rich cultivated farmland. It was an important centre of the fur trade. Via the St. Lawrence, it provided an alternate route deep into the heart of the continent, now that the Americans dominated the Atlantic seaboard and the mouth of the Mississippi. It was a large market for British manufactures. Yet unlike the Atlantic provinces or the former Thirteen

Colonies, it was composed not of transplanted Englishmen but of conquered Frenchmen.

The British never ceased to regard the French Canadians as a potentially seditious race. They felt fortunate that the habitants had not joined the American Revolution despite Benedict Arnold's urging. They assumed that as long as the French nation existed in Quebec, British dominion there was insecure. They installed some parliamentary institutions of a very limited nature in the hope these would begin to anglicize the population. They enlisted the support of the church and the seigneurial class in return for major British concessions to those groups. They set a British mercantile oligarchy in place of the French merchant class which had existed before the Conquest. They gave these Englishmen great political power and attempted to build their numbers and influence. They set the governor in chief and commander in chief of the Canadas in Quebec City. And at the same time they built up Upper Canada.

Upper Canada was to be the true-blue counterbalance to Quebec, populated by English-speaking loyalists fleeing the American republic after the Revolution or emigrating from the mother country itself. It would reproduce British social and political institutions, including even a local aristocracy parallel to that mainstay of stability in the British Isles. Eventually it was hoped that Upper Canada would grow to rival, and then dominate Quebec. In the meantime it was to be protected from the French influence and nurtured in its loyalty.*

On the one side of their calculations over Upper Canada the British worried about the conquered French; on the other, they fretted constantly over the liberated Americans. The United States stood as the continuing alternative in the eyes of Upper

* The English stuck with this plan and eventually did attempt the absorption of French into English Canada. This happened on the basis of Durham's recommendations in the aftermath of the revolutionary movements of 1837-8. It was a bit ahead of schedule since in 1841 at the time of the Union of the Canadas the Quebecois still outnumbered the Upper Canadians. However within a decade, owing mostly to immigration, the English did outstrip the French. Nevertheless the submersion of the French (plainly and simply their cultural genocide) was unsuccessful and the result was the re-separation of the two national entities under the aegis of Confederation.

Sir Francis Bond Head, lieutenant governor in 1837.

Canadians: what they might become in the absence of the British connection. Despite enormous anti-American propaganda, the United States exerted a siren call. Upper Canadians were constantly abandoning the hardships of the colony for the more dynamic situation of the Western states. Nor were the Americans indifferent to Upper Canada. They had attempted to annex it during the War of 1812-14 and continued to indicate an interest in expanding into the Canadian province. Furthermore the most natural source of immigrants to Upper Canada was the spillover from the westward flow in the States. These were people who often brought with them republican predilections, anti-monarchism, or at the least an indifference to any politics outside their own personal ambitions. The U. S. was the great threat to Britain's entire North American empire, and Upper Canada was the most vulnerable point for American encroachment.

With the Americans threatening to move in from their side, and the French threatening to revolt on theirs, the British came to see Upper Canada as the lynchpin of the security of their North American domain. It was crucial to retain the loyalty of the small colony. Such intentions account for some odd behavior on the part of the Colonial Office, and even odder perceptions on the part of the Upper Canadians themselves. This is well seen in the case of Mackenzie's mission to England.

The Colonial Secretary, Lord Goderich, eagerly met with him. The cabinet discussed his briefs. The *London Morning Chronicle* printed a series of his articles on Canada. Instructions generally favourable to Mackenzie's position were forwarded by the Colonial Office to Lieutenant Governor Colborne in Upper Canada. And by March of 1833 Goderich had ordered the dismissal of two of Mackenzie's arch-foes from their official positions. All this for an *un*official visitor recently *expelled* from the colonial Assembly for impropriety.

The Upper Canadian Reformers, including Mackenzie himself, misinterpreted this behaviour on the part of the British as a sign of the growing strength of liberalism and reform within British politics and the extension of such principles to colonial policy. The recent defeat of the Duke of Wellington's government, the introduction of the Reform Bill, Reform victories in the subsequent election, the attempt by the House of Lords to block the Bill, and passage itself — to them the tilt toward reform in Canadian policy seemed part and parcel of this general trend.

The Upper Canadian Tories similarly misunderstood the reception. They were scandalized by it and determined it was based on either stupidity or perfidy to the interests of England herself. Their discomfiture was so vast they actually threatened to secede from the empire. Their leading newspaper railed:

> Instead of dwelling with delight and confidence upon their connection with the glorious Empire or their sires, with a determination to support that connection, as many of them have already supported it, with their fortunes or their blood, their affections are already more than half alienated from the Government of that country, and in the

> apprehension that the same insulting and degrading course of policy towards them is likely to be continued, they already begin to "cast about" in "their minds eye" for some new state of political existence, which shall effectually put the Colony beyond the reach of injury and insult from any and every ignoramus whom the political lottery of the day may chance to elevate to the Colonial Office.

In order to save the imperial connection, they were prepared to dissolve it.

Both sides, however, were mistaken in their assessment of the source of British behaviour. The Colonial Office was simply attempting to keep the lid on in Upper Canada at a time when they faced mounting confrontation in Quebec, and continuing danger from American expansion. It was their wisdom to attempt to mollify opposition in Upper Canada because it was the one place they did not need trouble at such a time. They were prepared to stretch quite far toward Mackenzie, if it maintained the solidity of their Upper Canadian lynchpin. When they saw they had gone overboard, unsettling the loyalty of their rockbottom retainers, they simply and neatly reversed field, reinstating Mackenzie's enemies and disregarding Mackenzie's own further representations. Similar accommodations were to be attempted with Quebec and, in both colonies, when the carrot failed, the British moved very firmly and harshly, dealing with opposition by severe repression. Shifts in personnel: the replacement of Goderich as Colonial Secretary or Bond Head as lieutenant governor merely marked the shifts in policy. For Mackenzie and the other Upper Canadian radicals, the whole experience taught them not to tie their hopes to the tail of apprehended political developments in England. For as long as they did so they were subject to vicissitudes into which they had limited insight, and over which they had no control.

At the same time as the British imposed their policies through governors, troops and directives; they also implemented policy within the colony itself more directly in such a way that something of England itself was transplanted into Upper Canada.

In the latter half of 1820 the British began to encourage the emigration of a certain number of relatively well-to-do Englishmen. Former aristocrats and landowners, for example, who had been displaced by the rise of the industrial class and the turn away from farming toward manufacturing in England; members of what has been called a "despiccable squirearchy", similarly shuffled off the land; retired warhorses of the Napoleonic age. These were individuals to whom England had little to offer, but who retained their class pretensions and their sense of social superiority. They flocked to Canada in response to the urging of the government. Large numbers of them received land grants in return for giving up pensions or military commissions. Others got land simply for the asking. Many had neither the will nor the skill to farm, and sold off their grants to speculators; afterwards they would find employment as government officials, militia officers, and the like through their connections in England and the colony.

They had little feeling for Canada and remained emotionally attached to England. One of them wrote, "The country bears evident marks of having incurred the Divine displeasure; the birds of Canada do not sing, the flowers emit no perfume, the men have no hearts, the women no virtue." They imported their haughtiness and their pianos to the woods north of Peterborough and did all they could to establish a "little England" in the midst of the new world. At the same time life in Canada afforded them opportunity to exercise that sense of social grandeur they could no longer affect at home. "I was a Queen in Canada," lamented one such woman who had returned to England, "but I am no one here." Unlike the poorer immigrants who tended to assimilate and remake themselves in the image of the new land, they were a virtual fifth column of the old.

In times of crisis, they represented England even more directly. Owing to the official positions many of them occupied, these people were instrumental in crushing the uprising in 1837 before it spread. Susanna Moodie and her husband were members of this group of emigrants. They failed at farming, but were financially rescued by the pay Moodie received as a militia officer during 1837-8. As soon as news of the outbreak arrived, he rode off to join the fighting even though both his legs were broken at the time. When the emergency ended, Susanna despaired at the prospect of going back to farming:

> I pondered over every plan that thought could devise; at last, I prayed to the Almighty to direct me as to what would be the best course for

> us to pursue. A sweet assurance stole over me, and soothed my spirit, that God would provide for us, as He had hitherto done — that a great deal of our distress arose from want of faith. I was just sinking into a calm sleep when the thought seemed whispered into my soul, "Write to the Governor; tell him candidly all you have suffered during your sojourn in this country, and trust to God for the rest."
>
> At first I paid little heed to this suggestion; but it became so importunate that at last I determined to act upon it as if it were a message sent from heaven. I rose from my bed, struck a light, sat down, and wrote a letter to the Lieutenant-governor, Sir George Arthur, a simple statement of facts, leaving it to his benevolence to pardon the liberty I had taken in addressing him.

Some time afterward:

> The potato crop was gathered in, and I had collected my store of dandelion-roots for our winter supply of coffee, when one day brought a letter to my husband from the Governor's secretary, offering him the situation of sheriff of the V—District. Though perfectly unacquainted with the difficulties and responsibilities of such an important office, my husband looked upon it as a gift sent from heaven to remove us from the sorrows and poverty with which we were surrounded in the woods.

The Moodies spent the rest of their life together in the pleasant precincts of Belleville, where Mr. Moodie served as sheriff and helped his wife in her literary endeavours.

Probably even more important to the English cause in Upper Canada than the implantation of such individuals was the implantation of English and pro-English attitudes. To a certain extent this happened naturally among a large number of the poorer immigrants. These were former paupers and landless labourers from the British Isles who had often been thrown off their land by the enclosure movement. In Upper Canada many of them suddenly became small landowners. Unlike the pseudo-aristocrats who resented Canada and idealized England, to many of these reborn farmers Canada was the Promised Land and they were full of a misplaced gratitude to the government for their new fortunes. They wrote home, "a poor man can do a great deal better here than he can at home . . . our dogs . . . live better than most of the farmers in England." The effect on their politics was understandable. A visitor wrote in 1833, "every acceptable individual of the Whig, and even the Radical party in England, with scarcely a solitary exception, becomes what the disaffected party terms a 'Tory' the moment he comes to Canada."

The experiences of such people could only reinforce the pro-monarchy, pro-empire attitudes which had been engrained in many of them from their earliest years. The accession of Victoria to the throne in the summer of 1837 increased yet again these pro-imperial predilections. How could one be disloyal to this virginal slip of a Queen? It would be dastardly; it would be unmanly. Such strains run very deep in people, irrational as they may be. During the encampment by government forces on the Niagara River, opposite Mackenzie's Provisional Government on Navy Island:

> One of the men serving the guns which had caused all this havoc lost a leg by a cannon ball, a fine fellow named Miller, an old Navy man. After the mangled member was cut off he desired to see it, gave three cheers for the Queen, and in a few hours was dead.

An account of the gathering of government forces in Toronto gives an idea of the emotional state of the ordinary people who answered to the government call:

> Sir Francis did not inspect us very minutely, which was very kind of him, considering the state of our wardrobe. He knew that the seat of honour and loyalty, the heart, was sound, and made us a speech accordingly, which we acknowledged by giving him three hearty British cheers, three more for the Queen, and three more for the British flag which from the summit of Government House waved proudly over our heads. Oh! we forgot in that moment all our weariness and fasting and raggedness. We thought only of our Fatherland, and many a sun-burnt and sun-dried cheek were wet with tears — the overflowings of truly honest, upright, and loyal hearts.

Of course not all those who rallied to the government side did so willingly. Many had no choice, given the positions of power the Tories held in local militias for example. Failure to join the loyalists could mean immediate arrest for treason. Many men on their way to join Mackenzie after the battle already had been lost were pressed into government service, or volunteered for it, in order to avoid suspicion of being on the wrong side. But the enormous advantage to the imperial government of the general, ingrained political attitudes held by the population cannot be understated.

Mackenzie called it the force of popular "opinion" and considered it more important in the balance than any aggregation of merely physical factors:

> It cannot be too often repeated, that Britain has no power here if opinion be concentrated against the measures of her agents. We are far from the Sea — for five months our shores are ice-bound; the great republic is on one side of us; the Lower Canadians on another; Michigan, and the wilderness, and lakes, are to the west and north of us. The whole physical power of the government, the mud garrison, red-coats and all, is not equal to that of the young men of one of our largest townships. But so long as opinion is on its side, or wavering, the government wields indeed a gigantic power, the nature and extent of which will form the groundwork of another article. Our object is to oblige all who wield the power of the people, to do so for the common good of the country.

However, not all the influence from England was on the side of the imperial government. The same social forces which were challenging the established order in England — the parliamentary radicals, the Chartist movement, trade unionism — rallied to the side of the Canadian revolutionary forces. In March of 1837, the London Workingmen's Association held a meeting attended by over 2,000 people. It was billed as "Democracy or Despotism. Meeting of the Workingmen's Association in favour of Canadian Rights." The meeting sent the following address of greeting to the Patriote Central Committee in Montreal:

> To our friends in the cause of liberty, our oppressed brothers. The cause of democracy is everywhere triumphant. Can there be rebellion in a country when the liberties of a million men are trampled underfoot by a contemptible invading minority? Brother Canadians, do not let yourselves be deceived by fair promises. Trust in the sacredness of your cause. You have the full approval of your distant brothers. Have faith in your leaders. We augur your triumph. May the sun of independence shine on your growing cities, your joyous hearths, your deep forests, and your frozen lakes — such is the ardent wish of the Workingmen's Association.

It was signed by a dozen workers in different trades.

The Patriote Central Committee in Montreal sent this reply:

> We desire, through your Association, to proclaim, that whatever

course we shall be compelled to adopt, we have no contest with the people of England. We war only against the aggressions of their and our tyrannical oppressors.

The United States

It had always been American policy, as well as an ardent wish, to annex the Canadas to the United States. General Benedict Arnold went to Quebec in 1775 to urge the French Canadians to join the revolt of the Thirteen Colonies. He very nearly succeeded. The battles of the War of 1812-14 fought along the Upper Canadian frontier were another instance of the outbreak of the struggle for possession of the Canadas. In 1818, ex-president Madison wrote to President Monroe (author of the doctrine of American hegemony in the Western Hemisphere) giving reasons why the British should be amenable to an American takeover of Canada. "As far as such a transfer would affect the relative power to the two nations, the most unfriendly jealousy could find no objection to the measure; for it would evidently take more weakness from Great Britain than it would add strength to the United States." When the struggles of 1837 broke out, the American government chose not to intercede militarily, but this was not because they had cooled on Canada; they simply felt the moment was inopportune, and Canada would soon fall their way by other means. One Canadian supporter wrote from Washington in 1838 that politicians from all parties opposed intervention because they felt that "the natural and rapid increase of population on the lakes, in Michigan and Wisconsin, must inevitably, within a few years, give them the Canadas with lighter sacrifice than at present." The undying tradition of American hunger for Canada was continued with the formation of the Hunters' Lodges in the years following 1837, and with the Fenian raids of a generation later.

But just as British interests in Upper Canada were represented not only by official policies and emissaries — they were also upheld by individuals and attitudes implanted within the colony itself — the same was true of the United States. American emigrants were the overwhelming majority of the population in the formative years of Upper Canada. After the earliest arrivals, the United Empire Loyalists, other, non-Loyalist, American settlers continued to pour into Upper Canada. Some stayed, some stayed awhile, others passed on through to the Western states. But more arrived. By 1812 it was estimated that four out of five inhabitants were Americans, and less than a fourth of these were Loyalists. During the 1820s and 1830s, American emigration proportionately lessened, while emigration from the British Isles rose. But former Americans were still a preponderant part of the population. They were especially numerous in the parts of the province west of Toronto, all the way down to the American border at Sandwich (near Windsor). In this section of the province almost all the innkeepers were American. The only book to be found in most of their inns was a volume called *The History of the United States* written by An American. Americanisms of speech were very common. People "guessed" and "calculated" and "expected." They said, "Hold yer horses," "if ye don't like it, ye can lump it," "let 'er rip," "by cracky," "What the Sam Hill," and "by General Jackson."

They also brought and held onto many of their political attitudes, such as republicanism and egalitarianism. Western Ontario was a hotbed of opposition to Family Compact rule. Even during the anti-Reform deluge of 1836, the districts around London returned a solid six Reform candidates, while only London itself, built up as a Tory fortress among the Americans, returned a Bond Head candidate. After the uprising, in June 1838, a local Anglican rector estimated that revolutionaries outnumbered loyalists three to two in the western part of the province. This is striking considering that, at the time of the beginning of the American Revolution it is estimated the population divided one third loyalist, one third for independence, and one third still uncommitted. Among the government forces, there was little doubt that this disaffection was a Yankee disease. One newspaper blamed the "Yankee loafers and Yankee schoolteachers" for the anti-British, pro-republican attitudes so evident.

Just as powerful a force as the physical presence of Americans was the impact of reports, rumours, and even popular myths about what life was like down in the States. It was the heyday of Jacksonian democracy in the United States. The first Westerner had been elected president. Westward expansion was proceeding at a great pace. Ohio, Michigan, Indiana — they seemed embodiments of the twin American virtues of economic prosperity and political equality. Universal manhood suffrage and the secret ballot were being adopted in most states, and the American political system was widely held responsible for the country's material well-being. Tales of America spilled over the border, and spread through the province. Upper Canadians wondered: is it true about the United States? If true, what makes it so? And if they can live so bountifully, why not us as well? Images of America became a potent political force in Upper Canadian life. Many left for the United States to share in what they had heard tell of. Others chafed under the limitations of the colony. And one farmer we know of was so driven by the reports that he travelled to the United States solely in order to compare the myths he had heard to reality.

The farmer's name was Robert Davis and in 1837, a year after his trip to the States, he published a remarkable book called *The Canadian Farmer's Travels in the United States of America.* On the title page he described his work as one "in which remarks are made on The Arbitrary Colonial Policy Practised in Canada and the Free and Equal Rights and happy effects of the Liberal Institutions and Astonishing Enterprise of the United States." Davis' small volume provides a wonderful insight into the stupendous effect the example of America had on farmers in Upper Canada in the 1830s.*

The Farmer's Travels

Davis describes how his despair at the political situation in Upper Canada after the election of 1836 led him to leave for the United States, in search of hope, and some reason to carry on:

> On the 5th September, 1836, I left the township of Nissouri, in the county of Oxford, London District, for the United States. I had long had a desire to see with my own eyes, what I had heard of; as actual observation must be better than report. I was the more anxious to go

* Robert Davis' book became the basis for a scene in the play *1837* in which a Canadian farmer travels to see the United States. For some reason, each time the play has been restaged by the original company — five times now — this particular scene gives by far the greatest difficulty. An example of the kind of "creative bog" — as some actors call it — occasioned by the scene is given in the essay, Preface to *1837,* included elsewhere in this book.

> at this time in consequence of the mighty stir which had been produced by Sir F. B. Head, our Lieutenant Governor. His political manoeuvres at the late election were too much for my nerves, and I wished to see whether the same games were played by the Governors in the United States, and whether a species of human creatures, called Orange-men, prevented the free election of Representatives in the Republic.

He describes his background as a working farmer:

> The author has been in Canada ever since he was a little boy, he has not had the privilege of a classical education at the King's College, or the less advantages derived from a District School. The greater part of his time has been spent in close confinement in the wilderness of Nissouri Township. Indeed it has been confinement enough, to watch over and provide for a tender and increasing family. He had in most instances to make his own roads and bridges, clear his own farm, educate himself and children, be his own mechanic, and except now and then, has had no society, but his own family. Has had his bones broken by the fall of trees, his feet lacerated by the axe, and suffered almost everything except death.

His bitterness expresses itself as he travels toward the western border of the colony:

> . . . in consequence of the roads being so much used, they are very bad in wet weather, and I really wished Sir F. B. Head had been stuck fast in one of the great mud holes on the Long Woods, inasmuch as he had refused to sign the road bill, passed by the two houses of parliament.

Even what prosperity exists in Upper Canada has an ironic aspect:

> Chatham is a thriving town, it has several respectable stores and taverns, and a steamboat leaves it once in two days for Sandwich; and another boat is expected to ply between the two places shortly, which argues that trade is on the increase. However, this trade is principally composed of persons and their luggage going to the far west. Many of these are from the eastern states, and many are flying from the "girdled tree" in Upper Canada. But why are they afraid of the "girdled tree?" Because they are afraid the root is rotting, and that the trunk will fall upon them and crush them to the earth. For, at the last election, many of the limbs fell on the reformers' heads, and nearly deprived some of life. Others had to retreat to their homes to

> save their lives. Therefore, after the election, many of these reformers sold their property, settled their affairs, and made their way to the Chatham steam boats, for the far west, where they might have elections without cudgels and bribery, and get rid of a detestable aristocracy, and where they would get education for their children, and enjoy all the blessings of civil and religious freedom.

At length he arrives at the last Canadian outpost. Ahead is the United States.

> I reached Sandwich, as it is called, though it is two miles from the real village, and is the place of crossing the river to Detroit. Sandwich is not a place of much business; however, there are a few stores, and I saw a small steam boat, a schooner and a few small craft. Sir F. B. Head's blasting political wind must have reached this place.

The contrast with Detroit, on the American side of the river, is overwhelming:

> The number of steam boats, schooners and other vessels was a proof that things were better managed in the States than in Canada. The Canadians are languid, disspirited, and almost in despair, while the States people are lively, energetic, enterprising, and with every hope of success. Every man appeared to have the eyes of an eagle, and the feet of a deer. The people in Detroit live, and they welcome others to live with them.

He begins his investigation of American reality with an account of the bustling city of Detroit:*

> After this digression I would observe that from two to eight steam boats come to Detroit and leave it every day, besides a great number of schooners and other craft. The flow of emigration through Detroit to the western states, is often, as nearly as I could ascertain, two thousand per day. One steam boat after another came in, and I thought they never would have done unloading. I asked on one of these boats how many passengers they had brought from Buffalo, and they said six hundred. All the houses of entertainment at Detroit are crowded to excess. This city is well laid out, and its buildings are of a magnificent description. The meat market both pleased and surprised me.

* The obvious ironies of this description of Detroit past in comparison with Detroit of today only increase the poignancy of Davis' account of his experience and his admiration. This irony was the basis of the stage interpretation of Davis' tale.

> The museum is a place of considerable interest. The curiosities are rare, and the statues of great persons are well executed.

Needless to say, these were sights not to be found in Upper Canada. Davis the farmer, however, is most interested in life in the countryside. He travels on, by steamboat, railroad, wagon, horse, canoe and foot. He passes through the frontier states of Ohio, Michigan and Indiana. Everywhere he is assaulted by visions of abundance:

> The Indian corn fields were numerous and extensive, and for the first time in fifteen years I saw fine peaches. Towards night I came to a place called Bloomfield, and it is rightly named: the fruit was abundant; I saw people taking away waggon loads of peaches; and the trees were bending and breaking under their fruit. . . .
>
> Mr. Reynolds was cutting his second crop of clover, which was as heavy as our first crop in Canada; the after grass was twelve inches high, and very thick on the ground. The orchards were loaded with apples and peaches:
>
> They make cheese to weigh sixty pounds, and some of the farmers sell immense droves of cattle; I was told that the owner of one farm sold five thousand. I met a drove of four hundred going to Philadelphia, Pennsylvania. Waggons fetch away their cheese and butter, so that they have plenty of sale for their produce. . . .
>
> I left Darby Plains for Urbana, and on the road the fruit was so plentiful that the hogs fed on it.

Everywhere people are travelling west to settle and work:

> We met a great number of canoes loaded with merchandise and emigrants. . . .
>
> A little below Perrysburg there is a ferry, where a horse boat takes over people, cattle, wagons, &c. Great numbers were on each side of the river waiting to go over; many of these were emigrants, whose respectability we could not help noticing, and we observed to each other what a country this would be fifty years to come.

Towns are exploding alongside the fields:

> In the evening we heard a deal of firing and found when we came to a small village called Gilead, that they had been blasting rocks for a mill race. It is astonishing how quickly villages rise up in the United States. One would wonder where all the people come from.

Davis, like many Upper Canadian Reformers, is very curious

about the well known freedom of religion, and the separation of church and state; he looks into the practice of religion:

> After breakfasting with the quaker on the Sabbath day morning I walked between one and two miles to Bucyrus that I might enjoy the means of grace; and was pleased to find the place free from intoxication and profanation. I visited the Lutheran Sunday School, which was managed with great propriety, it was kept in the court house. In this place there were no prisoners, the happy effects of free institutions. From the Sunday School I went to the Methodist Meeting House, which was full of people. This gave me a favorable opinion of the town. I afterwards went to the court house and heard a most excellent sermon from Rev. I. 2.

He investigates land policies:

> The land office was constantly full of land buyers, who bought their land, paid down their money, and took away their deeds with them. I thought this was the right way of doing business. . . .
>
> A small town lot in Wayne, two years ago, sold for two hundred dollars, and the same lot, without any buildings on it, was sold a few days before my arrival, for seven thousand dollars. A colored man sold eighty acres for nine hundred dollars; two years before, he bought it at government price. He had only cleared five acres.

Everything he discovers that is American contrasts favourably to what he knows so well as Upper Canadian:

> Land in Canada often decreases in value instead of increasing. When will people open their eyes? What man's property in Upper Canada, increases in the same ratio with the United States property?

In fact a sense of difference is his overwhelming experience. He compares obsessively:

> What a contrast between Ohio and Upper Canada! Ohio was first settled in 1788, and it now contains more than 1,300,000 inhabitants, has five hundred and fifty miles of canal navigation, which cost upwards of five millions of dollars, besides a vast length of rail road, and a great deal both of rail road and canal work going on. Ohio has also eight chartered colleges, three of which are universities well supported. Congress has appropriated for common schools in Ohio, 678,576 acres of land, worth one thousand five hundred dollars, besides a tax on all taxable property of three fourths of a mill upon the dollar. Now. Upper Canada has been settling much longer than Ohio and

> yet the population of Upper Canada is at present no more than 365,-312, and no canal worth mentioning, and no rail road, neither has it any college except one on partial principles, for the use of the Church of England folks, or the great folks, and which has created much dissatisfaction in the province. And as for common schools, the aristocracy hate them, and therefore, will not encourage them. My children are without education, and must remain so, unless I shift my quarters.

The contrasts he finds are not merely material, but extend to the attitudes held by the people in the two countries:

> The landlord of this house made some remarks in answer to a question of mine, that exactly pleased me. He said that he had no more than eighty acres of land, and he wanted no more, as he preferred the society of his fellow men to having large tracts of land, which was a principle on which they wished to settle the United States. How different is this man's principle from that of the aristocracy of Upper Canada, who would like to have in possession all the land, and the poor men as their vassals.

But things, he discovers, have not always been so fine. They are the result of a steady improvement:

> Groceries in Ohio were very dear in 1820, tea from two to four dollars per pound, and salt from two to four dollars a bushel; at present, tea half a dollar per pound, and salt two and a quarter dollars a barrel. Formerly it took four or five weeks to go to New-York or Philadelphia, which can be performed now in a week. So much for Yankee enterprise, and so much for mobocracy, as our Solicitor General terms it.

"Let Canadians judge," says Robert Davis, "why there is prosperity in the States and poverty in Canada." The answer to that question is the same no matter where he puts it in his travels:

> These people, like all I had seen, looked ahead for prosperity, and are seldom disappointed, as the legislature encourage the people; but we are very differently treated by our Canadian legislature.

American governments look to the welfare of American farmers, not to their detriment, as in Upper Canada:

> Pork can be sent cheaper from Ohio to Montreal than from the London District. The States people can take their produce into our

> markets without duty, while a heavy duty is imposed on our produce if taken to the States. This is some of the Legislative managements of Canada, and Downing-street policy, to the detriment of the Canadian farmers.
>
> I mentioned this to an American who said, it was not fair play; but said he, we will protect our farmers, and if the British government will not protect theirs, that is not our fault: at the same time we will make hay while the sun shines. I felt a little touched at observing with what composure he uttered his remarks. He was going on to say, "we farmers choose our own governors, our own senators, our own legislators, to make laws, to encourage agriculture and protect our trade": at which I bid farewell, thinking on the bitterness of a Canadian's situation.

Prosperity in the end is traceable to politics. Everytime he examines a situation he comes to this conclusion:

> Indiana will be a flourishing state in a few years, as the legislature makes every exertion for the good of the people. Last year they granted a loan of fifteen millions and a half of dollars for public improvement, besides a million and a half of dollars of surplus revenue returned them by congress. When will the legislature of Upper Canada return a like sum to the people?

Davis had been through a powerful learning experience, but it was a painful one as well. For the more he saw the more he compared their situation with his own. And the more he did so, the more embarrassment he felt. He relates conversation with a farmer in Ohio who had expressed interest in moving to Canada, and proposed a trade of farms with Davis:

> Davis. Have you schools in this neighborhood for the education of your children?
>
> Friend. Yes sir, we are well provided with schools, Congress gives one section of land, that is 640 acres; besides one and a half mills on the dollar land valuation for the same purposes, and any man that will not give his children a good education is not much thought of here.
>
> Davis. Have you any ministers of the gospel to preach to you?
>
> Friend. Yes, we have Methodists, Baptists, Lutherans and others.
>
> Davis. And still you want to go to Canada. I have land in Canada and I will trade or exchange with you.
>
> Friend. I declare, and you are a Canadian. Now I want to hear all about it. But are you a man that can be depended on?

Davis. That is not for me to say, but if you will go over to Canada where I reside you can ask of my character.

Friend. Well is Canada a good country?

Davis. Yes sir, if it had fair play.

Friend. Why you make me stare. Has it not a good government?

Davis. As to that there is difference of opinion, but if you had been in London at the last election, you would have seen a set of government tools called Orange men, running up and down the streets crying five pounds for a liberal; and if a man said a word contrary to their opinion he was knocked down. Many were knocked down in this way and others threatened; and all this in the presence of Magistrates, Church of England Ministers and Judges, who made use of no means to prevent such outrages.

Friend. Well now Sir, I am done: and rather than get my head broken I will stay where I am. Here I can tell my thoughts without fear. And if the President should take a club and strike me, I guess I would make him rue it. He would be put into our County jail quicker than shot. If any man should strike me with a club, and I lived in a country where they would not give me justice I would settle matters with him myself; and yet I never struck a man in my life.

Americans taunted him:

> Canadian, you may look; are you getting angry? It is the truth and you cannot deny it. We can boast of our American institutions: look where you will, and you will find all activity and enterprise. Our internal improvements are without parallel in the world. Monarchical governments extend their dominions by conquests, but we by purchase and emigration. Since our Independence we have added to our territory East and West Florida, which cost us five millions of dollars, and Louisiana, which cost us fifteen millions of dollars: and we have paid the money. It costs more to support the English Church government, then it does to maintain the American civil government, with all her armies and navies: and what better does religion prosper in the British Empire than in the United States of America?

He had difficulty responding to many of these gibes:

> The captain of an American schooner said in my presence, that they had to dig their way through the Welland Canal, and then pay toll for it: but, said he, the day is coming when we shall have a ship canal of our own, and then we shall not be troubled. I felt a little roused to hear this captain talk as he did, and therefore reminded him that Upper Canada had given six hundred thousand dollars, besides those

> who have shares in our canal. But I had to confess that the money had been badly employed, or much of it embezzled. Indeed, no man can have his eyes blinded against the fact.

But the taunts ended in confirming him in his political convictions. "After these reflections I felt proud that we had such a number of independent men in my country who despised both Sir Francis and his bread and butter."* His frustration reached a peak, though, during a conversation he had with several American travellers as he journeyed back toward Detroit, and beyond it to Canada.

> One of the gentlemen present observed to them that there was a Canadian in the company who had been travelling in the United States, and who would undoubtedly give them information on the subjects of which they had been speaking. These gentlemen said, had they known of my being present they would not have entered so fully into the subjects themselves, as I must be a critic in Canadian politics if I had entered warmly into the late election. I answered that I did not take a very active part in them, but I had witnessed some who received hard blows, and that the first time I had seen men in anger draw blood from each other, was when I beheld it follow the clubs of the Orange men; and that I hoped that I should never see the like again, rather than see which I would sooner be transported to the Rocky Mountains. Governor Colbourne told us, he would cause emigrants to come from Europe that would infuse British principles into the people of Upper Canada, but if that be the mode of planting, I hoped my head would never be ploughed up to receive such seed, and that by such a mode of planting, I was sure it would not grow. I had always thought that I was a British subject, but I found that I could not be one, without breaking my neighbour's bones, and therefore gave up the thoughts, as I cannot be an Orange club man.
>
> These plain and broad expressions, spoken in an earnest manner, caused a general burst of laughter, for which the gentlemen apologized, and asked my pardon for their want of decorum. I proceeded: Ladies and gentlemen, you may laugh, but I am in earnest.

The people Davis was travelling with urged him to stay in the United States, to bring down his family, and to share in all the benefits he had observed on his journey. If Davis was tempted, he does not let on:

* For this reference, see the script of *1837* the scene titled The Head.

> I thanked them for their invitation to live in their country, but told them I had been laboring hard by my axe and other ways, to make Canada my home, and after all, my children were without education, and my industry and hopes were nullified. But if I could not get education for my children in Canada, I would go to the United States, and work as a day laborer before they should go without it. At this expression, the whole cabin resounded with approbation.

He finished his travels in the United States in the same city in which he began them, and his last moments evoked similar feelings to those he'd had on arriving:

> I walked through the city, and admired the enterprize of its inhabitants and the immense business transacted, after which I crossed the river into Upper Canada accompanied by Col. Adams. While walking down the river we observed to each other, what a beautiful situation the Canada side was for a city, yet all was dull: the Colonel observed, all was still as Sunday; and that he did not blame me for being dissatisfied with such a government. Here was one steam boat, but without passengers. — No pleasure trips on the Lake, or any thing that showed life and activity.

After arriving home, on October 10, 1836, he summed up what he had learned:

> The United States of America will ere long be the most wealthy, the most powerful, and the most happy country in the whole world. In the short period since their independence, they have made more rapid progress in internal improvements, foreign and domestic trade and commerce, arts and sciences, jurisprudence, religion, and the great secret of making a nation free and happy, of any country in the history of the world. The United States are now become the wonder, the envy, and terror of Europe.
>
> If it be asked what is the chief cause of prosperity in the United States? the answer is, their Elective Institutions, the Democratic Principle, which runs through all their projects. They have no Hereditary rulers, no titled drones, no useless tax-eaters, no union of church and state; and as they are not jealous of the people becoming too wise to be governed, they encourage Education.

For Davis, as for so many Upper Canadians, the United States was a massive, looming, goading presence. Myths of its magnificence and its maleficence were palpable forces in the minds of the inhabitants of the colony. So strong were those myths that to some extent the United States Davis sees on his travels is more a projection of his hopes and expectations than any sober empirical reality. He seemed incapable of seeing anything American as less than ideal. His tolerance of slavery and his praise of the way the American government dealt with the Indians are particularly off. On the other hand the western states of those years were undoubtedly impressive, particularly in comparison with Upper Canada. They probably came as close to concretizing the American dream as ever happened in the history of that country. The United States expanded, its economy boomed, and Upper Canada stagnated.

The comparison, in fact, was the point for Davis. He looked to the States for hope and for assurance that his own ambitions and standards as an Upper Canadian were not vain. Demoralization in a situation like his was a grave danger. The U.S. — what he saw of it and for that matter wanted to see of it — apparently pulled him free of despair. He published his book within a year of his return. That same year when the war for independence and democracy finally broke out in Upper Canada, Davis went off to fight. In December 1837 he was wounded near Amherstburg, south of Sandwich on Lake Erie. He died of those wounds. He had put his literary conclusions into practice, but that should be no surprise. As he said at one of those points in his journey when Americans were taunting him about the deficiencies of his homeland, "It is not to be supposed that Upper Canada is to be a laughing stock forever."

Chapter 5

The Canadian revolution and its aftermath

Organization

The summer and fall of 1837 was a time of intense preparation for the Radical Reformers of Upper Canada. They felt that every possibility of peaceful change had been exhausted. Elections, legislation, petitions to the local government or the imperial government had all been tried and failed. Direct action with popular backing was the only route open to them. In addition, events in Lower Canada were moving very quickly toward a crisis which would probably involve armed revolt. The Upper Canadian radicals were in close and regular contact with the French-Canadian Patriots and realized that their own success depended on coordination and joint action with the French. Accordingly they had to be prepared to move when things came to a head in Quebec.

They organized on two levels. On the public level, two hundred "monster meetings" or mass rallies were held throughout the province during the summer and fall of 1837. These amounted to independence rallies, and served to prepare the people for armed struggle, if this should become necessary. At the same time they proceeded secretively on a different level. In late July of 1837 Mackenzie presented a plan to his small inner circle of colleagues proposing a network of "societies" throughout Upper Canada. Each was to be a small, discreet unit of reliable individuals: "In order to avoid the mixture of persons unknown to each other, no Society is to consist of less than twelve or more than forty persons, and those to be resident as nearly as possible in the same neighbourhood." The societies were to be in touch with one another, and coordinated at a higher level by representatives who would comprise township committees. This pyramiding organization would continue at still higher levels with the formation of county committees and district committees. All of Upper Canada was to be organized in this manner into "four grand Divisions" which Mackenzie enumerated. The societies amounted to revolutionary cells scattered throughout local communities in Upper Canada, a disciplined force ready to be mobilized in opposition to the government authorities. The crucial element in the plan was that each society could be converted into a paramilitary unit at the moment of crisis. Mackenzie wrote:

> A plan, as I have suggested, could be easily transferred without change of its structure to military purposes. The secretary of each subordinate Society of twelve might easily be transformed into a sergeant or corporal; the delegate of five Societies to a Township Committee, into a captain with sixty men under his command; and the delegate of ten Township Committees to a District Committee into a colonel at the head of a battalion of six hundred men.

This disciplined, small scale organization proceeded alongside the popular agitational work of the meetings and the public pamphleteering such as the July 31 Declaration of Independence. By November, Mackenzie had a secret list of 1,500 men pledged to fight, if necessary, for the goals of self-government and independence.* A revolutionary organization had been set in motion; it was to be tested in the events that followed.

Doel's Brewery

Perhaps the most significant event of 1837 was one which did not happen. In early November, an opportunity for a *coup d'etat* in Toronto presented itself. The British had sent all their forces to Lower Canada to prepare for the war that everyone knew was imminent there. There were *no* British soldiers left in Upper Canada. Even Fort Henry in Kingston had been deserted. The British knew they were taking a risk, however they apparently considered the situation in Quebec sufficiently perilous to justify the transfer. A huge store of new muskets had arrived in Toronto for the army and had not yet been distributed. Considering that

* This was a substantial number to be formally committed to insurrection out of a population of about 300,000. It would be equivalent to a force of about 25,000 in the Ontario of today.

Drilling north of Toronto.

only one in five of the 1,500 men pledged to revolutionary action had weapons, this was a tremendous opportunity. Power was ready to be seized, with the means to do it at hand.

Mackenzie called a meeting of radical reform leaders at Doel's Brewery, at the corner of Bay and Adelaide streets, to urge action. Among those present were Dr. T. D. Morrison, John

Armstrong, a Scots axemaker, several merchants, a carpenter and a lawyer. Mackenzie began by explaining the political developments which had brought them to the current pass. He concluded his summary by asking "if the proper change could be obtained in any possible way short of revolution?" To this there was, as he says, "no answer."

He then moved swiftly to his proposal:

> I stated that there were two ways of effecting a revolution: one of them by organizing the farmers, who were quite prepared for resistance, and bringing them into Toronto, to unite with the Toronto people; and the other, by immediate action.
>
> Dr. Morrison made some deprecatory or dissenting remark, but I continued.
>
> I said, that the troops had left; that those who had persuaded Head to place four thousand stand of arms in the midst of an unarmed people in the City Hall, seemed evidently not opposed to their being used; that Fort Henry was open and empty, and a steamer had only to sail down to the wharf and take possession; that I had sent two trusty persons, separately, to the garrison, that day, and it was also 'to let'; that the Lieutenant Governor had just come in from his ride, and was now at home, guarded by one sentinel; and that my judgment was that we should instantly send for Dutcher's foundry-men and Armstrong's axe-makers, all of whom could be depended on, and, with them, go promptly to the Government House, seize Sir Francis, carry him to the City Hall, a fortress in itself, seize the arms and ammunition there, and the artillery, etc., in the old garrison; rouse our innumerable friends in town and country, proclaim a Provisional Government, send off the steamer of that evening to secure Fort Henry, and either induce Sir Francis to give the country an Executive Council responsible to a new and fairly chosen Assembly to be forthwith elected, after packing off the usurpers in the 'Bread and Butter Parliament,' such new Assembly to be convened immediately; or if he refused to comply, go at once for Independence, and take the proper steps to obtain and secure it.
>
> I also communicated, in the course of my remarks, important facts relative to Lower Canada, and the disposition of her leading men.
>
> Dr. Morrison manifested great astonishment and impatience toward the close of my discourse, and at length hastily rose and exclaimed that this was treason, if I was really serious, and that if I thought I could entrap him into any such mad scheme, I would find that he was not my man. I tried to argue with him, but finding that he was resolute and determined, soon desisted.

John Doel's Brewery and homestead at the corner of Bay and Adelaide, Toronto.

> That the proposition I made could have been easily and thoroughly carried into effect, I have never for a moment doubted; and I would have gone about it promptly, in preference to the course afterwards agreed upon, but for the indecision or hesitancy of those who longed for a change, but disliked risking anything on such issues.

This sounds like a somewhat restrained account by Mackenzie of what probably was said at this meeting. He was, after all, proposing to a group of basically very 'respectable' citizens that they take arms against the empire. The last Canadians to do so were those who joined the invaders in the War of 1812. A goodly number of them had been hanged, drawn and quartered at the "bloody assizes" at Ancaster in 1814. He was not only suggesting that they instigate a revolution, but that they personally carry it out. Even the signers of the Declaration of Independence in 1776 were not called on to personally overthrow the King's representative. Not surprisingly, the group gathered at Doel's declined.

This is one of the great "What might have beens" of Canadian history. Had they moved and seized power, the British would have been forced to divert a large portion of their forces back to Upper Canada. This in turn would have afforded the French Canadian revolutionaries a much greater chance of victory against the British in the heavy fighting that occurred in Quebec. And in Upper Canada an initial clear victory might well have ignited the revolutionary cause. Whether or not the Upper Canadian Radicals could have held out against the British and Tory forces cannot of course be known, but the history of the Revolutions of 1837 — and very probably the history of Canada — might have been vastly different.

So much for what might have been. The meeting at Doel's Brewery produced no action. A short time later, on November 18, a similar gathering did decide on a plan of action. They chose Mackenzie's alternate strategy: bring down the farmers. The purpose was the same: overthrow the government and seize the arms, but the method was to be by armed attack on the city. The members of the societies would be brought to Toronto as secretly as possible, assemble north of the city at Montgomery's Tavern on Yonge St., and advance and occupy the capital. The followup: a provisional government, demands for constitutional reform *etc.*, were to proceed as Mackenzie had outlined in his earlier proposal. It was expected that four to five thousand men could be gathered for such an attack, and since organization would take some time, the date for the assembly and advance was set as December 7. The man in overall charge of the operation was to be Dr. John Rolph, who was also selected to head the provisional government that would be established. Rolph would stay in Toronto while the rest of the conspirators, including Mackenzie, scattered through the colony, spreading the word and making preparations. No changes in the plan of any sort — above all in the date — were to be allowed except by agreement of all those who had initiated the program.

The Battle of Toronto

The siege and battle of Toronto was the most important single event — or series of events — of the revolution of 1837 in Upper Canada. For about a week between Saturday December 2 and Thursday December 7, the purposes and actions of partisans on both sides swirled around Toronto. The city at the time was a sleepy provincial capital with a population between ten and twelve thousand; now it was being besieged by a force of from five hundred to one thousand men. The government authorities were justly fearful; in addition to the rebel force proper, they did not know the extent of revolutionary sentiment within the city. The fate of this army would determine the fate of Upper Canada.

After the battle of Toronto, fighting went on for over a year but with the exception of Duncombe's army in the western part of the province, it was all initiated from the other side of the American border. Only during these first weeks did the Upper Canadian revolutionaries base themselves within the colony, where they had the greatest chance of arousing supporters.

The reasons for the defeat at Toronto are numerous, but most important was an ill-advised change of date made by Rolph on his own initiative and then inadequately communicated to those outside Toronto. Because of this alteration men did not arrive simultaneously and the full force never did gather; the commander-in-chief arrived later than his troops; the only other experienced military leader was killed in a freak accident very early in the siege; the cannon the revolutionaries had expected was lost and their lack of artillery was crucial in the battle; food and lodging arrangements were inadequate; the revolutionaries lost the initiative and surprise while the government authorities were informed and prepared. Yet such foulups are common in the early stages of revolutionary struggles. Control over such things as organization and communication is what the fight is *about,* and at the start the revolutionary forces are bound to be in some disarray. The main thing was that insurrection had finally broken out. There was no way of knowing then which way it would break. Here is an account of those days in and around Toronto:

● Saturday afternoon December 2. A special meeting of the Executive Council, which Rolph, the only rebel leader still left in Toronto, hears of. It is reported that the Council has learned of the attack planned for the 7th, and that a warrant for treason is out on Mackenzie. Rolph decides to change the day of the meeting to Monday the 4th. That night he sends a verbal message to David Gibson, four miles north of Montgomery's Tavern. Gibson sends it on to Samuel Lount's home at Holland Landing. Lount is away but Mrs. Lount takes the message.

● Sunday night. Lount returns and his wife gives him the message. Says he, "Rolph will be the ruin of us all." But he confers with Anthony Anderson and they begin to inform their men.

● Sunday night. Mackenzie hears of the change at David Gibson's house, is incensed and sends one of Gibson's servants to tell Lount not to march.

● Sunday night in Toronto. Rumours abound: that armed men are assembling at Holland Landing and Newmarket; that the rebels have lists of houses in Toronto they are going to burn; that Lount has been forging pikes for them at his smithy; and that a Yankee invasion is imminent. Businesses begin to close up.

● Monday morning. Lloydtown. Men begin to assemble in small groups and move out to work their way by various routes to Montgomery's Tavern. Many come unarmed so as not to attract attention. They expect there will be arms at Montgomery's.

● Monday afternoon. Mackenzie, Rolph and Gibson meet north of Montgomery's on Yonge St. Gibson's servant returns with word it is too late to stop the uprising — the entire north knows of it. Mackenzie is in favour of moving that night as soon as the men arrive. Gibson is opposed. The final decision is left for Lount to make when he arrives. In the meantime, they decide to set a picket across Yonge St. at Montgomery's to make sure news doesn't reach the city. Then Mackenzie and Gibson go off to Shepard's mill near the Humber, where bullets are being run.

● Monday 7 p.m. Twenty men from Lloydtown are the first to arrive at Montgomery's Tavern. Then comes Anderson's group. Finally Lount, with ninety men from around Holland Landing. Altogether there are about 150 men at the tavern. But, owing to the change in date, there is a shortage of arms and provisions, and the men are discouraged to hear of the defeat of the Lower Canadians at St. Charles. They are too tired to continue that night. Mackenzie's proposal to move on is defeated.

● Monday 8 to 9 p.m. Mackenzie, Anderson and Shepard set out by horse down Yonge St. to scout the city, prepare their allies for an attack the next day, and bring Rolph and Morrison back with them. At the top of Gallows Hill, just below St. Clair, they meet Tory alderman John Powell, patrolling out from the city. They take him prisoner. Powell swears he is unarmed and Mackenzie takes his word as a gentleman. Mackenzie sends him back toward Montgomery's with Anderson and Shepard and continues on. But Powell has lied and has two pistols concealed. He falls behind Anderson, draws one pistol and shoots Anderson through the back of the neck. Anderson falls from his horse, breaks his neck and dies. Powell rides back toward Toronto. Mackenzie, hearing the shot, starts back. He sees Powell coming, fires at him, but misses. Then Powell fires at Mackenzie at close range, but his gun flashes in the pan. He gallops on. Mackenzie rides back to Montgomery's. Anderson is dead, the only rebel leader present with military experience.

● Monday evening about the same time. Col. Robert Moodie of Richmond Hill has gathered prominent Tories at his house and determined to send word to the city of the troop movements they have seen all day. He sets out by horse with three others. As they approach Montgomery's there are three pickets set out across the road. Moodie fires his pistol at the first picket and charges through. A guard in the second picket raises his rifle and shoots Moodie. He is dead before he hits the ground. Rumour of his death begins almost immediately to circulate among the Loyalists in the area.

Meanwhile Powell has reached Davenport, where he abandons his horse. He proceeds by foot down to Queen's Park, across Queen's Park and down to Government House. Meanwhile in the city, Colonel James FitzGibbon, head of the militia, rouses Sir Francis at 10 p.m., but Sir Francis goes right back to sleep. "Good Lord, what an old woman I have to deal with," thinks FitzGibbon. At 11 p.m., Powell reaches Government House, rouses Sir Francis again and reports what he has seen. This time Sir Francis orders his family placed on a steamer in the harbour and the bells rung in the city as a sign of crisis.

● Monday midnight. The home of William Copland, just east of Yonge, one quarter mile north of the Bloor tollgate. "At about 12 o'clock, I was awakened by the report of two guns fired in a wood in front of my house; I listened for some time, but could hear nothing more and went to sleep. At about half past one, however, I was called up by a neighbour, who said that the rebels had got into the city and had killed one gentleman on the road. I thought no time was to be lost; and as soon as we knew the road was clear we packed up our plate and such other things as we could carry on foot, buried my account books in the garden, went off to town, and took refuge in my brother-in-law's house."

● Monday midnight. In the city Samuel Thompson hears the sound of hoofbeats and goes out to Ridouts' Corner, at King and Yonge, where Powell has dismounted and is telling of his capture and escape.

● Monday midnight. More rebel forces arrive at Montgomery's. Mackenzie again wants to march on the city but is overruled.

● Tuesday morning. At Montgomery's there are between seven and eight hundred men, poorly armed. Many leave immediately when they hear there are no arms for them.

● Tuesday morning in Toronto. Out of a population of over 10,000,

Head has managed to raise a force of only 300 during the night. In order to gain time while reinforcements are on the way, he decides to send a flag of truce to Mackenzie. He asks Rolph to go and Rolph at first refuses. Bond Head suggests that this refusal might be the act of a rebel, and Rolph agrees to go. The truce commission consists of Rolph, Baldwin and Hugh Carmichael, a carpenter, who carries the flag. Groups of children follow them up Yonge St.

Mackenzie and Lount start south from Montgomery's about noon with their force. They include 50 or 60 prisoners to swell their numbers. At the top of Gallows Hill, the truce party comes in sight.

They tell Mackenzie and Lount that Head will pardon everyone if they lay down their arms, Mackenzie replies his terms are, "Independence, and a convention to arrange details." The truce party returns to the governor for his answer. An hour later they return with the governor's refusal to bargain further. Rolph indicates to Lount in an aside that the forces should follow him into the city. The men, unaware of the role Rolph is playing, are confused and demoralized at the sight of him in a neutral position.

Dr. Rolph goes back, and into John Elliot's tavern, at the corner of Yonge and Queen, where many Reformers are gathered. He tells them that the rebel army is coming up right behind him. He then goes to a meeting at Doel's Brewery. But the army does not appear.

During the afternoon, Mackenzie sets fire to the house of Dr. Robert Horne, on the east side of Yonge, south of Sheriff Jarvis's estate in Rosedale. Horne's house was a centre for Tory spies. The smoke is visible in Toronto.

● At 5:45 p.m. Mackenzie assembles his men at the Bloor tollgate and addresses them. He tells them there will be no difficulty taking the city, that the Lieutenant Governor has been able to assemble only a small force, including boys from Upper Canada College, and that Head's family are already on a steamer in the harbour. They move down Yonge St., Lount and his riflemen in the lead, followed by men with pikes, followed by men armed only with sticks and cudgels. It is now very dark.

● At McGill St. Sheriff Jarvis has stationed 27 men of the Queen's York Rangers behind a fence. When the force is very close, they fire, and three rebels are hit. Lount's riflemen fire back, then kneel down to let those behind them shoot. Both sides are completely unfamiliar with battle. In the total darkness they panic. Each side flees, Jarvis' men head toward Toronto.

Mackenzie's men rush back toward the tollgate. Mackenzie tries to stop them, tells them this is their chance and by tomorrow it might be gone; he volunteers to continue if only twenty men will join him, but the men say they will not go on until daylight, and return to Montgomery's. One member of the rebel force, James Henderson, dies in the battle.

● Tuesday night in Toronto. A three pound cannon, just dry from the painting, is seized by the government at Norton's Foundry. It was meant for the rebels. Loyalist reinforcements begin to arrive. The first are 100 men from Scarborough under Captain Maclean, then Alan MacNab arrives on a steamer from Hamilton with 65 men. All day there is a great military stir at the market. Muskets are being issued to citizens.

At Montgomery's, there are rumours that the Tories in the city will shoot down from their windows protected by mattresses and feather beds. Many of the men leave for home, but about 200 more arrive. By Wednesday there are 550 men at Montgomery's.

● Wednesday morning in Toronto. Dr. Rolph flees to the United States. Between 6 and 7 a.m., a force takes Mackenzie's printing office. Dr. Morrison is arrested and charged with treason. The principal buildings — the City Hall, the Upper Canada Bank, the Parliament Buildings, Osgoode Hall, Government House, the Canada Company Office — and many private dwellings and shops are barricaded with two inch planks. Stores are closed and bread, potatoes and meat rise to famine prices. At 3 p.m. 400 men under MacNab parade Morrison through the streets. A loaded cannon precedes them. The militia are called out and put on pay and rations.

● Wednesday morning at Montgomery's. Mackenzie, Lount and others set out on horseback to intercept the western mail coach. They meet it at the Peacock Inn, on Dundas St., four miles west of Toronto. They seize the letters, including one from Robinson announcing a government plan for an offensive against Montgomery's. They take the stage, driver, and passengers back to Montgomery's.

At Montgomery's, two men wounded in Tuesday night's battle, die from loss of blood. In Toronto that night, the Loyalist leaders hold a council of war in Archdeacon Strachan's house overlooking the bay, in order to prepare the next day's battle.

● Thursday morning. Anthony van Egmond, the former cavalry colonel under Napoleon, arrives at 8 a.m. at Montgomery's and takes control of the rebel forces. A council of war is held. They decide to try and avoid a battle that day by sending a diversionary force under Peter Matthews east of the city. The rest wait for reinforcements at

Montgomery's. 550 men are reported on the way.

Meanwhile in Toronto, more government reinforcements have arrived. They draw up in battle order in the street and esplanade in front of Strachan's residence on Front St. The Lieutenant Governor is there in his everyday suit, with one double barrelled gun in his hand, another leaning against his breast, and a brace of pistols in his leather belt. Also Chief Justice Robinson, Judges Macaulay, Jones, and Maclean, the Attorney General, and the Solicitor General, all standing in the ranks as private soldiers under the command of Colonel FitzGibbon. At noon they begin to move north. Many unarmed citizens, including Archdeacon Strachan, march behind.

To the east, Matthews and his force stop the Montreal mailcoach, then cross the Don River and move west on King St. till they meet a militia detachment under George Ridout. They retreat over the bridge, attempting to burn it. On the east side of the river they burn a tavern and tollgate. During an exchange of fire a hostler is fatally shot in the throat. The bridge itself is saved.

But the main loyalist army is already moving toward Montgomery's. They have 920 men. In the centre are 600, lead by Sir Francis, FitzGibbon, and MacNab. They proceed up Yonge St. They have two cannons. On their left, 200 men under Colonel Chisholm move up College St., through Queen's Park, and on up various side roads. The right wing, under Colonel Jarvis, marches through ploughed fields to the east of Yonge St. Two military bands play Yankee Doodle as a satirical comment on the revolutionaries.

● One o'clock at the top of Gallows Hill. Rebel sentinels see the government force and a scout carries the news back to Montgomery's. Mackenzie himself rides out to check, rides back, and asks the 400 men still at Montgomery's if they are ready to fight a force larger and better armed than they are. They answer — Yes. A force of 150 under Van Egmond and Lount move into a small wood south of the tavern west of Yonge. Another 60 position behind rail fences in an open field across the road. A small force moves into the Paul Pry Inn, east of Yonge. 200 men who do not have arms remain at the tavern. When FitzGibbon's main force reaches the brow of the hill, they set their two nine-pounders west of Yonge and fire into the wood. A veteran of that engagement on the rebel side recalls: "We had no arms but our rifles and some had only rude pikes and pitchforks; the troops, besides their muskets and plenty of ammunition, had two small field pieces — one controlled by a friend of ours and the other by an enemy. The friend fired grapeshot and fired over us into the tops of the trees, cutting the dead and dry limbs of the hemlocks

The battle of Montgomery's Tavern.

which, falling thickly among us, scared the boys as much as if cannon balls had been rattling around us. The other gun was fired low, and so careless that I did not like it. One of the balls struck a sandbank by my feet and filled my eyes with sand, nearly blinding me. Capt. Wideman was killed on my left side and F. Shell was shot through the shoulder to the left of the captain."

The left wing of the loyalist force moves in on the wood from the west. The fighting lasts a half hour. Then the main body moves on, fire their cannon into the Paul Pry Inn, dislodging the rebels there, and then fire into Montgomery's. The men there pour out like bees from a hive. Some are captured. Bond Head orders and supervises the burning to the ground of the Tavern. Eleven patriots have been wounded; four of them die afterward in the hospital. Capt. Ludwig Wideman is dead in the wood. Five loyalists are wounded. The battle of Montgomery's Tavern is over, and so is the struggle for Toronto.

Duncombe's Army

Along with Toronto and the area just north of it, the western part of the province was also a Reform and Radical stronghold. This was reflected when fighting broke out in Toronto. A sizeable rebel army was assembled in the west. Its leader was Dr. Charles

Duncombe, the American-born physician and parliamentarian. Communications again proved treacherous. It was only on December 6 that Duncombe heard of the initial plan for an attack on Toronto on the 7th. On that same day, Mackenzie dispatched messengers from Toronto to tell Duncombe of the engagement on Yonge St. the night before, and to ask for immediate support.

The next day, the 7th, while the main battle was being fought in Toronto, a Patriot meeting was held at Joseph Beemer's Inn in the town of Scotland, fifteen miles west of Brantford. Volunteers were called for to assist the forces in Toronto. Half the men there offered to go. Officers were appointed to collect arms and a provisional committee was formed. The meeting concluded with cries of "Down With The King," and "Damn The Tories." Reports had meanwhile reached the authorities in Toronto of what was brewing in London District. Following the battle at Montgomery's Tavern, Bond Head ordered Alan MacNab to take 400 men and march into the district.

On December 8, in London, a group of Reformers gathered in Flanagan's Hotel to prepare defensive measures against attacks they anticipated from Tories. They were not long in waiting. Tories and government officials used the meeting itself as a reason for arresting those who had attended on charges of treason. The next day, December 9, brought the arrival of the messengers Mackenzie had sent out on the 6th. For the first time Duncombe learned of the speedup in schedule at Toronto. He still did not know that the main battle had already been fought and lost. He speeded up his own plan, which was to assemble his supporters in Scotland, march through the Oakland Plains to Brantford, from there descend on Hamilton, consolidating control of all these places and then join Mackenzie's forces in Toronto. Had government forces been defeated, or even just pinned down in Toronto, it would have been a feasible plan.

Finally on December 10, the forces began to gather. One or two hundred men were with Duncombe himself in Sodom in Norwich Township, and another sixty to seventy in Scotland under under Eliakim Malcolm. Farmers and innkeepers sympathetic to the revolt began sending supplies for the army to Scotland. On December 12 Duncombe's contingent reached Scotland.

Others were arriving from farther away, such as Joshua Doan's Spartan Rangers from Yarmouth. By December 13 there were four to five hundred rebel troops in Scotland. On that same day MacNab's government force reached Brantford, fifteen miles to the east. There Macnab added another two hundred and fifty to his force, including one hundred Indians from the reservation near Brantford. In Brantford, MacNab learned of the rebel concentration in Scotland, and sent messengers telling other loyalists to converge on that town. MacNab had by now assumed the role of chief government figure in putting down the uprising. It was a task that demanded energy, organization and ruthlessness and MacNab did it well. He was later knighted for his role.

A rebel scout, who happened to be a doctor, was captured by MacNab's troops near Brantford. He persuaded his captors he was on a sick call, and managed to escape and ride to Duncombe with the news of the army he had seen. When he arrived, the rebel army was drawn up in a line and Duncombe, on horseback, was addressing them. At almost the same time, news finally reached Duncombe of the defeat at Montgomery's Tavern, a full six days before. It was obvious the initial plan was not viable. Rather than an unimpeded advance, they faced a government force which was forewarned, flushed with victory and well-supplied with that decisive element — artillery. Duncombe decided to "retreat and conquer" into Norwich, that is to carry the struggle back toward where he knew support was still firm. Some of his men disagreed; they wanted to stay and fight in the pine woods to the south. About thirty of them remained.

At noon on December 14, MacNab moved out from Brantford toward Scotland. He sent one hundred men to attack from the north while the Indians were to move through the woods to the south. Their instructions were to capture anyone without a badge of red flannel in his cap — a sort of improvised Tory uniform — and to shoot those who tried to escape. When MacNab and his main force reached Scotland, he found Duncombe and most of his troops had left. There was a battle with the small force remaining. Fifteen were captured, and three shot trying to escape into the woods. MacNab camped there; reinforcements kept joining him until by nightfall his army numbered 1,900.

On December 15, Duncombe's army reached Sodom, where

they had started from. Duncomb assessed the situation and decided there was no hope of success, so he dispersed his army. By this time Mackenzie had reached Buffalo and was planning to return with a force to join *Duncombe's* army. But the dispersal of the force by Duncombe, who of course did not know this was Mackenzie's intention ended the possibility of a regrouping within Upper Canada itself. Further rebel military organization would have to take place on American soil. As for MacNab, he left three hundred men in Scotland, announced prices on the heads of the rebel leaders, and focussed on Norwich, which he, like Duncombe, considered "the most disaffected part of this district". He embarked on a vindictive march through the area "for the purpose of scowering the very hotbed of treason."

Mackenzie's Escape

The initial attempts to overthrow the government — in Toronto and in the London district — had failed. The revolutionaries were in disarray and their leaders were in flight. Dr. Rolph had escaped to the United States during the siege itself. Dr. Morrison had been arrested during the same siege and paraded through the streets of Toronto on his way to jail. Marshall Bidwell had been deported by the government though he had taken no part in the revolutionary initiatives. Those leaders who had actually wielded arms faced an even more urgent need to escape, and even greater obstacles to doing so. Rewards were publicly offered for them and they were hunted down by search parties.

Duncombe fled using various devices and disguises. One friendly farm couple kept him in their bed between them at night to conceal him from searchers. Another farmer disguised him as a sleeping "granny" and government soldiers actually overlooked him. Finally, dressed as a woman complete with a curl on his forehead, he crossed the western border into Michigan. The United States was the goal for all the refugees. Samuel Lount hid for days, made his way to Lake Erie, and tried to cross it in a small boat with two companions. Just as they were about to land on the American side after two days of agonizing rowing, a sudden wind drove them back to the mouth of the Grand River on the Canadian side. A local farmer took Lount into custody under

Eliakim Malcolm, a leader in the west.

suspicion of smuggling. A magistrate recognized Lount and from there the way led to the gallows. The farmer who turned Lount in received 500 pounds reward and the disgust of his neighbours. Peter Matthews, who was hanged with Lount in Toronto, was overpowered by militia while he slept in a farmhouse. The most incredible tale of escape, though, was Mackenzie's.

A price of 1,000 pounds was put on Mackenzie's head. A circular described him as "a short man, wears a sandy-coloured wig, has small twinkling eyes that can look no man in the face." Yet Mackenzie passed through the most densely populated section of Upper Canada, and no one turned him in. His account of his escape, written from the United States ten years later has the flavour of the flight in defeat of another heroic Scot, Bonnie Prince Charlie. Mackenzie said that he "gloried" in his highland "rebel" blood. Both his grandfathers had fought for "the true king" at the battle of Culloden, and one of them had accompanied the Scottish prince into exile. Mackenzie makes explicit reference to that flight, in his description of his own, following the Canadian battle for national independence.

> It evidently appearing that success for the insurgents was, at that time, impossible, the Colonel and many others gave way, and crossed the field to the parallel line of road west of Yonge Street. I endeavored to get my cloak, which I had left at the hotel, through which Capt. FitzGibbon's men were just then sending their six-pound shots with good effect, but too late. Strange to tell, that cloak was sent to me years afterwards, while in prison, but by whom I know not.
>
> Perceiving that we were not yet pursued, I passed on to Yonge Street, beyond Lawyer Price's, and the first farmer I met, being a friend, readily gave me his horse — a trusty, sure-footed creature, which that day did me good service. Before I had ridden a mile the smoke rose in clouds behind me, and the flames of the extensive hotel and outbuildings arrested my attention, as also another cloud of smoke which I then supposed to be from the Don Bridge, in the city, which we had sent a party to destroy or take possession of. Colonel Fletcher, now of Chautauque county, N.B., handed me an overcoat, and told me he would make for the States, but not by the head of Lake Ontario.
>
> Although it was known that we had been worsted, no one interrupted us, save in friendship. Dr. ———, from above Newmarket, informed me that sixty armed friends were on their way, close by. I assured him it was too late to retrieve our loss in that way, and bade him to tell them to scatter. Some, however, went on, as volunteers for Sir Francis Bond Head; the rest returned to their homes.
>
> At the Golden Line, ten miles above the city, I overtook Col. Anthony Van Egmond, a Dutch officer, of many years' experience under Napoleon. He agreed with me that we should at once make for the Niagara frontier, but was taken, almost immediately after, by a party who had set out from Governor Head's camp, to gain the

rewards then offered there.

The Colonel was a man of large property, old, and known to be opposed to Head's party. Though not found in arms, he was placed in a cell, so cold that they had very soon to take him to the hospital — on his way to the grave.

Finding myself closely pursued and repeatedly fired at, I left the high road with one friend (Mr. J. R.) and made for Shepard's Mills. The fleetest horsemen of the official party were so close upon us that I had only time to jump off my horse, and ask the miller (himself a Tory) whether a large body of men, then on the heights, were friends or foes, before our pursuers were climbing up the steep ascent almost beside me.

When I overtook Col. Lount, he had, I think, about ninety men with him, who were partly armed. We took some refreshment at a friendly farmer's near by. Lount was for dispersing — I proposed that we should keep in a body, and make for the United States, via the head of Lake Ontario, as our opponents had the steamers; but only sixteen persons went with me. I had no other arms than a single-barrel pistol, taken from Capt. Duggan during our Tuesday's scuffle, and we were all on foot. Some of my companions had no weapons at all.

We made for Humber Bridge, through Vaughan, but found it strongly guarded; went up the river a long way, got some supper at the house of a farmer, crossed the stream on a foot bridge, and by two next morning reached the hospitable mansion of a worthy settler on Dundas Street, utterly exhausted with cold and fatigue.

Blankets were hung over the windows to avoid suspicion, food and beds prepared, and while the Tories were carefully searching for us, we were sleeping soundly. Next morning (Friday) those who had arms buried them, and after sending to inquire whether a friend a mile below had been dangerously wounded, we agreed to separate and make for the frontier, two and two together. A lad in his nineteenth or twentieth year accompanied me, and such was my confidence in the honesty and friendship of the country folks, Protestant and Catholic, European and American, that I went undisguised and on foot, my only weapon at the time being Duggan's pistol, and it not loaded. Address was now wanted more than brute force.

We followed the Concession Parallel, and next to the great Western Road saw and talked with numbers of people, but with none who wanted the Government reward. About three in the afternoon, we reached Comfort's Mills, near Streetsville; we were there told that Col. Chisholm and three hundred of the hottest Orangemen, and other most violent partisans, were divided into parties searching for us. Even from some of these there was no real danger. They were at heart friendly.

Mr. Comfort was an American by birth, but a resident of Canada. I asked his wife for some bread and cheese, while a young Irishman in his employ was harnessing up his wagon for our use. She insisted on our staying to dinner, which we did. Mr. Comfort knew nothing of the intended revolt, and had taken no part in it, but he assured me that no fear of consequences should prevent him from being a friend in the hour of danger. After conversing with a number of people there, not one of whom said an unkind word to us, my companion and I got into the wagon and the young Emeralder drove us down the Streetsville road, through the Credit Village (Springfield) in broad daylight, and along Dundas Street, bills being then duly posted for my apprehension, and I not yet out of the county which I had been seven times chosen by its freeholders to represent. Yet, though known to everybody, we proceeded a long way west before danger approached. At length, however, we were hotly pursued by a party of mounted troops; our driver became alarmed, and with reason, and I took the reins and pushed onward at full speed over a rough, hard-frozen road, without snow. Our pursuers, nevertheless, gained on us, and when near the Sixteen-Mile Creek we ascertained that my countryman, Col. Chalmers, had a party guarding the bridge. The creek swells up at times into a rapid river; it was now swollen by the November rains. What was to be done? Young W—— and I jumped from the wagon, made toward the forest, asked a laborer the road to Esquesing to put our pursuers off our track, and were soon in the thickest of the patch of woods near the deep ravine, in which flows the creek named and numbered arithmetically as the Sixteen.

The men in chase came up with our driver almost immediately after we left, took him prisoner, seized his team, gave the alarm to all the Tories and Orangemen in that part of Trafalgar, and in an hour or thereabouts, we were annoyed by the reports of rifles and the barking of dogs near by the place where we were hidden.

Some who saw me at Comfort's Mills went and told the armed Tories of Streetsville, who instantly went to the worthy man's house, insulted and threatened his intrepid and true-hearted wife, proposed to make a bonfire of his premises, handcuffed and chained him, threw him into a wagon, and dragged him off to Toronto jail, and, as they said, to the gallows. He lay long in prison untried, and was only released to find his excellent wife (who had been in the family way) in her grave, the victim of that system of persecution and terror which often classes men in America, as in Europe, not according to their personal deserts, but with reference to their politics, birth-place, faction, or religious profession. . . .

Faces of revolution. John Montgomery: his tavern burned. Charles Duncombe: his army dispersed. Samuel Chandler: he guided Mackenzie. Peter Matthews: hanged in Toronto.

Trafalgar was a hot-bed of Orangeism, and as I had always set my face against it, and British nativeism, I could hope for no friendship or favor, if here apprehended. There was but one chance for escape, however, surrounded as we were — for the young man had refused to leave me — and that was to stem the stream, and cross the swollen creek. We accordingly stripped ourselves naked, and with the surface ice beating against us, and holding our garments over our heads, in a bitter cold December night, buffeted the current, and were soon up to our necks. I hit my foot against a stone, let fall some of my clothes, (which my companion caught,) and cried aloud with pain. The cold in that stream caused me the most cruel and intense sensation of pain I ever endured, but we got through, though with a better chance for drowning, and the frozen sand on the bank seemed to warm our feet when we once more trod on it.

In an hour and a half we were under the hospitable roof of one of the innumerable agricultural friends I could then count in the country. I had a supply of dry flannels, and food, and an hour's rest, and have often wished since, (not to embark again on the tempestuous ocean of politics,) but that I might have an opportunity to express my grateful feelings to those who proved my faithful friends in the hour when most required.

I had risked much for Canadians, and served them long, and as faithfully as I could — and now, when a fugitive, I found them ready to risk life and property to aid me — far more ready to risk the dungeon, by harboring me, than to accept Sir Francis Head's thousand pounds. The sons and daughters of the Nelson farmer kept a silent watch outside, in the cold, while I and my companions slept.

We crossed Dundas Street about 11 o'clock, P.M., and the Twelve-Mile Creek, I think, on a fallen tree, about midnight. By four, on Saturday morning, we had reached Wellington Square, by the middle road. The farmer's dogs began to bark loudly, the heavy tramp of a party of horsemen was heard behind us — we retired a little way into the woods — saw that the men were armed — entered the road again — and half an hour before twilight reached the door of an upright Magistrate, which an English boy at once opened to us. I sent up my name, was requested to walk up stairs (in the dark,) and told that the house, barns, and every part of the premises, had been twice searched for me that morning, and that McNab's men, from Hamilton, were scouring the country in all directions, in hope of taking me. I asked if I had the least chance to pass downward by the way of Burlington Beach, but was answered that both roads were guarded, and that Dr. Rolph was, by that time, safe in Lewiston.

Believing it safest, we went behind our friend's house to a thicket

— he dressed himself, followed us, gave a shrill whistle, which was answered, and all three of us were greatly puzzled as to what safe course I could possibly take. As my companion was not known, and felt the chill of the water and fatigue, he was strongly advised to seek shelter in a certain house not far off. He did so, reached the frontier safely, and continued for four months thereafter very sick.

At dawn of day it began to snow, and leaving footmarks behind me, I concluded to go to a farm near by. Its owner thought I would be quite safe in his barn, but I thought not. A peas-rick, which the pigs had undermined all round, stood on a high knoll, and I chose it for a hiding-place. For ten or twelve days I had slept, when I could get any sleep, in my clothes, and my limbs had swelled so that I had to leave my boots and wear a pair of slippers; my feet were wet, I was very weary, and the cold and drift annoyed me much. Breakfast I had had none, and in due time, Colonel McDonell, the High Sheriff, and his posse, stood before me. House, barns, cellars, and garret were searched, and I the while quietly looking on. The Colonel was afterwards second in command to Sir Allan McNab, opposite Navy Island; and when I lived in William Street, some years ago, he called on me, and we had a hearty laugh over his ineffectual exertions to catch a rebel in 1837.

When the coast seemed clear, my terrified host, a wealthy Canadian, came up the hill as if to feed his pigs, brought me two bottles of hot water for my feet, a bottle of tea, and several slices of bread and butter; told me that the neighborhood was literally harassed with bodies of armed men in search of me, and advised that I should leave that place at dark, but where to go he could not tell me.

When night had set in, I knocked at the next farmer's door — a small boy who lived, I think, with one of the brothers Chisholm, (strong Government men, collectors, colonels, &c.,) or who was their nephew or other relative, came to me. I sent in a private message by him, but the house had been searched so often for me that the indwellers dreaded consequences, and would not see me. The boy, however, volunteered to go with me, and we proceeded by a by-path to Mr. King's, who lived on the next farm to Col. John Chisholm's, which was then head-quarters for our Tory militia. The boy kept my secret; I had supper with Mr. King's family, rested for an hour, and then walked with him toward my early residence, Dundas village, at the head of Lake Ontario. We saw a small party of armed men on the road, near the mills of an Englishman, but they did not perceive us. Mr. King is now dead, but the kind attention I met with under his hospitable roof I shall not forget. Why should such a people as I tried and proved in those days ever know hardship or suffer from foreign or domestic misrule?

We went to the dwelling of an old friend, to whom I stated that I thought I would now make a more speedy, yet equally sure, progress on horseback. He risked at once, and that too most willingly, not only his horse, but also the knowledge it might convey that he had aided me. Mr. King returned home and I entered the village alone in the night, and was hailed by some person who speedily passed on. I wanted to take a friend with me, but durst not go to wake him up; there was a guard on duty at the hotel, and I had to cross the creek close by a house I had built in the public square; I then made for the mountain country above Hamilton, called at Lewis Horning's, but found a stranger there, passed on to the dwellings of some old Dutch friends, who told me that all the passes were guarded — Terryberry's, Albion Mills, every place.

I got a fresh horse near Ancaster, from an old comrade — a noble animal who did me excellent service — pursued my journey in a concession parallel to the Mountain Road above Hamilton, till I came near to a house well lighted up, and where a guard was evidently posted to question wayfarers — and, as it then seemed the safest course, pulled down the worm fence, and tried to find my way through the Binbrook and Glanford woods, a hard task in daylight, but far worse in the dark.

For several weary hours did I toil through the primeval forest, leading my horse, and unable to get out or find a path. The barking of a dog brought me, when near daylight, to a solitary cottage, and its inhabitant, a negro, pointed out to me the Twenty-Mile Creek, where it was fordable. Before I had ridden a mile, I came to a small hamlet, which I had not known before — entered a house, and, to my surprise, was instantly called by name, which, for once, I really hesitated to own, not at all liking the manner of him who addressed me, though I now know that all was well intended.

Quite carelessly, to appearance, I remounted my horse and rode off very leisurely — but turned the first angle and then galloped on, turned again, and galloped still faster. At some ten miles distance, perhaps, a farm newly cleared, and situated in a by-place, seemed a safe haven. I entered the house, called for breakfast, and found in the owner a stout Hibernian farmer, an Orangeman from the North of Ireland, with a wife and five fine curly-headed children. The beam of a balance, marked 'Charles Waters, Maker,' had been hung up in a conspicuous place, and I soon ascertained that said Charles resided in Montreal, and that my entertainer was his brother.

I took breakfast very much at my leisure, saw my horse watered, and fed with oats in the sheaf, and then asked Mr. Waters to be so kind as to put me in the way to the Mountain Road, opposite Stony Creek, which he agreed to do, but evidently with the utmost reluctance.

After we had travelled about a quarter of a mile in the woods, he turned round at a right angle, and said that that was the way. 'Not to the road,' said I. 'No, but to Mr. McIntyre, the magistrate,' said he. Here we came to a full stop. He was stout and burly; I, small and slight made.

I soon found that he had not even dreamed of me as a rebel; his leading idea was, that I had a habit of borrowing other men's horses without their express leave — in other words, that I was a horse-thief. Horses had been stolen; and he only did his duty by carrying a doubtful case before the nearest justice, whom I inferred to be one of McNab's cronies, as he was a new man of whom I had never before heard, though a freeholder of that district, and long and intimately acquainted with its affairs.

This was a real puzzle. Should I tell Waters who I was, it was ten to one but he would seize me for the heavy reward, or out of mere party zeal or prejudice. If I went before his neighbor, the new made justice, he would doubtless know and detain me on a charge of high treason. I asked Mr. Waters to explain.

He said that I had come, in great haste, to his house, on a December Sunday morning, though it was on no public road, with my clothes torn, my face badly scratched, and my horse all in a foam; that I had refused to say who I was, or where I came from, had paid him a dollar for a very humble breakfast, been in no haste to leave, and was riding one of the finest horses in Canada, making at the same time for the frontier by the most unfrequented paths, and that many horses had been recently borrowed. My manner, he admitted, did not indicate anything wrong, but why did I studiously conceal my name and business? And if all was right with me, what had I to fear from a visit to the house of the nearest magistrate?

On the Tuesday night, in the suburbs of Toronto, when a needless panic had seized both parties, Sheriff Jarvis left his horse in his haste—it was one of the best in Canada, a beautiful animal—and I rode him till Thursday, wearing the cap of J. Latimer, one of my young men, my hat being knocked off in a skirmish in which one or two of our men were shot. This bonnet-rouge, my torn homespun, sorry slippers, weary gait, and unshaven beard, were assuredly not much in keeping with the charger I was riding, and I had unfortunately given no reply whatever to several of his good wife's home questions.

My chance to be tried and condemned in the hall where I had

often sat in judgment upon others, and taken a share in the shapeless drudgery of Colonial legislation, was now seemingly very good—but I did not quite despair.

To escape from Waters in that dense forest was entirely hopeless—to blow out his brains, and he acting quite conscientiously, with his five pretty children at home awaiting his early return, I could have done it with ease, as far as opportunity went, for he evidently had no suspicion of that, and my pistol was now loaded and sure fire. Captain Powell, when my prisoner ten days before, and in no personal danger, had shot the brave Captain Anderson dead, and thus left eight children fatherless. No matter; I could not do it, come what might; so I held a parley with my detainer, talked to him about religion, the civil broils, Mackenzie, party spirit, and Dr. Strachan; and found to my great surprise and real delight that, though averse to the object of the revolt he spoke of myself in terms of good-will. Mr. McCabe, his next neighbor, had lived near me in 1823, at Queenstown, and had spoken so well of myself and family to him as to have interested him, though he had not met me before.

'I am an old magistrate,' said I, 'but at present in a situation of some difficulty. If I can satisfy you as to who I am, and why I am here, would you desire to gain the price of any man's blood?' He seemed to shudder at the very idea of such a thing. I then administered an oath to him, (and with more solemnity than I had ever done the like when acting judicially,) he holding up his right hand as we Irish and Scottish Presbyterians usually do.

When he had ascertained my name, which I showed him on my watch and seals, in my pocket-book and on my linen, he expressed real sorrow on account of the dangerous situation in which I stood, pledged himself to keep silence for twenty-four hours, as I requested; directed me how to get into the main road, and feelingly urged me to accept his personal guidance to the frontier. Farmer Waters had none of the Judas blood in his veins. His innate sense of right led him at once to the just conclusion to do to his fellow-creature, as he would be done by. I perceived, from his remarks, that he had previously associated with my name the idea of a much larger and stouter man than I am.

When I was fairly out of danger he told the whole story to his neighbors—it was repeated and spread all over—he was soon seized and taken to Hamilton, and there thrown into prison, but afterward released.

When I was passing the houses of two men, Kerr and Sidney, who were getting ready, I supposed, to go to church, I asked some questions as to the road, again crossed the Twenty-Mile Creek, and at

The others. Sir Allan MacNab: he commanded. Sir John Robinson: he sentenced. John Rolph: he wavered. Robert Baldwin: he sat it out.

length re-entered the mountain path, a little below where a military guard was then stationed. While in sight of this guard I moved on very slowly, as if going to meeting, but afterward used the rowels to some advantage in the way of propellers. Some persons whom I passed on the road I knew, and some I didn't. Many whom I met evidently knew me, and well was it for me that day that I had a good name. I could have been arrested fifty times before I reached Smithville, had the Governor's person and proclamation been generally respected.

Samuel Chandler, a wagon-maker, resides in the Western States, but I do not now know where. He was forty-eight years of age when he volunteered, without fee or reward, to see me safe to Buffalo — had a wife and eleven children, and resided in Chippewa. He is a native of Enfield, Conn., had had no connection whatever with the civil broils in the Canadas; but when told, in strict confidence, of the risk I ran, he preferred to hazard transportation, or loss of life, by aiding my escape, to accepting the freehold of eight thousand acres of land which would have been the reward of my betrayers.

It was about 8 o'clock on Sunday night, when Chandler and I left Smithville. We turned our horses' heads toward Buffalo, crossed the Twenty, ventured to take a comfortable supper with a friend, whose house was on our way, crossed the Welland Canal and the Chippewa River, steering clear of the officials in arms in these parts, and got safe into Crowland before daylight. We soon awoke Mr. C——, left our horses in his pasture, and he immediately accompanied us, on our way to the Niagara River on foot.

On inquiry, he found that all the boats on the river (except those at the ferries, which were well guarded) had been seized and taken care of by the officers of Government. There was but one exception. Captain M'Afee, of Bertie, who resided on the banks of the Niagara, opposite the head of Grand Island, was believed to have kept one of his boats locked up beside his carriages. I hesitated not a moment in advising Mr. C—— to state the difficulty I was in to him, in case he had a boat, for, although he had no knowledge of, or belief and participation in, the outbreak, yet he was well known to be a strictly upright man, benevolent, not covetous, a member of the Methodist Episcopal Church, very religious, and in all he said or did, very sincere.

The brothers De Witt are censured, for giving up to Charles II, (who had been himself a fugitive,) and to a cruel death, three of his father's Judges; and the poor and gallant Scotch Highlanders, whom a mammoth bribe of £30,000 could not tempt to betray the heir to the Crown, when a wandering fugitive in the native land of his royal ancestors, are held in honor. The Irish peasants who refused to give up Lord Edward Fitzgerald to his country's oppressors, for gold, the poor sailors who enabled Archibald Hamilton Rowan to escape from Ireland and an untimely fate, with the proclaimed reward on a hand-bill in their boat, and the three bold Englishmen who saved the life of the doomed Labedoyere, have the merited applause of an admiring world. Are these noble citizens of Upper and Lower Canada, whom wealth could not tempt to give up, nor danger deter from aiding and saving, their fellow men, though many of them were opposed to them in politics, and at a time of the strongest political excitement, are they less deserving of the meed of public approbation?

Mr. Samuel M'Afee is now over sixty years of age, and, I think, he is of the New Hampshire family of that name, who played their part like men, in 1776. Our movement had proved a failure, and he knew it. He was wealthy — had a large family — and risked everything by assisting me; yet he did not hesitate, no, not even for a moment.

As well as I can now remember, it was about nine on Monday morning when I reached his farm, which was one of the finest on the river — an excellent breakfast had been prepared for us, and I was much fatigued and also hungry. But there was a military patrol on the river, and before sitting down to a repast, I thought it safe to step out and see if the coast was clear. Well for me it was that I did so. Old Colonel Kerby, the Custom House officer opposite Black Rock, and his troop of mounted dragoons, in their green uniforms, and with their carbines ready, were so close upon us, riding up by the bank of the river, that had I not then observed their approach, they would have caught me at breakfast.

Nine men out of ten, in such an emergency, would have hesitated to assist me; and to escape by land was, at that time, evidently impossible; Mr. M'Afee lost not a moment — his boat was hauled across the road and launched in the stream with all possible speed — and he and Chandler and I were scarcely afloat in it, and out a little way, below the bank, when the old Tory Colonel, and his green-coated troop of horse, with their waving plumes, were parading in front of Mr. M'Afee's dwelling.

How we escaped here, is to me almost a miracle. I had resided long in the district, and was known by everybody. A boat was in the river, against official orders; it was near the shore, and the carbines of the military, controlled by the collector, would have compelled us to return, or have killed us for disobedience.

The colonel assuredly did not see us; that was evident: he turned round at the moment to talk to Mrs. M. and her daughters, who were standing in the parterre in front of their house, full of anxiety on our account. But of his companions, not a few must have seen the whole movement, and yet we were allowed to steer for the head of Grand Island with all the expedition in our power, without interruption; nor was there a whisper said about the matter for many months thereafter.

In an hour we were safe on the American shore; and that night I slept under the venerable Colonel Chapin's hospitable roof, with a volunteer guard.

Navy Island

Mackenzie arrived in Buffalo on December 11th. His intention was to return to Upper Canada as soon as possible, and continue the fight. His first plan apparently involved gathering a force of refugees like himself, crossing Lake Erie back into Upper Canada, and joining Duncombe's army. At a number of public meetings he addressed large, enthusiastic crowds. Two Americans (Thomas Jefferson Sutherland, and Rensselaer van Rensselaer, the latter the son of a Dutch military officer, who had ambitions for a military career himself) joined Mackenzie to aid in organizing a continuation of the war against the regime in Upper Canada. Rather than cross back directly, it was agreed to set up a base on Navy Island in the Niagara River. On the 14th, three days after he reached Buffalo, Mackenzie landed there on Canadian territory again with a force of twenty four men, and declared a provisional government. He still intended to rejoin the battle on the mainland, but the news of the dispersal of Duncombe's force several days later eliminated that possibility. Instead, Navy Island itself became during the coming month the site of the next confrontation over the future of Upper Canada.

It was a small wooded piece of land, inhabited by only one family, who were compensated and moved to Grand Island upriver. Since it was Canadian territory its occupation could, at least symbolically, represent the liberation of Canada from British control. At the same time, it was near enough to the United States, to allow use of American soil as a staging ground for recruits and supplies, and also as a potential escape hatch. In the expectation of an attack by Upper Canadian government forces, a buildup of fortifications was begun. Reinforcements arrived and within several days of the initial landing there were sixty

The sinking of the Caroline: a very approximate artist's conception. In reality Navy Island is over a mile upriver from the falls.

men on the island, along with several cannons. Mackenzie issued a call to arms to the inhabitants of Upper Canada. He also announced a reward of $500 for Bond Head, considerably less than the reward Bond Head had offered for Mackenzie. Americans along the frontier in New York state warmed to the cause of the Patriots, as they were now generally known, and sent supplies, weapons, money and recruits to the island.

A government force of 1,800 militia encamped at Chippewa opposite the island on the Canadian side. After routing Duncombe's army, Alan MacNab moved over to take command of this force, and under his command it grew to 2,500 by the last week in December. Since both sides had cannons this time, there was some irregular artillery duelling, as well as the occasional spying foray from either shore. By that final week of 1837 the Patriot force had increased to 150, and was operating a ferry service between the American shore and the island, using a steamship called the Caroline. The Patriot cause continued to gain popularity in the United States and there were men and supplies to transport to the island. The government force, frustrated by inactivity and by the sight of the Patriot flag (two silver stars on a field of blue representing the peoples of Upper and Lower Canada) flying on Canadian ground, sent a raiding party to put the Caroline out of service. Fifty to sixty men including, as Bond Head put it, a number of "Elegant Extracts," *i.e.,* the sons of respectable Upper Canadian families, went over in three small boats under cover of night. They discovered the Caroline was moored not at the island, but at a wharf on the American shore. Despite the fact — or because of it — that this meant invading American territory, they boarded the ship and fought a battle with the crew on hand, killing five or six and driving the others off. Then they set fire to the Caroline, pushed it into the river, and watched it drift downstream toward the falls as they returned to base. As one of the participants in the raid recalled, "Her pipe got red hot and stood upright till the last. At the commencement of the rapids, she appeared hesitating a moment when she plunged, rose once, then a sea struck her, she keeled over, sunk in the falls, and disappeared forever."

The sinking of the Caroline prompted a heated reaction in the United States.

Interest in the Patriots soared and American recruits poured onto the island. At the height about 450 men were there. Americans on the island came to outnumber Canadians.

At that point, the thrust of the movement began to shift from Upper Canadians fighting for their own independence, to Americans fighting Englishmen on behalf of Upper Canadians — a quite different struggle and one in which the Patriot leadership could not hope to win as much support from their countrymen still in the colony. The shift was reflected in increasing conflict between Mackenzie and the Americans who had joined him in the leadership. At the same time the heightened involvement of Americans alerted the American government to the danger of igniting a war with Britain. Federal officials began a stricter enforcement of the neutrality laws, which prohibited any involvement of American territory or resources in any military action outside government policy. This is what eventually landed Mackenzie in an American jail. The United States army did its part to hinder Patriot plans by taking over steamboats the Patriots had planned on using themselves.

In early January, with the increase of men on both sides, the artillery battle heated up. One man was killed on Navy Island, and three died on the Chippewa side of the river. Nevertheless neither side tried to cross. The situation was stalemated and seemed likely to worsen for the Patriots. So, on January 13, 1838, they abandoned Navy Island, and on the 15th Canadian government forces occupied it. Mackenzie was no longer in charge of the Patriot troops and they scattered in various directions. A number proceeded west to Detroit, where they were to participate in some of the border raids and battles that constituted the next stage in the struggle.

The Border War

In spite of the initial setbacks of Montgomery's Tavern, Duncombe's army, and Navy Island, the revolutionary movement did not disappear. War continued against the Upper Canadian government and the imperial authorities for over a year. But as time passed, the struggle assumed more and more the character of a border war, with Patriot forces stationed in the United States making periodic landings and raids into Upper Canada. The movement lacked a foothold in Upper Canada itself, and it became very difficult for supporters still within the province to participate. At the same time this American emphasis provided propaganda ammunition for the Tories. Perhaps most important, leadership began to shift from Upper Canadians to Americans, some well-meaning, others differently motivated. During the early engagements of this border war for Canadian independence, most of the soldiers were Upper Canadian refugees, but even at this early stage a number of the leaders were American.

In January 1838, a force gathered on the western border of the province to attack Fort Malden at Amherstburg. This force proceeded in two sections, half on a schooner called the Anne under the command of an Irish-American named Alexander Theller; the other under Thomas Jefferson Sutherland who had been with Mackenzie on Navy Island. Theller and Sutherland both referred to themselves as generals, though neither had any military rank.

While Theller's force went ahead on the Anne and engaged a force of Canadian militia, Sutherland camped with his men on an island still in American territory. When the schooner ran aground, the militia boarded it, killing one man, wounding eight and taking twenty-two prisoners. Though Sutherland's men, mostly Canadians, wanted to go to the aid of the Anne, Sutherland held them back, then left the island for the United States mainland. Some of those captured were held in jail, others were pardoned and deported. Theller himself was taken as a prisoner as far as the citadel in Quebec City, from which he and several others escaped and made their way back to Maine.

A month later, in February of 1838, a force of Patriots from Detroit went down the St. Clair river toward Fighting Island, just below Sandwich. They were joined by other troops from Detroit and Cleveland, and were led by Donald Macleod, a former British soldier who had run a school in Prescott, Upper Canada. When American army troops from Detroit approached to disperse the Patriot force they crossed to the island, which was in Upper Canadian territory. They were poorly armed, but Dr. Duncombe, in Detroit at the time, rounded up some muskets and got them to the men on the island. A force of regular British troops, along with some militia, attacked, but were beaten off. An artillery duel commenced, as the Patriots had a cannon. Residents of Detroit came down to watch the battle and cheer on the Patriots from the American side. (This odd scene: American "fans" of the Canadian Revolution cheering it on, was repeated a number of times that year — at Pelee Island, Prescott and Windsor.) On the second British attack the Patriots retreated. Several were wounded, but they made it back to the American shore, where they were scattered by the American troops waiting there.

In March another, larger battle, was fought, this time at Pelee Island in southern Lake Erie, about 18 miles from the Canadian shore. Four hundred and fifty men from Ohio had crossed the ice and occupied the island. Reinforcements joined them and their numbers grew to about 1,000. The British brought up regular troops, artillery and cavalry from Amherstburg and crossed the ice to meet the invaders. The British attacked, the Patriots retreated, were cut off by the cavalry, and retreated in another direction, heading back to the American side over ice so thin that the British chose not to follow. In the fighting half a dozen British soldiers were killed and a dozen Patriots. It was the largest battle of the border war so far and it seemed to sap the energies of both sides temporarily. The British were taking the situation seriously enough that they reassigned regular troops to Upper Canada, no longer relying on local militia as they had during the early stages of the uprising. A kind of lull set in, which lasted until June of 1838, when the scene of confrontation shifted eastward to the Short Hills area of the Niagara peninsula.

This time the confrontation came not in a battle but in a raid. A mainly Canadian force of 26 men sneaked across the border. They had information that on their arrival hundreds of Upper Canadians would join them in an uprising. This move represented a return to the earlier strategy of mounting an indigenous revolution, rather than an overthrow by invasion. The leaders of the raid were James Morreau, an American, and Samuel Chandler, the wagonmaker who had guided Mackenzie to safety during his escape.* For almost a week and a half this force moved stealthily through the peninsula, hiding with farmers and remaining unknown to the authorities. By then they had enlisted 100 locals and they attacked a tavern where a detachment of British lancers were quartered. They succeeded, took the lancers prisoner, but could not decide what to do next, so they finally released the soldiers. Neither their presence nor their action had evoked the kind of response they had hoped for in the country and for lack of any further plan they decided to disband and retreat to the border separately. By this time though the authorities had been alerted, and the hunt for the raiders was on. As often happened in Upper Canada at this time, the searchers used the situation as an excuse to break into the homes of suspected rebel sympathizers, harrass them, settle old grudges and loot or destroy homes. Most of the infiltrators, including Chandler, were captured. Morreau was hung at Niagara. Seventeen others were condemned to death but had their sentences commuted to life in the prison colony of Van Diemen's Land off the coast of Australia. Raids also took place across the western border on Sarnia and Goderich. The raids soon impelled both the British and American armies to step up patrols on either side of the border in order to stop such activities.

By the summer of 1838 the Patriot movements had developed a new centre: the Hunters' Lodges. These were secret societies, on the order of fraternal lodges, apparently named after an Upper Canadian refugee who had settled in Vermont. They were dedi-

* This is the same Chandler whose small, neglected monument is referred to in the essay Preface to *1837*.

cated to expelling the British and annexing Canada to the United States by force of arms. They were a substantial force; estimates of their membership run from 15,000 to 200,000. As late as spring of 1839, when the main battles were over, they claimed with some credibility to have 3,250 men ready to fight. Canadians were members but were in a minority; a further shift had occurred toward American predominance in the movement for Canadian liberation.

On November 11, 1838, over 400 Hunters set out from Sackett's Harbour, on the eastern shore of Lake Ontario in New York State. They headed north for the Upper Canadian town of Prescott on the northern shore of the St. Lawrence. Their party became separated, but Colonel Nils von Schoultz, a young Polish military man, landed a group of about 170 a mile and a half below Prescott near a large windmill. They hauled three cannon ashore with them and soon others of the original force joined them. A small British naval crew tried to prevent the landings but failed. A more or less pitched battle occurred over the next four days.

A British naval contingent from Kingston soon arrived and, along with a number of militia units, attacked the invaders who retreated into the windmill. It was a stout structure, 100 feet in circumference and 80 feet high; its walls were three and a half feet thick and the naval guns of the British didn't dent them. After this first round, a truce was declared to allow time to clear the field of dead and wounded. Both sides had received casualties but the Hunters seemed to have the advantage. After several days in the windmill, the raiders knew their situation was hopeless. The British had brought up heavy artillery and were bombarding the mill to bits. Twice the occupants raised a white flag which the British ignored. Eventually, after the British had closed in, they accepted a surrender. Sixteen British soldiers had been killed, and sixty wounded; the Patriot losses were greater. Von Schoultz himself was executed (the young John A. Macdonald defended him in his court-martial) and ten others were hanged later. Another sixty were transported to Van Diemen's Land.

The focus of activity had been shifting eastward during the year, from the western frontier near Detroit, through Lake Erie, to the Niagara peninsula and finally Prescott on the St.

The battle of the Windmill, near Prescott, seen from the American side of the St. Lawrence.

Lawrence. For the last major confrontation of the year, and of the border war itself, the focus swung back west to Windsor, a small town of several hundred at the time across the St. Clair River from Detroit. In December of 1838, a number of Hunters' Lodges commandeered a steamer in Detroit harbour, crossed to the Canadian side and landed 135 men who marched on Windsor. They attacked the town hall where the British garrison was quartered. They burned the hall, killing some of those inside, and shooting others as they emerged. Shortly after, Canadian militia under the command of a very stern figure, Colonel John Prince, moved on the town and joined battle with the invading force. The Hunters broke and ran. Four of the militia were killed and four wounded. Twenty-one of the invaders were killed; a number were forced to run a sort of gauntlet which ended in their shooting and on Prince's orders, five were shot on the spot. In the aftermath, six of the prisoners were hanged in London, and eighteen others sentenced to Van Diemen's Land.

This battle in December marked the last major clash of the border war, though other sorts of Patriot and Hunter activity had been going on and contined. William Johnston, for example, a Canadian removed to the States, was active as a kind of inland pirate in the Thousand Islands of Lake Ontario near Kingston. In

May of 1838, he and a group under his command looted and burned the steamship, Sir Robert Peel, a very large passenger vessel. Bank robberies, mailcoach holdups, abductions, burnings of farms and churches, and the odd murder continued for some time even when overt military operations had ceased. As late as April 1840, Hunters blew up the monument to General Brock, English hero of the War of 1812, at Queenston Heights.* Over a year later, in September of 1841, an attempt to destroy the locks of the Welland Canal failed; the border war had ended, but not with a bang.

Reprisals

During the year that followed the outbreak of fighting in Upper Canada, 885 people were arrested or sought on charges of insurrection or treason in the province. A small number of these fled to the United States and remained in exile there. The others were jailed, pending trial. Conditions in the jails were deplorable. Prisoners were jammed together, with inadequate food and clothing during those winter months. A number of men took sick, usually from the cold, and died either in jail or in hospital. Among these was Anthony van Egmond who, at 67 years old, contracted pneumonia in Toronto City Jail. By fall of 1838 most of the charges had been dealt with; in November only 27 of the charged men remained in Upper Canadian jails. The majority — over 600 — were acquitted or had their charges dismissed. Another 150 or so were pardoned. These however often had to provide considerable bail. A large group were deported to the prison colony of Van Diemen's Land. Twenty men were hanged across the province: Lount and Matthews in Toronto on April 12, 1838 for the battle of Montgomery's Tavern; Morreau in Niagara for the Short Hills raid; Von Schoultz and ten others in Kingston for the battle of the Windmill; and six in London for the raid on Windsor. The lesson of the hangings — which were public events — was taught across the province, from east to west.

* In 1824, while the monument was being erected, a bottle containing a copy of the first issue of Mackenzie's *Colonial Advocate* was placed in its base as a kind of time capsule. When the lieutenant governor learned of this, he actually ordered the dismantling of what had been built so far, in order to remove the newspaper.

Of those 885 men, most came from around Toronto and London. A breakdown of the list in terms of occupation shows almost equal numbers of yeomen or small farmers (375) and labourers (345). There were 80 carpenters and other tradesmen, and 85 "others", including teachers, lawyers, merchants, artists, and two preachers, a Baptist and a Methodist. The list provides evidence that the movement in its most serious phase — its armed phase — was carried out chiefly by working people.

The defeat was the occasion across the colony for a great deal of witch-hunting and personal score-settling. Groups of government supporters, sometimes official, sometimes quasi-official and sometimes merely gangs of Orangemen broke into homes, harassed families, and stole property. In many cases the most bitter events occurred after the insurrection itself had been crushed. A typical incident occurred during the search for Samuel Lount. The tale is told by his nephew:

> One cold night in December, 35 or 40 men, dressed in blanket coats, burst in our door. Their blanket coats and cappotes drawn close over their heads made them appear like Indians. None being up at the time but my mother, she was very much frightened and begged of them not to murder us. My father got up and demanded by what authority they broke into his house in such a manner. The warrant was shown him, and their further authority that should they be met with serious opposition they were to shoot down all but the wife and her son. After looting the place of all the light goods, such as socks, mittens, handkerchiefs, collars, shirts, and other similar things, and after partaking of a hearty meal of boiled pork, bread cakes, pies, butter, preserves and milk, they said they were quite satisfied Lount was not there. In the confusion I had been pricked with a bayonet because I would not turn over and satisfy a drunken fool that my uncle was not in bed behind me and I felt that if I had the strength of a Samson I would annihilate every one of them. I was told by my mother to visit the barn, which I did, and I could see through a crack that they were thrusting their bayonets deep into the hay and straw, frequently repeating, "I wonder if the d—d rebel might be here."
>
> Unexpectedly at this juncture Moses Hayter* put in an appearance. He enquired if there was a gun in the house, took the old piece and loaded it, and took his stand at the door. He told us to go back to

* Hayter later became sheriff in Toronto.

> bed. They marched up with torches, shouting "Down with the d—d rebel's house," and mingled with fearful imprecations. Hayter, standing on the platform in the front sang out in a loud commanding voice, "Halt!" which was instinctively obeyed, as the command was quite unexpected. He thus addressed the mob: "Do you call yourselves Englishmen? I am an Englishman from the city of London, was an usher to the Duke of Wellington, where I was taught to know no fear when in a just cause. I most sacredly declare that before you enter this house, with the intention of burning it down over the head of a defenceless woman and her children, you will have to walk over the dead body of an Englishman, but not before I will take good account of at least one of you. If you only knew the character of the man who you are seeking for his life as well as I do, you would retire with shame. Once he saved me and my family from starvation when that fate stared us in the face. And hundreds can testify that he has reached out a helping hand to those who were in great need." On hearing these words, every man threw down his torch and went slinking away down to the tavern. . . .*

One major effect of these systematic as well as spontaneous forms of repression was a massive emigration to the United States in the year following the failure of revolution. It is estimated that 25,000 people left Upper Canada. This is an enormous drain from a population of between 300,000 and 350,000. Nor were those who left mainly transients who would have passed on anyway. The majority were almost certainly people who believed in the country and had pinned their hopes on change. In the aftermath of the attempt at revolution, all hope was dashed and Upper Canada lost perhaps the best of its citizens to the western States.

* Sympathy for Lount, by the way, was prominent, from all sides. He was a highly respected blacksmith and Reformer, from a Quaker family at Holland Landing. A petition urging the lieutenant governor to grant Lount clemency received thousands of signatures, at a time when signing such a document could easily be called an act of sedition. The same Moses Hayter mentioned above is said to have ridden his horse directly across Lake Simcoe at the time of the spring breakup, leaping from floe to floe, in order to save time in the gathering of the signatures. The new lieutenant governor, Sir George Arthur, rejected the petition, as Lount had predicted. ("It's no use David. Every name you get on that petition makes my death more sure.") Lount had correctly understood that he was chosen for execution precisely because he had so much respect and sympathy from his fellow citizens. The British showed a thorough ruthlessness in every aspect of the suppression of the rebellion.

Prisoners on their way to jail: a frequent event in both Upper and Lower Canada during 1837-8.

Ninety-two of those arrested were sent to Van Diemen's Land. This was a British prison colony off the southeastern corner of Australia. Today it is called Tasmania. During the first half of the nineteenth century, 100,000 convicts from various parts of the British empire were transported to the prison island. On the average during those years, there were 37,000 convicts on the island, along with 30,000 settlers and inhabitants who were not convicts. The governor of this bizarre society between 1824 and 1836 was Sir George Arthur, who had made a reputation with his viciousness and a fortune in land investment. On leaving Van Diemen's Land he was appropriately appointed to the post of lieutenant governor of Upper Canada. He replaced Bond Head and superintended the repression of the revolutionary movement. Prisoners of Van Diemen's Land, after their long ocean voyage and forced marches to various encampments on the island, spent most of their time in hard labour on the roads. Some were rented out to settlers. They were subjected to solitary confinement for minor violations of the rules; many died of disease or exhaustion. Escape attempts were common, but in the history of the colony only two prisoners are said to have succeeded. One of the punishments for attempted escape was the treadmill:

> An immense wheel about thirty feet in diameter and sixty feet in length was kept in constant motion fourteen hours of twenty-four by thirty prisoners. Every four minutes one of the men descended from the wheel at one end while another mounted it at the other, each man upon the wheel thus periodically shifting two feet towards the place of descent, which was reached in two hours.

After several years, prisoners were eligible for parole. This meant they were no longer shackled or confined in the prison camps themselves, but they were forbidden to leave the island or to move about except in their particular district of parole. This led to a very strange in-between existence. There was little work to be found, and many paroled prisoners became outlaws, or bush-rangers as they were known. Other prisoners also on parole were employed to pursue these outlaws, with the promise of pardon if they brought them in dead or alive. In this way one portion of the paroled prisoners became hunted by another portion, and both groups kept busy. Escape from parole was a little easier than from direct imprisonment, and Samuel Chandler along with two others did escape from parole in 1842. They arrived back in North America that summer, the first prisoners to return from Van Diemen's Land.

For most though, the last step toward release from the island was pardon, which might come several years after parole. The majority of the Patriot prisoners were pardoned in 1844, largely due to the efforts of the American ambassador to England and the American consul in Van Diemen's Land, on behalf of the Americans in the group. But pardon did not include transportation home, and the exiles had to find means of making their own way back. One Upper Canadian did not make it back to his home town until 1860, when the local newspaper reported, "Last Monday [John] Berry landed in Brockville after an absence of 22 years." Of the 72 prisoners known to have gone to Van Diemen's Land, and there may have been more, thirteen are certain to have died there; of another forty or so there is no record that they ever returned; the rest made it back to North America and some, on the basis of amnesties, returned to Canada.

In sum, the repression of the revolution in Upper Canada was very severe. There were arrests, harassment, persecution, trials, deportation, flights into exile, expropriations, hangings, and sentences to a prison colony on the other side of the world. So harsh were the British in the aftermath that they seem to have destroyed the movement for independence root and branch. Never since has there been a movement for Canadian independence which reached the point of armed revolt against the imperial master.

Chapter 6

Epilogue: Mackenzie after 1837

In March of 1838, two months after the evacuation of Navy Island, Mackenzie turned forty-two years old. He was a youthful and vigorous individual. His first revolution had failed, and was behind him; but many years of public life still lay ahead.

Exile

From Navy Island, Mackenzie went to Rochester, east of Buffalo on the southern shore of Lake Ontario. He still favoured an invasion in the hope that it would spark an uprising within the province. Strategically, he wanted to aim at Fort Henry, the key British naval base on the Great Lakes. A plan was set afoot but Van Renssalaer gained command of the proposed expedition. Mackenzie felt that after Navy Island he could take no part in any movement in which Van Renssalaer played a leading role. Accordingly Mackenzie severed his connections with the forming army and played no significant role in the battles that were ahead.

Instead he began to tour, pursuing the cause of Canadian independence by other means. He travelled to Plattsburg, in upstate New York, where he met with the Lower Canadian leaders in exile. Then, in Philadelphia and New York, he addressed rallies. Until this point his wife had been with him, the rest of his immediate family remained in Upper Canada. In May 1838 his mother and his six children joined them in New York city. That month Mackenzie put out the first issue of a new Patriot newspaper, *Mackenzie's Gazette.* It was meant to be a source of information and a rallying-point for Canadians in political exile in the United States; and also a way of keeping the "Canadian question" before the American public. Mackenzie continued to publish it until the end of 1840, even during the eleven months he spent in jail.

During the latter part of 1838, he found himself in increasing conflict with the direction the Patriot movement was taking. He apparently opposed the raid at Short Hills on the Niagara frontier, and the invasions at Prescott and Windsor. He did not participate in the formation of the Hunters' Lodges in the summer, nor did he become a member. He tried, by taking a different set of initiatives, to give the movement an alternative thrust. In the closing months of 1838 he held Independence meetings in a number of American cities. The Prescott battle had led to a sharpening of American government opposition to Patriot activity and it was made known that any rally in Washington was officially frowned upon. Nevertheless Mackenzie went ahead with a meeting there which the government ordered its employees to boycott. In February of 1839 Mackenzie moved to Rochester in order to be near the fighting and the centres of decision. He was more determined than ever to recapture leadership of the movement and change its direction. He wrote of the necessity "to set up such a [new] organization here and now on the other side [i.e. in Canada] and to make such use of that already in operation, as will probably somewhat change the aspect of Canadian affairs. The material is before us if we choose to make use of it."

In March of 1839, Mackenzie organized a Convention "to be composed of Canadians or persons connected with Canada, who are favorable to the attainment of its political independence, and the entire separation of its government from the political power of Great Britain." The Convention met in Rochester. Its membership was primarily Canadian and its leadership was thoroughly Canadian. It asserted that Canadian independence would have to be initiated by Canadians *in Canada,* not by well-meaning Americans and exiles, and only thereafter would outside help be appropriate. It called for active opposition to "hasty and ill-planned expeditions or attacks upon parts of the Canadas, designed or begun by, or in the name of, Canadian refugees or persons in Canada." An organization called the Association of Canadian Refugees was formed. This was the beginning of a Canadian-led alternative to the Hunters' Lodges. Duncombe started a branch in Cincinatti. There is no way of knowing whether this attempt to remould the movement and recentre it on Canada and Canadians would have succeeded. In June of 1839 Mackenzie was forcibly removed from the political scene.

He had been indicted in an American court about a year before for alleged violation of the neutrality laws. These dated from 1794 and prohibited violation of American neutrality, or actions which contravened the treaty obligations of the United States. The law had never before been invoked, nor was it now applied to any American citizens. Mackenzie was charged with violations stemming from the Navy Island period. He felt that the charge was primarily an attempt by the American government to placate the British for the border troubles and head off any political or military conflict with England. But, having laid the charge, the government was reluctant to proceed to trial because of Mackenzie's personal popularity and the popularity of his cause, among the American population. The trial was delayed a year. Finally, in June 1839 Mackenzie demanded that he be tried; he had, he said, never yet shrunk from a charge. The trial was held in Rochester in June and lasted two days. Mackenzie defended himself. He accused the American government of hypocrisy: history demonstrated America's perpetual desire to absorb Canada, yet out of a temporary concern to appease the British, they pretended to neutrality, and offered the trial of Mackenzie as proof. The jury found him guilty and the judge sentenced him to eighteen months in jail and a ten dollar fine. Mackenzie was taken immediately to the Rochester jail.

This effectively removed him from the political arena, though he continued to supervise publication of his newspaper from the jail. It was a difficult period for Mackenzie. He was the sole support of his wife, mother and children. The jailers treated him with harshness in spite of the fact that his crime was not considered to involve, in the phrase of the time, moral turpitude. He was not allowed to exercise outdoors. He received visitors but they were often treated abusively by the jail staff. His family brought him meals so that he did not have to eat jail fare. The dampness of the jail site, and the lack of air and exercise made him ill and feverish. He worried constantly for his family's welfare: a daughter was ill; in his lifetime five of his children had previously died. Still, a popular movement for Mackenzie's release was underway.

Toronto jail, where prisoners were held, Van Egmond died, and Lount and Matthews were hanged.

By mid-November fifty to sixty thousand people had petitioned for his freedom.

In December Mackenzie's ninety-year-old mother took seriously ill. He had always been extraordinarily devoted to her. He was not permitted to visit her and she could not come to him. From his cell he wrote, "Our last meeting here in the jail was a long and happy one. I did not think it would be the last, but I fear the hard-hearted Americans will grant no relief." John Montgomery, of Montgomery's Tavern, was running a hotel in Rochester at the time. He concocted a strategem whereby one of his lodgers sued another, and named Mackenzie as a material witness. It was necessary to subpoena Mackenzie from the jail and the court authorities conspired to hold the trial in Mackenzie's house. In this way he was able to visit his mother on her deathbed. When she died soon after, however, he was not permitted to attend the funeral; he watched the procession through his cell window.

He was a public man removed from the public arena. Private crises and anxieties replaced political ones. In late April he wrote in a letter:

> This is the eleventh month of my confinement. For about three months I never crossed the threshold of one solitary prison room for a day. For the last three months I have not been allowed to go downstairs, even inside, but am kept continually in the upper story of the building. The door of my apartment opens within five feet of the door of the female dungeon; and the women's cells are close by. The howling and yelling of twelve or eighteen unhappy creatures at all hours, night and day, I shall never forget. I am locked up, as usual, like the felons in Newgate.

Pressure was growing for his release. The Secretary of State intervened for better conditions, and at the end of April he was permitted to exercise in the yard of the jail. By this time the number of names on the petition to President van Buren had reached 300,000. On May 10, 1840 the release of Mackenzie was ordered. The imprisonment undoubtedly played a powerful role in Mackenzie's increasing disillusionment with the United States. Half a year after his release he wrote, "Over three years' residence in the United States, and a closer observation of the condition of society here, have lessened my regrets at the results of the opposition raised to England in Canada in 1837-8." But his bitterness over the jail experience was not merely personal. He saw his case as typifying American political hypocrisy: he had been prosecuted not for violation of the law, but in order to mollify the British. The American government had sacrificed the principle of freedom for the Canadas to political expediency in its foreign relations, with Mackenzie as the convenient scapegoat. It indicated to Mackenzie a rottenness at the core of the American system which he had not expected to find there.

Meanwhile the Canadian government (uniting Upper and Lower Canada in early 1841, according to Durham's recommendation) continued to regard Mackenzie as a threat. While he was in jail they had proposed an exchange of one hundred prisoners captured at Prescott and Windsor for Mackenzie. The government of New York state replied that the trade was impossible because public opinion in the state would not stand for it. While he was in jail Mackenzie was the target of an assassination attempt: one day as he stood by his cell window, a bullet passed by his head and lodged in the cell wall. On his release the reward for him had been renewed and increased. In the fall of 1840, a kidnap plot to snatch him on board a ship in the harbour failed because Mackenzie was informed of it.

But while these attempts on his life and liberty failed, poverty was closing in. In December 1840 he closed the *Gazette* and sold its equipment for the money to buy food and fuel for his family. He applied for permission to practice law but this was rejected. In the spring of 1841, he began another newspaper, *The Volunteer,* struggled with it for a year, then closed it in the spring of 1842 because of lack of public interest in "the Canadian question." He still had his cause, but he had no constituency for it. His financial need was so great that he melted down the massive gold medal the electors of York had given him after his first expulsion and re-election, and sold it; the proceeds went mainly to pay off a debt. In March of 1842 his home in Rochester caught fire and many of the family's belongings were lost. He wrote, "After an utterly ineffectual attempt to live here with my family, I'm starved out." In June of 1842 he moved the family to New York City, with $2.50 in his pocket and the hope of better times. They remained there until 1850.

By now Mackenzie had almost no active connection with Upper Canada or Patriot politics. He opposed any schemes and movements for reopening the battle, but these were largely spent anyway. In 1843 an amnesty was granted to most of the leaders of the Rebellion, including Rolph, Duncombe and Montgomery, and these were permitted to return to Canada. All but Duncombe did so. In 1844 Papineau was pardoned and in 1845 he returned. Mackenzie however was excluded. He was now isolated even from his fellow exiles. Whatever his feelings about Upper Canada, there was no way at all to exercise them; he turned his energies to the support and survival of his family and, increasingly, to American politics.

His first job in New York was as actuary at the New York Mechanics' Institute. He stayed at this about a year, during which he began a book about Irish heroes; he never finished the work. Then he gained a position as temporary clerk in the New York Custom House. In the course of his work there he came across a correspondence that revealed embezzlement by a former Chief of Customs to the tune of $250,000. Mackenzie secured possession of the documents and in 1845 published a book based on the scandal which became a bestseller, until a court order banned further printings. In order to prove his purposes were beyond question, Mackenzie turned over all proceeds from the book to the publisher. Then, using the same material from the Custom House, he published a biography of President van Buren, who had been implicated in the affair. This book was one of the factors in ending Van Buren's political career. Although it was under Van Buren's administration that Mackenzie had been jailed, revenge was not a motive. In fact Mackenzie had become a strong Van Buren supporter, only reversing himself because of the evidence of corruption he had found. In 1846 he began writing for the New York Tribune under editor Horace Greeley.* He had reached a very low ebb personally. In October of that year he wrote, "I am more of a misanthrope than I once was; I never attend or speak at public meetings, and creep as it were through the afternoon of life."

Mackenzie continued to support himself by writing for the *Tribune* during the remainder of his stay in the United States. But it was evident America had little to offer him economically and, far more important to his sustenance, politically. He longed to return to Canada. He was the last remaining exile. The earliest amnesty had come in 1838; fifty nine leaders had been excluded. Then came the amnesties for leaders of 1843 and 1844. There had since been numerous vain addresses to the British government on Mackenzie's behalf. However in 1849 a general amnesty proposed by a Canadian government led by Robert Baldwin was passed by the British parliament, and it became possible for Mackenzie to return home. By this time his attitudes toward the United States and Canada's relation to it had changed greatly, and were acceptable to the British and Canadian authorities.

Before the revolutionary attempt, the United States had stood as a beacon to many Upper Canadians, of what was possible, what they stood to gain. The United States represented success as a national society; the key to that success was American-style democracy, and the prerequisite for such a political system was national independence. There were some Upper Canadians who

* Six years later another political exile, Karl Marx, based in England, began a ten-year career as correspondent for the same American newspaper.

wanted outright annexation to the United States, but for most it was an example to be emulated, not an irresistible magnet. Before December 1837, Mackenzie and his colleagues put their major effort into breaking the British connection and ending colonial status. The status quo was the one option definitely *un*acceptable to them. In their calls and declarations concerning independence, they nowhere recommended joining the United States. Their goal, "the prize" as Mackenzie put it, was national independence. Perhaps a debate on relations with the States might have ensued thereafter, but winning freedom *from* the British was their preoccupation.

It is true that in 1840 Mackenzie wrote, "My darling wish for twenty years was to see one great federal union of the nations of North America. . . ." But the statement is not to be taken literally; a mere sixteen years before, in the first number of *The Colonial Advocate,* he had stated, "We like American liberty well, but prefer British liberty." The "darling wish" of union with the United States was a rhetorical flourish meant to emphasize by contrast a definitive critique of American democracy and rejection of annexation. For Mackenzie after two years in the United States, the dream — dreamed among others by Robert Davis, the Canadian farmer — was over.

In September 1838 Mackenzie had declared his intention to become an American citizen. But then had followed his experience with the cynicism of American policy toward Canada, his incarceration, and his close, searing scrutiny of the American political and social fabric. In January 1840, he addressed his former countrymen on the subject:

> TO THE PEOPLE OF
> UPPER CANADA!
>
> Since crossing the Niagara in January, 1838, I have ascertained — that the republican forms of the government of these United States serve as a mantle to conceal from the people the aristocratic machinery which, as in England more openly, moves the vessel of the state. In this great country of New York, the lawyers protect their monopoly by seven years apprenticeships, and at least as many varieties of rules of life, taken from England, her colonies, state legislation, congress statutes, foreign treaties, and British common law, as are in use among yourselves. The administration of justice is exclusively in

the hands of those monopolists, the judges being often selected by the Banking influence, from among the most intolerant and exclusive of the members of the bar. Equal rights and the truths of the Declaration of Independence are not and cannot be enjoyed in the midst of a thousand city, village, clerical, manufacturing, railroad, canal, and worst of all, banking corporations, every one of them more exclusive than another. They are the props of the British monarchy beyond the sea; they are England's fortresses on the continent of America. The influence of the press upon the people here is very great; and the tongues of the lawyers and the pens of the editors move in implicit obedience to the same monied power which has prostrated the last remains of freedom in Britain.

England has a standing army, and the government here is quietly increasing the efficiency of a like prop of monarchy. The State Legislature, whether whig or democrat, meets but to increase the burthen (*sic*) of the people, rich capitalists pass laws for poor laborers.

As far as I can judge, the two great parties of ins and outs whose leaders move the people as if they were two contending armies, are the very counterparts of the British Whigs and Tories, and equally *honest* and *disinterested* in all they say and do! The ballot, of which I was much in favor when with you, would be no adequate protection to the poor voter in the present state of society in England, neither does it protect the people here. Corruption is powerful in England and with you, but beyond its influence here I should think that nothing could go. . . .

Yet the conclusions he drew from this devastating look behind the American facade were very positive ones for Canadians:

The sooner we get rid of English power, the nature of which this Almanack faithfully describes, the better. While England keeps five millions of her home subjects in poor-house bastiles or for factory work, we can have nothing to hope from her sense of justice; and it would be no enviable condition to become miserable dependents of the slaveowners of the south and the usurers of the north, by exchanging the yoke of Victoria for that of Congress. . . .

Canadians would have to go it alone; they could not rely on foreign patrons, British or American. Whatever unstated views of the United States he might have held, he had not pinned all his hopes on it, and on absorption into it, and he could survive disillusionment.

"Why did you try to revolt, if this is so?" will be asked by the Canadian Loyalist.

> Because the people CAN afford a remedy here, while in Canada they dare not even attempt it.

This is as prescient a statement as has been made on the value of national independence. The independence, which a nation such as the United States enjoyed, was no guarantee of a truly democratic and just society. Nevertheless independence was a prerequisite for such a society. Under foreign domination even the possibility of building such a society did not exist. Once free and ostensibly democratic, a nation could still go awry as Mackenzie had witnessed in the U.S. But without national freedom not even the possibility was there.

Mackenzie reached this conclusion in January of 1842. The harshness of his private life was meanwhile taking its toll. American society as he now experienced it offered no compensation for what he had given up by leading a revolution which failed. He wrote:

> Perhaps the privations of the last three years, exceeding all I ever knew before, have blinded my vision in some of the beauties of American Democracy, and made the comparison with limited and absolute Monarchy and the Colonial yoke, less favorable to the former than heretofore.

His cause had failed, and he was personally *worse* off than before. The consolation prize of living in a democratic society had not materialized for him. In March of 1842, as poverty closed in further, he wrote to his son, "The more I see of this country the more do I repent the attempt at Revolution at Toronto and St. Charles." This statement seems to contradict the one of several months earlier that affirmed the validity of the revolutionary attempt in order that "the people CAN afford a remedy." Yet the "regret" Mackenzie expresses here at his action is an odd mixture of the personal and political. The disillusionment with the United States had become almost indistinguishable from his personal misery, and he began to despair of revolutionary possibilities in general, in exactly the same way he had lost hope of improving his family's lot. As his economic situation worsened in the coming years he fell further into personal bitterness and political despair. When the other exiles left, he lost even the gratifications of a struggle shared and lost together. In October of 1846 as we have seen, he felt he was creeping through the afternoon of life.

In March of 1847, he wrote to his son, "After what I have seen here, I frankly confess to you that, had I passed nine years in the U.S. before, instead of after, the outbreak, I am very sure I would have been the last man in America to be engaged in it." A definitive repudiation of his earlier course, it seems. Yet it is as much of a product of political isolation and personal misery, as it is of cool analysis. For, once he had returned to Upper Canada and re-entered politics there, he very soon joined the old battles again and ceased to apologize for his pre-exile days.

For the time being though, his greatest yearning was to return home, and his current mood enabled him to address a request for pardon to the Colonial Secretary, which could be favourably viewed in London. In 1849, he wrote to Earl Grey:

> There is not a living man on this Continent who more sincerely desires that British Government in Canada may long continue, and give a home and a welcome to the old countrymen than myself. Did I say so, or ask an amnesty, seven or eight years ago, till under the convictions of more recent experience? No; I studied earnestly the workings of the institutions before me, and the manners of the people, and looked at what had been done, until few men, even natives, had been better schooled. The result is — not a desire to attain power and influence here — but to help, if I can, and all I can, the country of my birth.

Return

The general amnesty of 1849 for all participants in the revolutions twelve years before, in reality applied only to Mackenzie. He was the only exile left. Immediately following its passage, he decided to return. He made a preliminary visit, coming to Montreal first in March 1849. On a trip to the library of the House of Assembly, now located in Montreal for the combined government of the Canadas, Mackenzie was insulted and ordered to leave by Colonel John Prince, the militia commander responsible for the summary executions at the battle of Windsor. As Mackenzie passed through Kingston on his way to Toronto from Montreal, he was burned in effigy, and on his arrival in Toronto, he was the occasion for a Tory-inspired mob riot. Nevertheless, a year later in May 1850, he returned with his family to settle in Toronto. While in the United States he had buried his mother and a daughter; now there were wife and five children.

He re-entered politics almost immediately, with a kind of indecent haste. He didn't even wait for a general election; instead he stood for the first vacant seat in a by-election. It happened to be Haldimand, in Western Ontario farm country; the farmers elected Mackenzie over George Brown, editor of *The Globe*, and later to become a key political leader. Inside the House of Assembly, Mackenzie did not align with any of the parties; he played the independent role of watchdog and critic. Within weeks of his election he called for an investigation into the operation of the Court of Chancery. His motion implied a criticism of the government, and it received so much support that Robert Baldwin resigned as Prime Minister; shortly after Baldwin left politics for good. Mackenzie increasingly recaptured his old stride. In 1853 he founded a newspaper, *Mackenzie's Weekly Message*, which continued publication until the fall of 1860, shortly before his death.

What he rediscovered was his constituency — the people, the working farmers, the mass of ordinary Upper Canadians. It was the lack of this constituency, and of the interaction with them, that had oppressed him most during the years in exile. While in the States, he had remained committed to the abstract *cause* of freedom and justice in Canada, but he missed the people he served that cause *for*. Their support had carried him through every crisis between 1824 and 1837. When he finally returned to them he was like a duck back in water. He expressed his joy in recovering his constituency as a journalist: "I have worked hard since I had the pleasure of asking you to take hold of the subscription lists of the last six winter months, — and I think that cheered on as I am by thousands whose worth I have long known, I can work still harder during the summer months." He also expressed it as a politician happy to be out on the hustings again:

> I attended Mr. Hincks' meetings at Ingersoll, Mount Elgin, Otterville, and Norwich — held other meetings in the forenoons at Tillsonburg &c. — did my best to give South Oxford into Hincks' true character, and was most attentively listened to by very large audiences, many of the hearers in which were old and sincere friends.

As late as 1859, after he had resigned his seat in the House,

Mackenzie remained committed to the necessity of being a *representative*:

> To the Great Conference in St. Lawrence Hall, recently, I was invited as an Editor, and the moment they named me on the committee to propose special committees, I stated my determination to take no part, seeing I had been the choice of no constituency, I took the place of an observer. . . .

He thrived on this sense of constituency, and his possession of one of his own. The years in the States, when he had none, or at least no sense of one, must have been an inordinate trial for him.

Buoyed by this return to people he could feel responsible to, Mackenzie took up the battles of the time. He considered Canada of the late 1850s to be in a state of "emergency" and he did what he could to get at the causes of it. He rooted out corruption as he had always done. He had started with the challenge concerning the Court of Chancery. He attacked the privileges being granted to the new Trust and Loan Company. In 1854 he chaired an inquiry into government operations. But the great arena for government corruption in the 1850s was the railroad boom. Mackenzie was not opposed to railroads; on the contrary, he felt them so valuable to national development that he was ready to accept a considerable amount of wastage and even graft for the sake of the results. He did, however, draw the line at certain points. Much of the business of Canadian parliaments in those years consisted of legislators' granting charters, subsidies, concessions and land to railroad companies, which were themselves usually run by the very same legislators doing the gift-giving. The most blatant case of all was the Grand Trunk Railway, a line intended to run from Montreal, through Kingston to Toronto. This line was financially anchored in some of the great banking houses of England; its construction was given over to a huge British firm; and a number of senior Canadian government officials sat on its board, handing over the funds and assets of the Canadian people to, in effect, themselves and their British patrons. "This is a dishonest scheme to take control of $12 million, borrowed in Britain on the security of every house and farm in Canada, away from the country and give it to a few crafty land jobbers, bankers, sharpers etc." charged Mackenzie in 1853, and he was to be proven more than right. Within a decade the Grand Trunk had fallen into such a financial morass, that its directors had to invent and perpetrate Confederation to bail themselves out. As (the by then Sir) Alan MacNab said, "Railroads are my politics."

Many of the self-serving financial shenanigans of the time were carried out under the holy slogan of union, or unity, between political parties, and eventually between the provinces of British North America. Mackenzie described the real worth of this rhetoric:

> "Let us be united!" is the cry of the leaders of two factions, struggling for the control of places and pelf, and for nothing else — "let us rally round our principles." The poor fellows who follow these cunning rogues find that when one set of sharpers get the patronage, they unblushingly betray their trust, while the knaves they have ousted, promptly take up the cries of their predecessors or invent additional plausible stories. As Sir A. MacNab said "there is no principle involved."

Confederation was merely another float in this parade of specious proposals ostensibly to create "unity" in the colonies, and Mackenzie gave it short shrift in its early forms, though he died before it had really got off the ground.

As for the much-lauded advent of "responsible government," Mackenzie had long since labelled it a sham because of the absence of "independence of foreign control." Now, viewing it from close range, he considered it to be merely a new form of patronage: the largesse of power was being shared by a group considerably expanded beyond the old Family Compact. In 1858, he reported on a meeting held to consider the widespread poverty in Toronto:

> Mayor Boulton presided; and Sheriff Jarvis (candidate for the Legislative Council), J. Hilliard Cameron (would be candidate for the Assembly), Bishop Strachan, several other preachers, and Messr. John Duggan, Heward, &c, were present.
>
> It appears that there is no poor rate, but that, out of the enormous income of the city, $2000 were voted to the poor, to be expended by an Association called the House of Industry. Six hundred to eight hundred respectable mechanics have nothing to do, and many of them families to support, while a stranger from Europe, a mere transient person, demands nearly thirty-two thousand dollars and a palace, tax free, for propping up misrule. Henry John Boulton boasts that he has acquired a greater influence over His Excellency than

> even Madame Killaly exercises with Her Excellency. Dr. Strachan's income is enormous; R. Baldwin wallows in wealth; the Robinsons, Boultons, Cawthras, &c, are very rich.

There were old names and new: John A. Macdonald and "the official and judicial upstart tribe" are mentioned later in the same article. There had been some redistribution of roles but the basic division of the society into a small class of rulers and the mass of the people remained as it had been; and the British still held firm control of it all at the top.

Just as the composition at the top of the social pyramid had altered, a change had occurred on the lower levels. In the years since 1837, an urban industrial working class had started to emerge. Their growth had come with the need for workers to build the railroads, and at a time when new farmland in Upper Canada had become scarce. The "labourers and mechanics" formed a natural addition to Mackenzie's old constituency of "honest hard-working farmers." He supported these workers in their struggle for a ten-hour working day. He argued that rises in the cost of living hit these wage-earners harder than they hit farmers or professionals; accordingly they had the right to demand higher wages when staples such as food and housing rose in cost. Mackenzie even wrote a poem, "The Workman's Strike," quite appropriate to the mood of a newly self-conscious working class:

> In numbers strong, in reason bold
> Let justice equalize the powers
> If theirs the gold,
> Let them be told
> The work that yields it them is ours.

Mackenzie however never came anywhere near to being a socialist. He always remained a devotee of laissez-faire capitalism — a follower of Adam Smith from the days when Smith was still the leading revolutionary thinker in the world of political economy.

The return to Canada, to his constituency and to the political and journalistic arenas emboldened Mackenzie, and through the 1850s, he grew less and less apologetic about his revolutionary past. He once again took to the attack, and was as radical in his criticisms as he had ever been. He increasingly focussed on imperial ambitions as one of the main evils of the world. He came to consider that one of the roots of the degeneration of the United

States was the ambition to expand; he urged the Americans to "cease to grasp at more widely extended Empire, and govern well the patrimony they have in charge." He considered British imperialism still to be the great scourge of the world: "their hordes, naval and military, invading, annexing and enslaving many lands, in order that weaver-princes and Jew usurers may wallow in wealth won by the blood and sweat of outraged humanity, and offices be created for the idle scions of the privileged." He had long castigated the British role in Ireland, and he now harped on India as well: "Who can wonder that when 200,000 Indian troopers are employed by a mercenary organization of covetous storekeepers in London to rivet the yoke on India, they sometimes rebel, and sigh for at least national independence of the stranger!" The analysis led where it had before, and by 1859 he was again calling for independence, "a Republican Constitution for Upper Canada," a limit on public loans, free land to indigent settlers, an end to British use of Canadian taxes, and proportional representation. The apology and despair of the years in exile were gone. His was a lonely voice in the Upper Canada of the 1850s, but he was one of the few to continue to raise and grapple with the most serious political issues facing Canadians.

In 1858 he resigned his seat in the legislature over what he considered to be an irreconciliable difference between himself and his constituents. He continued to publish *Mackenzie's Message* until 1860. He was still threatened by poverty and in addition troubled by sickness. By 1861 he was confined to his house, and then to his bed. On August 28, 1861, he died. A line of mourners half a mile long followed his coffin to the cemetery.

During a visit to a Toronto high school several years ago, I asked some students what they knew about 1837.

"Eighteen thirty-seven . . ." they said. "Act of . . .? Repeal of . . .?"

"No," I said.

"Give us a hint," they said.

"Mackenzie," I said.

"Mackenzie King?"

I grimaced.

"Aha," said one. "William *Lyle* Mackenzie."

Mackenzie was not our George Washington, our Gandhi or

our Mao. He failed, but what can you do — he was the best we've had so far. When the country is finally free, it will be because we've had better heroes. In the meantime, as Dennis Lee says:

> Mackenzie was a crazy man,
> He wore his wig askew.
> He donned three bulky overcoats
> In case the bullets flew.
> Mackenzie talked of fighting
> While the fight went down the drain.
> But who will speak for Canada?
> Mackenzie, come again. *

* From ''1838'' by Dennis Lee, *Nicholas Knock and Other People*, Macmillan of Canada Ltd., Toronto, 1974.

NOTE ON SOURCES

The material referred to in *1837: Mackenzie and Revolution* can be found, for the most part, in the following sources.

Chapter 1

Craig, Gerald M., *Upper Canada: The Formative Years* (McClelland & Stewart, Toronto, 1963).
Creighton, Donald, *The Empire of the St. Lawrence* (Macmillan, Toronto, 1972).
Fink, Dean, *Life in Upper Canada, 1781-1841* (McClelland & Stewart, Toronto, 1971).
Myers, Gustavus, *A History of Canadian Wealth* (James Lorimer & Co., Toronto, 1972).
Ryerson, Stanley, *Unequal Union* (Progress Books, Toronto, 1968).
Teeple, Gary (ed.), *Capitalism and the National Question in Canada* (University of Toronto Press, 1972).

Chapter 2

Dunham, Aileen, *Political Unrest in Upper Canada, 1815-1836* (McClelland and Stewart, Toronto, 1963).
Earl, David W. L. (ed.), *The Family Compact: Aristocracy or Oligarchy?* (Copp Clark, Toronto, 1967).
Graham, W. H., *The Tiger of Canada West* (Clarke Irwin, Toronto, 1962).
MacFarlane Lizers, Robina and Kathleen, *In the Days of The Canada Company* (Mika, Belleville, 1973).

Chapter 3

Fairley, Margaret (ed.), *The Selected Writings of William Lyon Mackenzie* (Oxford University Press, Toronto, 1960).
Kilbourn, William, *The Firebrand* (Clarke Irwin, Toronto, 1956).
Lindsey, Charles, *The Life and Times of William Lyon Mackenzie* (Coles, Rexdale, 1971).
Rasporich, Anthony W., *William Lyon Mackenzie* (Holt, Toronto, 1972).

Chapter 4

Bergeron, Léandre, *The History of Quebec: A Patriote's Handbook* (NC Press, 1971).

Burroughs, Peter, *The Canadian Crisis and British Colonial Policy 1828-1841* (Macmillan, Toronto, 1972).

Davis, Robert, *The Canadian Farmer's Travels in the United States of America* (Steeles Press, Buffalo, 1837).

Moodie, Susanna, *Roughing it in the Bush* (McClelland & Stewart, Toronto, 1962).

Chapter 5

Many of the above and,

Guillet, Edwin C., *The Lives and Times of the Patriots* (University of Toronto Press, 1968).

Chapter 6

Same as source materials for Chapter 3.

PART II

1837: The Farmers' Revolt

Rick Salutin and Theatre Passe Muraille

Preface

1837 was first produced at Theatre Passe Muraille in Toronto in January, 1973. Here is a "diary" of that production.

Fall, 1972

Last year, while I was in rehearsal with a play called *Fanshen,* about the Chinese Revolution, the director said, "Now what we ought to do *next* year is — Quebec!"

Oh no, I thought. No more getting off on these exotic foreign revolutions. Next year if we do a revolution it will be right here in Ontario.

Sunday, Dec. 3

Drove out to the Niagara Peninsula with Paul (director) and Williams (designer). On a winding narrow road that once was the thoroughfare between Hamilton and the frontier we found a neglected monument, high as my waist and shaped like a gravestone. Divided into crescents, it read:

> Up the hill 50 feet stood the home of Samuel Chandler Patriot
> He guided Mackenzie to Buffalo
> And here they had supper
> Dec. 10, 1837

It is encouraging. With all the denigration spattered on the rebellion during our schooldays and since, I was beginning to ponder whether we were the first who had ever thought to treat it as a serious national event.

Wednesday, Dec. 6

Rehearsals begin tomorrow, the 7th, the anniversary of the Battle of Montgomery's Tavern. The 7th was also a Thursday in 1837. Odd how those things fuel you. We have no script yet, only general ideas of why and how we want to do it. I've tried too. In September, I sketched out scenes, then showed it to L. "Looks just the way we learned it in school," she said. Back to the drawing board. Paul is delighted. He's said all along we're better off without a script, that it makes the actors lazy. Even if we had one, he'd be for hiding it. Fine — but what do they need *me* for?

Thursday Dec 7

We have six actors. Three men and three women. Two I know from *Fanshen.* The rest are strangers. I brought in a few goodies: maps and pictures of Old Toronto. Great stir at finding the *history* of places we've all lived around. We're starting very far back: other countries may have to relive or reinterpret their past, but they know they *have* a past. In Quebec they may hate it, but it's sure as hell there. English Canadians, at least around here, must be convinced there *is* a past that is their own.

We paraded to Mackenzie House on Bond St. in midafternoon where little Wasp women in period dress served us tea and apple butter. I nearly choked on it, and the rest of what they've wreaked on our only militant independantiste. Our work is cut out.

Before splitting up, we asked each of the actors to present an 1837 object. The best was Clare. She set herself before us and said:

> I'm William Lyon Mackenzie's house. My feet are spread wide apart and are firmly planted. My hands are on my hips and I look straight ahead. I have *lots* of windows and any question you ask me, I'm not afraid to answer.

It's already apparent that Paul is right. The absence of a script is drawing material out of the actors. After all, they have more theatre experience than anyone, and they're almost never asked to draw on it.

Friday Dec 8

We gave the actors anger exercises today. Each had to simulate anger around 1837. For some it was agony — or constipation. Neil was superb. "Nobody," he roared, "is going to make me speak with an English accent." That is a true Canadian actor's anti-imperialism. Theatre is one of the few areas left in Canada where the main imperial oppressor remains England and not the U.S. They run every regional theatre in the country; Englishmen waft over and drown in role offers. Stratford — our *national* theatre — gobbling public money to become an acknowledged *second* best in *another* country's national playwright. Neil was one of Stratford's golden boys — an apprentice — in its early years. Then he rebelled by going to act for twelve years in New York, instead of London. He's been back about two years now.

Last spring, when Paul and I first talked about this play, I said it was to be an anti-imperialist piece. He leaped joyfully and cried, "Right — we'll really smash the Brits" — making me wince, but in theatre he was right.

Monday Dec 11

First resistance. From Clare. She looked to me and said, "*There's* all the research — bottled up in your head — and we can't get at it."

Actors have been so infantilized. Writers tell them what to say and directors tell them where to stand and no one asks them to think for themselves. They come to work with Paul because they want to break that pattern, but then they freeze up. I remember my first horrified encounter with actors, during *Fanshen.* They were treating this play exactly as they would any other; it might have been *Barefoot in the Park.* Like the mailman, they'd deliver anything. It shocked me that they were like any other group in the country, politically, that is. But the actors are also the real proletariat of the theatre; that too was clear from the first rehearsal. They are the bottom rung. They take shit from everyone else, and *their* labour holds it all up: reproduces it all, night after night.

This matter of research: the material on 1837 is endless, to my surprise. The collective method takes the pressure off me for digesting all of it. Everyone reads like crazy. Mornings, before we start, the rehearsal room looks like a library.

Tuesday Dec 12

We're still concentrating on texture, and haven't begun to build scenes.

The woman problem remains completely unsolved, although we are ignoring it at this point. Paul originally wanted only one woman. I insisted on at least two and claimed we could show the class conflict through two women. He went along, and since Suzette became available, we now have three, in addition to the three men. But what will we do with them, given the paucity of the sources on women? I've ransacked the records, talked with historians, writers, feminists. All we find are interminable journals by the *gentle*women of the time, who complain of their hard life in the Bush, and how tough it is to get servants. Women didn't fight, and they didn't legislate. Clearly they worked. But what they did, and how they felt, in specifics. . .? Every time I go back over it, I end up nowhere. In *Fanshen,* the woman issue was so *clear*.

Wednesday Dec 13

Williams brought in the set — that is, a mockup in a shoebox. What a triumph. A series of four platforms ranging from 2 to 8 feet off the floor connected by ramps which will be corduroyed. Plus five enormous trees set throughout the theatre that will tower up through the roof.

The effect of the platforms will be to give us the possibility of isolation and concentration — *plus* the possibility of movement (between the platforms); it is the best of all possible worlds, in terms of design. Instantly all our thinking about the play is transformed. I keep wandering by it and conjuring miniature people on the ramps.

Thursday Dec 14

We tried Mackenzie's newspaper piece on the Family Compact today. It's a fine hatchet job. He numbers them from one to thirty, and cross references them by number. We did it with five people taking all the roles — switching — and Neil reading. It will, I hope, become the definitive version of the Family Compact. I suppose I like it because I have been writing political satire for radio three years now and see Mackenzie's piece as the start of a Canadian tradition.

I gave Miles *The Canadian Farmer's Travels in the U.S.A.* to read. Written by an Upper Canadian farmer named Davis in 1836. I discovered it in the rare book room of the public library. Heartsick at the election of '36, he went travelling in the U.S., was thrilled by the abundance he saw everywhere and the efficacy of the democratic system, and resolved to return home and struggle for improvement here. He published the book, and died in the fighting in 1838. It's a very naive book — he's so overwhelmed by what he saw, that he loves *everything* — slavery, Indians — all of it. It's a trip scene and should work well, especially with the kind of energy Miles can give it.

More texturing: we've given everyone a minor character to do from the time. Someone who's barely mentioned in the records. Sally Jordan, who worked for Anne Langton, who wrote a journal. Ira Anderson, innkeeper, who's on the arrest record. A name mentioned in Mackenzie's paper as seconding a motion at a meeting. They must build their character according to what they know of the time. We'll quiz the actors in coming days on what these characters were about at various times in 1837. Some scenes may come out of it, but more important is the *thickness* — to pour into and onto whatever and whoever we end up using. We have to build the reality of the ordinary people of the time. They are the core of our past we have to get through to; they must be the centre of the play — not any of the "great" individuals who hog most of the records.

Friday Dec 15

Blizzard. After the break Janet said, "Can I go home?" and Paul said, "If you walk all the way up Yonge St. and do it in character." Upshot was we bundled up and trekked through Old Toronto. Down to the site of the hangings on King St., along King to Berkeley, up Parliament and over to the cemetery where Mackenzie, Lount and Matthews are buried. It was locked when we arrived. One thing we concluded: December was a hell of a time to make a revolution here.

Monday Dec 18

A row at the end of the day. "I'm sick of our Canadian politeness," Paul complained. We'd been doing break-ins by loyalists at the homes of rebels after the battle. The traditional Canadian knock at the door. Our intruders had tied themselves in knots trying not to be too, too nasty.

It is a crux: the ability to *really* identify with the main struggles and passions of the people at the time; else it will be just play-acting, better or worse. Clare dealt it back the strongest. "One of the nicest things about Canadians is that they *don't* get angry," she yelled.

I argued — academically I fear — that this "typical" Canadian reserve is not genetically rooted; that Canadians did fight and shout in 1837; and that our esteemed diffidence is the result of the failure and repression of such moments of resistance and assertion. If it is that historically based, we're not going to shake it loose by doing a passionate play; still, we may gain an inch or two.

Wednesday Dec. 20

Pictures: we give the actors five minutes to rummage through books, choose an image, and give it back.

David plunged: "Now sir, when we moved onto that plot, there was nothing there. All I'm asking is . . ." Suzette hauled a table and chair in front of him, and leaned back like a contemptuous land agent. As he stammered on, about how he and his family had worked, the others filled in behind, chopping and clearing. Hewers of wood and drawers of water. Very strong. David is our staunchest, in a way. Our oak — (and we have Miles chop him down in a scene). He grew up in Kirkland Lake, taught high school ten years in Brantford, and did his first professional acting this past summer.

Janet did a brilliant picture. Back to us, passed her palm above her head, saying, "A smooth broad forehead." Then she stood Suzette and Neil side by side facing us as, "Two piercing eyes." Drew their inner arms forward together as, "A classic nose." Got Clare in to make a mouth; and announced it was John Beverley Robinson, one of the leading members of the Compact. Now to find a way of integrating it into the production so that it becomes more than a *tour de force* of theatricality.

(The "Head" developed this way: Paul felt we had to make it the head of Lieutenant Governor Francis Bond Head, not Robinson, since Mackenzie had been so fond of punning on Head's name. Neil found a speech by Bond Head that was the quintessence of the Imperial attitude; as one of the eyes he also delivered it. It fit perfectly as the prelude to the Canadian Farmer's Travels to the U.S. The whole didn't come together until weeks after

Janet had given us the original image.)

Friday Dec. 22

There was no point trying to rehearse today. Everyone is gripped with job insecurity, because Actors' Equity is about to shut down Factory Theatre Lab, and is preparing an offensive against the other small Canadian theatres like ourselves. Ostensibly the issue is kickbacks. Equity actors who work at the small theatres must sign contracts at Equity rates, but since these are unrealistic for the small theatres, they often return a part of what they are paid. We have four Equity actors and they've all received threatening letters from *their* union. (They can't seem to get the incongruity of this through their heads.) They fear they'll be expelled. We talked all day, mostly about American unions and how typical this is of the way they operate in Canada — and about other forms of imperialism, especially American. I am the only one with a thoroughly paranoid interpretation: that Equity's real purpose is to shut down the small Canadian theatres because they provide increasing competition and audience drain from the downtown mausoleums that house touring Broadway shows, American-mounted productions, to which Equity gives its main allegiance. I was alone in deeming it a conspiracy, but various forms of fear and indignation reign among the rest. They're tired of yearly questionnaires from Equity asking how many hours they've worked on-Broadway, off-Broadway etc. There is certainly no way of avoiding this discussion in the context of the play we are making.

Boxing Day

Finally tried Ventriloquism. Inspired by a handbill for an 1830's travelling show (". . . and featuring — VENTRILOQUISM") It's a perfect metaphor for colonialism — maybe too perfect? Divided our actors into teams of dummy and master; David and Clare were far the best technically. Now to work on the problem of what they're to say.

Thursday Dec. 28

We had our good day today, as Janet said.

For his anger homework, David came in with a team stuck in

the mud. Got off his wagon, stuffed his shoulder against a wheel, shoved and cursed. Others moved in as horses etc., and Janet sang God Save the Queen. *Finally* we got behind the academicism of the "roads" issue. Each time someone uses it, it sounds plucked from the section of the textbook called Causes of the Rebellion. We've taken to barking "Cause Three" when they mention roads, and "Cause Four" to the Clergy Reserves. But this was real and *felt*.

Neil began musing about the secret meeting at Doel's Brewery in Toronto before the rebellion — the night when the city was unguarded and Mackenzie urged his fellow reformers to seize it and the four thousand arms that were there. I've yearned to do it from the start. It was the time to act, but they stalled till they could bring down the farmers to take the risks for them. Had they acted there is no doubt our history would have been different. The British would have been forced to return half their forces from Quebec, where fighting had already begun; the French just might then have succeeded; in Ontario there'd have been arms and impetus. . . . Still, dreams aside, the point of the scene is not to show what might have been, but the unreliability and timidity of bourgeois leadership in a struggle for Canadian independence. Then as now. Paul felt it was too programmatic to get out of the actors, but Neil was so keen on it that we both gulped, "Let's try it." It went not badly, broad lines emerged, and in this one case, I am going to write it up as a scene, based on the improved work. My first chance to be a playwright. Now they get a chance to judge my work.

We finally got the Davis scene, the Canadian farmer travelling in the U.S. Miles had had an anxiety attack each time he moved into it. Today we literally sat on him, holding him down, and by the time he finally escaped he'd gathered so much energy it carried him right through the trip. The key is to satirize the farmer's enthusiasm for all things American. To put through our eyes what we saw through his. On one side lethargic Windsor (yawns) and then — Industrious Detroit — everyone pumping and rushing and HAPPY. He adores it all: Neil ran up and said, "Excuse me sir, I'm a runaway slave, which way is Canada?" and he said — "No, don't go, it'll get better here." Got quite wild, snatches of Aquarius, etc. Very exciting. I'm still excited about it.

Friday Dec. 29

I've got a last line. Talking with Suzette about Canadian plays and what downers they are — always about losers. Yet what to do? Our past is negative. The country has remained a colony; the struggle in 1837 did not succeed. I've thought of changing the ending, having the rebels win (Stop that Hanging!); or cutting off before the battle and the defeat, at, say, the high point in October '37. But finally we have to wrestle with what actually happened and wring something positive out of that. Losing, I argued, does not have to make you a "Loser"; there are winners who lose. It is the difference between saying, "We lost", and saying, "No, we just haven't won yet." There it is.

Saturday Dec. 30

The Family Compact is turning into a hell, more demoralizing each time we run it. The novelty of the numbering has worn off, they are reaching for ever more corn to cover their changes. We're down to staging numbers 21-25 as a bloody cricket match. Paul can't get it. Damn. Paul's strength — his genius — is working with people and eliciting their creativity. I try to help — but I'm no director. Christ what a loss it would be — it's right there!

Sunday Dec. 31

They showed me a scene Suzette had improvised yesterday while I was out. An English gentlewoman doing the tour of the colonies gets stuck in her coach on the road from Toronto to Niagara, blusters at the driver, fidgets about her manservant, yammers endlessly, but together they push free and suddenly she is ecstatic about the "adventure" they've just had. ("My cousin Stephanie was one experience up on me, you know.") I loathed her — extolling "Nature's cathedral" which only she and not the gruff coachman could appreciate, bidding "Goodbye Brave Bush," before she'd climb back in the coach. I grabbed for one of our stage rifles and would gladly have plugged her through her "jaded, civilized eyes." But she is so right and brilliant and hilarious — I suppose there will be no way of keeping it out of the play.

We are starting to think about how to shape these things. About time. It is New Year's Eve. We open on the 17th.

Tuesday Jan. 2

Working with Mackenzie's newspaper again. Divided them, as usual, into an upper class, and a dirt poor family, each reacting to the same articles differently. Today though, they fell into interrupting each other's readings and emerged in fullblown battle. All the good arguments were with the reactionaries. And all the articulateness. "My dear man, you can't expect illiterate farmers to actually *govern?*" "What do *you* know about economics?" "Are you admitting then that you are *disloyal?*" On and on, Neil and his gathering steam; David and his, being ground down. Miles (for the rich) made some patronizing analogy, to which David tried pathetically to respond. Janet got closer to the class reality, barging in with, "That's a stupid argument!" Suzette cooed, "Why can't we all get *along?*" in a perfect Rosedale tone. Janet tore through the paper looking for counterarguments, looking to us — what she really felt was — If only Mac was here, *he'd* tell them. We suddenly saw Mackenzie's real importance for these people. The oppressed never control the ideological apparatus; it is always used by the ruling classes to confuse and demoralize them. Mackenzie took the ideological skills he possessed and put them at the disposal of the oppressed instead of the oppressors, doing for them what they had not been given the resources to do for themselves. He really served the people. What nonsense the way we learned it — as if it was Mackenzie against the Family Compact in personal combat. It was the working people against the Empire. They were the centre, but they needed him.

Wednesday Jan. 3

I distributed the script for the brewery scene today; reaction was astounding. They blinked and wouldn't believe — a real script — went berserk with gratitude and joy. Much feigned, of course, but it came from somewhere. The pressure and demands on them in this method of work are vast. That we knew; but not quite how *much.*

Most striking was how the presence of a script shot everyone into an instant role. They became actors, underlining their speeches and saying bitchy things like, "Let me feel my way into this, will you?" Paul became a director urging interpretations and line readings on them ("Let me coach you.") And I became a writer, skulking in back, gritting my teeth at what they were doing to "my" lines, nodding when they "got it", and not intervening except to occasionally whisper to Paul. Till now, roles have been loose; everyone was writing, directing and acting, though of course not all to the same extent. With the script, compartmentalization set in like terminal cancer. I'm glad we did it — just this one scene — to watch it happen.

Toward the end of the day, with everyone tired and loathe to take on a bummer like the Compact, Paul spied a length of rope in the corner, looped it six times, put it over their heads and told them they were prisoners being returned to Toronto after the rebellion. They trudged and told us what they felt and saw. Too much self-pity at the moment, but a strong image and one that will work on our set. Where did that come from? I asked Paul. Desperation, he said.

Friday Jan. 5

Last night I read through seven or eight accounts of the Seige of Toronto between Dec. 4 and 7, culminating with the Battle, and typed a composite account, very long and detailed. Then I cut it up with scissors into thirty different pieces, numbered, and this morning gave five pieces to each actor. Each has to say his section, as they come up in sequence, though everyone acts out the events. It will take lots of choreography and coordination, and we will be at it once a day till we open — like taking vitamins, says Paul. I think our audiences will be captivated — all those warlike events up and down Yonge St.

I feel less guilt about my contribution, now that I've done some scripting. And I think I can see the shape of Act II. From Doel's, through the Battle, the march of the prisoners, the hangings. We'll be leaping right into the maw of the defeat, and see what kind of victory we can bring from it. But as for Act I, God only knows. . . .

Monday Jan. 8

Awful. Just awful. I can't say how bad. There is nothing there. And they will not work, will not give. The Family Compact is a horror; we haven't dared touch it in five days. Miles is stumped on his Farmer's Travels. We all see what a good scene it is; we've seen him do it brilliantly; but he's clogged up, he makes excuses and accuses Paul of not directing him. Paul fires back that Miles won't commit himself. I stalk around the theatre — we moved in today out of the rehearsal room — wanting to rip Miles into bits for his stingy withholding. I know that's false, but it's what I feel. Paul and I confer hostilely, and they pick it up and sulk or fling back angry glares — Janet is doing that more and more. We are at a dead halt — no, we are careening backwards. There is no giving, no expansiveness — and no script to fall back on!

Christ, I said to Paul, is it this way every time?

I don't know, he sighed. I can't remember. I guess so.

How do you stand it?

I must forget. If I remembered, I would never do it again.

Tuesday Jan. 9

Today it was Clare. She has no lines in the Doel's scene, but is a brewery hand who sets it up and works away in the background while the leaders of the rebellion are conspiring below. She is the lurking presence of the ordinary working people who will have to take all the chances while most of their "leaders" sit tight. But she's been a lump. I challenged her on it and she maintained that since she knows nothing about brewing beer, she can't act it. I said she should figure out something that seemed to her like brewing and do that. She pouted that she'd take off the rest of the day and go research brewing in the library. More tight-assed withholding — I stormed off. Paul? I don't know where he gets the patience. Like a shrink fighting through layers of resistance, he patiently counters argument after argument of hers till she admits she just doesn't want to take a chance. Then she went ahead and did it — beautifully. I don't know what the hell *she* thought she was doing, but at the least it didn't look like *not* brewing beer.

Wednesday Jan. 10

The Ventriloquism is in trouble. We haven't figured out how to use it — is it metaphor, is it to the audience, is it within the play itself? David and Clare are balking, say it's no fun, no point. I'll try and script it as a two minute skit — as if I were writing for radio.

We did get the Family Compact. We'd written it off regretfully but I was looking at the set today — ramps running down from platform to platform — and said, Why don't we try it on the ramps, unwinding the Compact from top to bottom? So we did, and we have a scene.

Thursday Jan. 11

Came up with an Act I closing. Our anger exercises. Spread our people over the set, doing bursts of anger one after another. They made them up on the spot; some were extraordinary.

Miles: (climbing off the floor onto the set) I don't care who you are and what your name is. From now on you can clean the muck out from under your own damned English footbridge.

Neil: See this cabinet. Took me six months. Know why I can't sell it? Because it was made in (an awful angry whine) Torrrrooonnnttoooo-

Janet: So I sez to her — Milk your *own* cow!

And finally a chance to use Suzette's Quebec half: Moé-la, j'aimais plus je'n chant'rai pour les Anglais!

It is the boiling point of 1837, where grievances and resentments are irrepressible and have to burst into the action of the rebellion itself — in Act II.

Friday Jan. 12

Just what we'd considered our strongest suit — the pictures — just won't work down here in the theatre. They were grand in the little rehearsal room with the low ceiling but — ah well, they served their purpose: got us into the texture of the time.

Saturday Jan. 13

Worked with David on his (Lount's) gallows speech. He's been to the provincial archives mornings this week, reading accounts of the trial of Lount and Matthews.

Finally found a use for those lists I like so much — the names of those arrested or charged in the aftermath of the rebellion. 885 men, their homes, and occupations. Fine names — Caleb Kipp, Josiah Dent, Joshua Doan: yeoman, labourer, tanner, etc. When I have been stymied by this work both before and then during rehearsals, I've taken to reading through those names. I've wanted to employ them as a sort of litany. They work well into the rope scene, the march of the prisoners. Each gives his name and when they've gone round once, they go round again, and then again, creating with the six an endless line of captured revolutionaries. I gave a page of names to each actor; they can choose the ones they'll use each night.

The final form is now clear. Act I will be fairly diffuse, a view of the life of the times — our blessed texture — though building to the inevitability of the outbreak. It should end high, with the feeling, This Can't Miss. After intermission we change pace completely.

Act II drives right through with the line of the rebellion, defeat and aftermath. It will have the guts of our politics, what we make of this event and why we are returning to it now.

Monday Jan. 15

We hit the crunch today with the Farmer's Travels. Miles capsized again midway. He tried to get Paul to call it off, cut the scene, give it to someone else — do *some*thing. I could see Paul struggling with the offer; then he leapt up on the set and refused. Said he would not become the paternalistic director at this point. If Miles really wanted to do the scene, Paul would stand by him no matter how much it seemed to lack — and he was sure the audience would accept it. Or — if Miles really didn't want to do it, *he* would have to say so. It was a trap for Paul and he was magnificent in avoiding it. Suzette, bless her, said, "I vote to have it in," not pressing but making the point that, if not Miles, then someone else should do it. Miles wrestled with it, started the trip again, stalled, slumped down, and said, "I don't want to do it like this." "O.K." said Paul, "Janet — will you try it?"

Janet looked to Miles, he nodded generously, she launched it, and was fine. When we tried it again later, Miles came in as the wife, urging the farmer not to leave for the States. It works, and I think it also means we've solved the women problem as far as we can. Clare argued with me the other day that one of the men on the scaffold should be played by a woman, and I argued back that it would be so obtrusive that we would end up with a scene about the equality of women, not about 1837. It might be right politically, but if it doesn't work as theatre there is no point in doing it in a play. Janet plays a man because it has become dramatically necessary in the travel scene. We have women playing men in the battle and the brewery scene for the same reason and it is unobtrusive there. We've failed to find a centrality for women in 1837 terms. But we are *doing* the play in *our* terms — with an equal cast, fair distribution of parts, etc. It is an attempt to portray an oppressive reality in a liberated way.

Tuesday Jan. 16

We've put the Ventriloquism unit as the introduction to the meeting Mackenzie addresses before the rebellion. As a skit presented by two farmers for their friends at the rally. Agitprop of '37. Allows the other actors to react to it as *its* audience, drains off the heavy symbolism, and clarifies that Clare is playing a real person who is *playing* a dummy.

Great consternation about the newspaper scene with which we'd wanted to open. It is important, for me 1) to open a play about Canadian history with a scene of class conflict, and 2) to show the centrality of Mackenzie's paper — its propaganda and education — for the movement. Paul's retort was — it's not doing either of those things as it is now. I had to agree. We put it to them and — wonder of wonders — they say they want to do it as we have it and are sure they can pull it off tomorrow night, though they'd like me to settle on four or five articles and choose an order for them. Instead of suggesting another cut, they propose an inclusion — a good, good sign.

The programs came today, and I like them. They are a piece with the rest of this work: single sheets with a map of Old Toronto and an alphabetical list of the people who made the play.

I think I see now Paul's vision of theatre and the value he places on improvisation. Without a script, there is real tension and the possibility of creative breakthrough on stage at any moment. It is not *set*. People come to plays thinking of them as movies or TV gone live, perfect realizations of a script or theme, and frozen at that point of perfect realization. But a play is made live each night, and its possibility is not frozen perfection but ongoing re-creation. The edge for an audience should not be awe at a perfect performance, but anxiety about something new and possibly better at any moment.

Opening Night

Two instructive things happened. When Clare started Act II with "Bay and Adelaide, the northwest corner," the audience laughed. If an actor said, "Montmartre, 4 a.m.," or "Piccadilly Circus, twelve noon," no audience anywhere would laugh. But we are so imbued with self-denial, so colonized, that the very thought of something historic happening *here,* at Bay and Adelaide, draws laughs.

Again, during the Battle, in the nighttime skirmish when both inexperienced sides broke ranks and fled, Miles lost his line for a moment, and the audience laughed. Miles — American Miles — said that moment made clear to him for the first time what I'd been saying about the problem of Canadian history for a Canadian audience. There was nothing funny about the moment. It was terrifying or should have been.

Three Weeks Later

The actors have come to take it as a challenge to deliver those lines so that the audience can not laugh at them. At the same time, Janet says the response to *1837* is different from any play she's ever appeared in. It is not just appreciation. It's something warmer.

It is, I think, identification. Beyond the identification you get in any good theatre. It is a meeting with ourselves.

Over a year later, the play was reworked. The result — amounting to a new play — was called *1837: The Farmers' Revolt.* It was produced in the spring, summer, and fall of 1974 — first in the auction barns of southwestern Ontario, then in the Victoria Playhouse in Petrolia, Ontario, and then in Toronto. It has since had many productions throughout the country. It is the script of this latter production which is included below.

1837: The Farmers' Revolt was developed in exactly the same way as the first version of the play. But it was meant for a tour of farming communities, instead of an urban theatre audience and it differed from the earlier play in the following ways.

It was not Toronto-centred. In the first *1837* we had made hay of the events and locales of early Toronto. We de-emphasized these in the country, and looked for elements that reflected what had happened out there, where we were planning to tour the show.

So, for instance, we cleared a larger space for Anthony van Egmond, the old colonel who led the revolutionary force at Montgomery's Tavern. Van Egmond had lived just outside Seaforth — in the village now called Egmondville. The family home is still standing, and local people are restoring it.

Instead of showing the entire four days of fighting around Toronto, we showed only the final battle there. For the first three days, we went out to the country, and followed Van Egmond, as he marched from his home down to Toronto, to take command of the forces there.

Numerous such changes in the script occurred. Another change which took place was, in a way, political.

The earlier play — beamed into the Toronto milieu — could assume a somewhat left-of-liberal politics on the part of its audience; more or less of a sympathy, or at least tolerance, for the revolutionary sentiments of the play. But the farming community is, at least in its explicit attitudes, far more conservative. So some of the rhetoric — what Miles called the "bombast" — came out. And more justification of the movement for change went in. For instance, we had *two* scenes, instead of one, depicting the bitterness of the farmers over the land policies of the 1830s.

The play also changed dramatically, or artistically.

It became much tighter than the earlier version. In the first version, for example, we served the battle up whole. In the second, by concentrating on the experience of Van Egmond, we gave the scene a dramatic focus it had lacked. In the end, I would say version two (the one included here) is a far better play.

This is largely so because on the first time round we were intent on getting clear *what* we were going to say about 1837. By round two, that most crucial of matters was basically settled; we could concentrate on *how* to say it most effectively, refining scenes, characters etc. The resulting script proves, I think, that the collective process can produce a play as dramatically tight as the more typical scripting approach.

In some ways though, I preferred the earlier version. It would not make as good reading, and it did not play as well. Yet it had a rawness and a timeliness. It felt to me when we first put this show up in January of 1973, that we were expressing something of what was happening in the country at the time: a determination to throw off colonial submissiveness in all areas. *1837* was a theatrical expression of that feeling, making it more of a political event, and not just, or even primarily, a theatrical one.

By the second time round, a mere year and a half later, things seemed to have changed, have slowed. The movement for Canadianization of trade unions had *not* yet taken off; the universities were more dominated than ever by Americans; the Waffle had been expelled from the NDP, largely for its nationalism; the cries for economic control had muted. The nationalist, anti-imperialist impetus was still present, and *more* necessary than ever; but it was less fresh, was in a bit of a withdrawal.

And so the play became more of a theatrical, and less of a political, event. That is why I preferred version one, though version two is no doubt superior "theatre."

1837: The Farmers' Revolt had an original cast of five: three men and two women. Men played women, and women men, or animals or objects or parts of the body — depending on the needs of the scene. There were very few props. I mention this because anyone reading the script will be tempted to imagine a well-equipped cast of thousands.

The actors who worked on the various productions were Janet Amos, Clare Coulter, Suzette Couture, Doris Cowan, David Fox, Eric Peterson, Miles Potter, Terry Tweed, and Neil Vipond. I had a notion of including a list with this script indicating which actors were primarily responsible for which scenes — but when it comes to the doing it is terrifically difficult to assign such credit. So I will just reiterate that the play is *entirely* a creation of the company in rehearsals and performance. The present script is an after-the-fact, somewhat composite, effort, assembled *following* the close of the fall 1974 run.

The director of *1837* was Paul Thompson. The designer was Paul Williams. I was the writer on — but not of — *1837.*

RICK SALUTIN

1837: The Farmers' Revolt

ACT I

WALKING

A man is walking on the set. He carries an axe and a sack. He walks and walks and walks, seeing the forests and the occasional cleared farm of Upper Canada pass by him as he goes. The audience are still entering. They are asking each other, Who is he? Where's he going? What's he got with him? *He keeps walking. This is a play about a time when people in Canada walked to get anywhere and do anything. Eventually two farmers enter, one stage left, and one stage right. They are taking a rest. They watch him go by their field.*

FIRST FARMER: Who is that fellow?

SECOND: Name's Thomas Campbell.

FIRST: Where's he from?

SECOND: Glasgow.

He walks. Enter two more farmers.

THIRD FARMER: Where's he going?

FOURTH: He's bought a plot of land near Coldwater.

They watch him awhile. They are all tired from hard work.

SECOND: How much did it cost him?

FIRST: Twenty dollars down — he'll work the rest out.

FOURTH: How long has he been walking?

THIRD: Four and a half days.

FIRST: *Feeling his own feet.* Ouch.

SECOND: Does he have any family?

FOURTH: Wife. Son. Three daughters. Younger brother. All back in Scotland. They'll be over later.

THIRD: What's he got with him?

FIRST: Everything he owns.

SECOND: Think he knows how to use that axe?

THIRD: If he doesn't, he'll learn.

FIRST: What does he see?

THIRD: Trees.

SECOND: Trees.

FOURTH: Trees.

FIRST: Trees and trees and trees and trees —

They all fill in the word "trees" as he speaks. They are planting a forest of trees with their voices. It mounts, then recedes and dies.

THIRD: What's he going to do when he gets there?

He gets there. He puts down his load, very weary. Looks around at the trees, up at the trees, tries to see through to the sky. He decides not to rest, raises his axe, and begins clearing his land.

BLACK.

CLEARING

Grunts and sounds of straining in the dark. Lights up slowly. Four people working around a great (imaginary) stump, hacking and hauling at it. With one mighty heave it comes loose and they fall away from it, spent.

VOICE: *Offstage.* Hallooooo —

STEADMAN: *Panting.* Hallooo —

VOICE: *Offstage.* Is there a Peter Steadman there?

They lie there, too exhausted to respond. Enter Magistrate Thompson, obviously an official. He approaches one of them.

MAGISTRATE: Peter Steadman?

He is motioned toward Steadman.

MAGISTRATE: Magistrate Thompson, from Richmond Hill.

STEADMAN: Magistrate, how do you do? *With distaste, the Magistrate shakes*

Steadman's sweaty hand. It's a long ride from Richmond Hill. Will you take something to drink? Sit down?

MAGISTRATE: Thank you, no.

STEADMAN'S WIFE: Can I get you anything?

MAGISTRATE: No. I was told I would find you here.

STEADMAN: We've been here a long time.

MAGISTRATE: How long, exactly?

STEADMAN: Close to two years.

MAGISTRATE: This is fine land. How much have you cleared?

STEADMAN: Eighteen acres.

STEADMAN'S BROTHER: Eighteen acres in two years!

STEADMAN'S WIFE: We've been working hard.

MAGISTRATE: Yes. Congratulations. That's a fine home.

STEADMAN'S WIFE: First one I've ever had that was my own.

STEADMAN: We were going to come up to Toronto to see you people pretty soon.

MAGISTRATE: Good, black, fertile soil.

STEADMAN: Yes, it's a good farm.

MAGISTRATE: Could I see your deed please, Mr. Steadman?

STEADMAN: I don't have a deed.

MAGISTRATE: Then your letter of license.

STEADMAN: Now I wouldn't have one of those without a deed, would I?

MAGISTRATE: Mr. Steadman, don't presume to tell me my business. *He unrolls a survey map, which looks to us like a Union Jack.* Your lot is number seventeen. On this government survey map, lot seventeen, here in this corner — I see no record whatever of the name Steadman. But it *is* part of a parcel of one thousand acres which was granted three weeks ago to Colonel Sparling of the Forty-Eighth Highlanders.

STEADMAN: Granted!

MAGISTRATE: By the Lieutenant-Governor.

STEADMAN'S SISTER IN LAW: This farm is not for sale!

STEADMAN'S BROTHER: You listen — we homesteaded this land.

MAGISTRATE: I choose to call it squatting.

STEADMAN'S BROTHER: Call it what you want. It's what everybody does when they don't have any money to start.

MAGISTRATE: And everybody who does it accepts the risk that something of this sort will happen.

STEADMAN: *Trying to be reasonable* I'll be glad to go down to Toronto and talk to this Colonel and buy the land from him.

MAGISTRATE: Mr. Steadman, I know with certainty that he simply does not want you on his land. He is not however an ungenerous man, and if you approach him on the right footing, he might be willing to recompense you for your labour on his land.

STEADMAN'S BROTHER: How's he going to pay us for two years of clearing?

MAGISTRATE: He wants you off the land. You have one week, Steadman.

STEADMAN: *Burning.* You have one minute, Magistrate — to get off my farm.

Steadman's brother picks up his axe. The Magistrate beats a retreat.

MAGISTRATE: *As he goes.* One week Steadman —

STEADMAN: *Calling after him.* We'll be here a week from now, Magistrate. We'll be here long after you're dead —

Left alone again, the anger quickly drops away and doubt sets in.

STEADMAN'S WIFE: What do we do now?

STEADMAN: *Ponders, then —* Go back to work. Come on —

They set in around the stump again, straining and grunting. Lights down slowly to black.

HAT

Lights up on Mackenzie.

MACKENZIE: My name is William Lyon Mackenzie. I run a small newspaper here in Toronto — it's called The Advocate. Used to be The Colonial Advocate, but I decided it was high time to get rid of the "Colonial" part. It's a good paper, pick one up if you get a chance. Now I was on my way down King Street to the office the other day — and it had rained just the night before. Well any time it rains here the roads turn into quagmires, and the only way you can use them is to pick your way from one high, dry spot to another. So I was picking my way along King — just outside here — when I noticed this hat lying in the mud in the middle of the road. Well it looked like a good hat and I decided it was worth muddying my boots to get it, so I picked my way over *(He is doing it)* best I could, and I picked up the hat.

As he lifts the hat he uncovers a man's head. The man spits out a mouthful of mud.

MACKENZIE: There was a man under it! *To Man.* It looks like you're in trouble.

MAN: Yes, I certainly am.

MACKENZIE: *Bending down to hoist him.* Here, let me give you a hand.

MAN: You're quite a little fellow. I think you'd better go for some help.

MACKENZIE: Oh I'm pretty tough. I think I can pull you out myself.

MAN: But it's not just me I'm worrying about. It's the wagon and the two oxen!

BLACK.

THE TAVERN

Onstage right: Isaac Casselman, Tavernkeeper; Emma, his wife; Ruth, a friend and customer; and Jamey, local drunk and part-time help at the tavern.

ISAAC: *Singing.* When I got up in the morning, my heart did give a wrench, For lying on the table was the captain and a wench —

Freeze. Enter Fred Bench, stage left. Addresses audience.

FRED: That's why you cut your roots and come thousands of miles across ocean — to buy your own land, be your own boss. I just got back from Toronto about that very thing —

Tavern action resumes.

ISAAC: *Singing.* And then one fine spring morning, I did a dancing jig —

Freeze.

FRED: This is Isaac Casselman's Inn. When I'm not working in the bush I spend most of my time right here.

Tavern resumes.

ISAAC: For lying on the table was the captain and —

Enter Fred.

ISAAC: Fred Bench! You're back —

EMMA: Fred — welcome home.

FRED: Hello Emma. Jamey! Hasn't Isaac fired you yet?

JAMEY: He can't fire me Fred.

FRED: Why not?

JAMEY: *Tottering into cellar.* I'm the only one who knows the inventory —

FRED: Ruth —

They embrace. Ruth is so excited she can't talk. Enter Jamey, carrying a keg.

JAMEY: In your honour Fred. The best keg of rum in Isaac's cellar.

FRED: How do you know that Jamey?

JAMEY: Because I tested four others before I found it. It's the best.

EMMA: Fred — come on and tell us some good stories about Toronto.

RUTH: And show us what you've got!

ISAAC: Now first things first. In honour of the traveller's return — a toast!

ALL: Hear hear; a toast; etc.

They all take mugs.

ISAAC: To Fred Bench — and his new land.

ALL BUT FRED: To Fred Bench and —

FRED: Hold it. That's not quite right. To Fred Bench — and his *almost* land.

ISAAC: Wha—?

EMMA: Have you been drinking Fred?

JAMEY: *Undaunted.* To Fred Bench and the almost land. *Down the hatch.*

RUTH: What do you mean?

FRED: Haven't touched a drop Emma. At least not yet. But now I'll tell you that story. Do you want to hear it?

ALL: Yes; etc.

FRED: It's a story about Toronto. What a city! For three days I walked through the bush. It was dark. Trees blocking out almost all the light. But when you get to the top of Yonge St., that bush just sweeps away. And there's Toronto. Morning fog coming in off the lake. Spires poking through here and there. It was like a dream. And I knew that day the city belonged to Fred Bench! Down into it I went — why do you know they've got it built up all the way to Queen St.? *Disbelief.* I walked right in alongside the gentlemen and ladies. Isaac — you should see the taverns they've got now. And the traffic. Right along the flagstone sidewalks of King Street to the Courthouse — that's where the Land Office is. Up the steps — just a whiff of fish coming in from the wharf — inside are pillars that lay the fear of God in you. And *there's* the Land Office. And behind its thick oak door sits the Commissioner of Crown Lands. *He is seized with an idea.* Jamey — c'mere. You want to help me show these fine people some of the facts of life?

JAMEY: *Stumbling to Fred's side.* Facts of life? You've come to the right man for the facts of life.

FRED: Stand over here Jamey. Peter Robinson, Commissioner of Crown Lands. *Jamey looks around.* No. That's you. Straight and tall. Fine satin shirt. Stiff collar. *Jamey begins to assume the role.* Velvet trousers. And boots that you can see your face in.

JAMEY: Shine my boots Fred! *He has become the Lands Commissioner.*

FRED: Oh yes sir! Because you see, you control all the government land in the province.

JAMEY: All the land in the province? Mine?

FRED: Lord Jamey!

JAMEY: That's me — Lord Jamey!

Fred moves away from Jamey.

FRED: Now on the other side of this oak door is the waiting room, three times the size of your tavern Isaac. And it's packed with people like me — all wanting land.

RUTH: Come on, let's help him out.

They all join Fred in the waiting room.

FRED: And we're packed in so tight — fifty or sixty of us — that we can't even sit down. Hey Jamey, we got no land, you got it all. What do you think of us?

JAMEY: *Swaggering.* I think you're all — pieces of dirt!

FRED: We just couldn't get past the door. We waited one, two, three, four days, and never saw the Commissioner. Then, on the fifth day, in walks a private land agent — a Mr. Bronlyn. *Isaac assumes the role as Fred talks.* A rich man, in a grey suit, with a bit of a paunch and cold grey eyes that look right through anything and anyone they —

Bronlyn barges right through the waiting room, slapping people out of his way. The Commissioner opens the door to him.

ISAAC *(As Bronlyn)*: Ah, Mr. Commissioner —

JAMEY: Mr. Bronlyn, come in. *To the others.* Slam!

EMMA: Fred — you mean he just walked in there — nice as you please!

FRED: Just like that.

EMMA: What'd you do?

FRED: What would you do?

Emma stalks up to the door and knocks.

EMMA: Mr. Commissioner! I want to talk to you. We were promised land. We've been waiting here for five days. Some of us are hungry. You've got to —

JAMEY: *Without opening door.* My dear woman — who do you think you're talking to? The Commissioner of Crown Lands — that's who you're talking to. Now can't you see I'm busy? Go away. I've got important business to discuss with my friend, Mr. Bronlyn. If you want, you can leave your names with my clerk.

FRED: So we left our names with his clerk, walked out of the waiting room, and stood around Toronto for another two days. And then, in comes Mr. Bronlyn.

ISAAC: Is there a Mr. Bench here? A Mr. Fred Bench?

FRED: Yeah?

ISAAC: Mr. Bench, I understand that you wish to purchase some land.

FRED: Oh yes, yes sir — you bet I do.

ISAAC: Well I have just the land for you. One hundred acres of good, fertile —

FRED: And I have the twenty dollars here to buy it.

ISAAC: You don't understand Mr. Bench. This land sells for two dollars an acre.

RUTH: What?

EMMA: But that's two hundred dollars —

ISAAC: That's correct, Madam. Well Mr. Bench —

FRED: Now hold on. I got the newspaper that says I can get one hundred acres of government land for twenty dollars.

ISAAC: That might be, Mr. Bench — though I rather doubt it. But I do not represent the government. I am a private land agent. I sell land for a profit.

FRED: *To Emma and Ruth.* Now where did he get my name?

JAMEY: *Still in his "office".* I gave it to him, Fred. I gave him all your names — for a little . . . consideration.

FRED: A little consideration. You see, they're in it together. Two crooks working hand in glove.

ISAAC: Well Mr. Bench? Do you or do you not want to buy the land? *Reverting to himself.* What'd you do, Fred?

FRED: I laughed in his face, grabbed him by his fancy shirt, and threw him out — because nobody makes a fool of Fred Bench!

EMMA: Good for you Fred!

JAMEY: You really did, did you Fred?

RUTH: You mean . . . you didn't get the land . . . there's nothing . . .

FRED: *Keeping up the bravado.* Well — no. But I've still got twenty dollars, and if it's not going for land, it's going for the biggest party we've ever had around here! Jamey — come on —

JAMEY: I'm with you Fred —

FRED: Isaac, more drinks —

All but Ruth cheer and raise their glasses. Freeze. Lights down on them. Ruth, alone on the other side of the stage, wails her disappointment.

BLACK.

THE FAMILY COMPACT

MACKENZIE: Ladies and gentlemen, this evening for your entertainment, and with the help of my charming assistant *(Enter charming assistant)* I would like to demonstrate for you a magical trick. Now the thing that interests me about magic is not so much the phenomenon of the trick itself, as how it is actually accomplished, and I shall try to perform this trick in such a way that you can share its secret with me. *To assistant.* We need the volunteers onstage. *To audience.* I would have got volunteers from the audience, but you're all far too respectable for that. *Enter the three volunteers. They are a sullen, brutish lot.* Now this trick will go down in the annals of conjuring history as one of the most remarkable ever performed anywhere in the world, for you are about to see this gang of thieves, rogues, villains and fools transformed before your very eyes into the ruling class of this province. Yes indeed — this band of criminals, by magical transformation, will become the government of Upper Canada. Now I've said I was going to do this trick slowly, so that you'll be able to see the positions they hold in the government, as well as the bonds that tie them together: bonds of blood, marriage, or greed — and in most cases it's all three. Anyway, on with the trick. Number one — *The assistant covers up the first volunteer with her cape.* Presto — Darcy Boulton Sr. *Cape is whisked away, revealing volunteer transformed into member of the Family Compact.* Retired pensioner, at a pension of five hundred pounds a year, paid by the people of Upper Canada. Number two — Presto — Henry Boulton, son to number one. *So on with the cape. After three she begins again with one.* Now Henry is the Attorney General for Upper Canada as well as being bank solicitor. Number three — Presto! — Darcy Boulton Jr. Auditor-General for Upper Canada as well as being Master in Chancery and a commissioner in the police. Numbers four and five — William and George Boulton — Presto! — also sons to number one, brothers to two and three, and holding various positions in the government. Number six — presto! — John Beverley Robinson. Now Robinson is a brother-in-law to the Boultons there. He is the Chief Justice for Upper

Canada. He's a member of the Legislative Council and the speaker of the Legislative Council. Number seven — Peter Robinson, brother to number six. He's a member of the Executive Council, he's a member of the Legislative Council, he's the Commissioner of Crown Lands, and Commissioner of the Clergy Reserves, as well as being the Surveyor-General of Woods. Number eight — William Robinson, brother to numbers six and seven. He's the Postmaster for Newmarket, he's a member of the Assembly for Simcoe, he's a government contractor, a colonel in the militia, and a Justice of the Peace. *Mackenzie claps his hands twice. This brings the volunteers out of their trance. They are dumbfounded.* We'll skip over nine, ten, eleven, twelve, thirteen, fourteen, and fifteen. They're just more of the same: they're all related to each other and they all hold various positions in the government. Which brings us to sixteen *He claps again, thrusting volunteers back into character. The assistant can barely keep the blistering pace.* — James B. Macaulay. Macaulay is a justice of the court of King's Bench. Number seventeen — Christopher Alexander Hagerman — presto! — Now Hagerman is a brother-in-law to Macaulay — *The cape is still in place, and a struggle is evidently taking place behind it. Mackenzie rushes across, and snatches it away to reveal Hagerman in an unseemly clinch with the assistant.* This man is the Solicitor-General of Upper Canada! Now we won't do eighteen to twenty-two for the same reason we skipped the earlier batch, which brings us to twenty-three, twenty-four and twenty-five — the Jarvis family: Samuel Peter Jarvis, Grant Jarvis — his son, and William Jarvis, his brother. They hold such varied positions between them as clerk of the Crown in Chancery, Secretary of the Province, bank solicitor, clerk of the Legislative Council, police justice, judge, Commissioner of Customs, and two high sheriffs. And that brings us to twenty-six, the biggest fish in this small pond of Upper Canada — archdeacon John Strachan, family tutor and political schoolmaster to this mob. This man is the archdeacon and rector of York. He's a member of the Executive Council, he's a member of the Legislative Council, he's president of the University, president of the Board of Education, and twenty other situations. *Mackenzie and Strachan glare at each other.* Oh I almost forgot — twenty-seven — Thomas Mercer Jones. He's the son-in-law to Strachan and he's the agent and director for the Canada Company land monopoly here in Upper Canada. And there you have it — the government of this fair colony. *They take a bow.* Now this family connection rules Upper Canada according to its own good pleasure. It has no effective check from the country to guard the people against its acts of tyranny and oppression. It includes the whole of the judges of the supreme civil and criminal tribunals; it includes the agents and directors for the Canada Company land monopoly; it includes the president and solicitor and members of the board of the Bank of Upper Canada; it includes half of the Executive Council and all of the Legislative Council. *They are chortling with self-satisfaction.* Now this is pretty impressive, I'd say — criminals into government. But there's one piece of magic even more mind-boggling than that you've already seen — and that is how this Family Compact of villainy stays in power in Upper Canada! *They laugh him off the stage.*

MARY MACDONALD

Edward Peters, a farmer, is stage left. He is waiting for someone to arrive. Enter Mary Macdonald, stage right. She is expecting to be met. She does not notice him. He approaches her nervously.

EDWARD: Excuse me, are you Miss Mary Macdonald?

MARY: I am. *She is very Scottish.*

EDWARD: Oh. I'm Edward Peters.

They are both horribly awkward.

MARY: I'm very pleased to make your acquaintance Mr. Peters.

EDWARD: I'm very pleased to meet you. *A painful silence.* You must be tired after such a long trip.

MARY: Yes, I am — a bit.

EDWARD: They have benches here for people if you'd care to — um —

MARY: Oh, thank you.

They cross and sit down.

EDWARD: *Plunging.* I wrote you a letter, Miss Macdonald. I don't know if you received it, proposing a date for the — um — for our wedding.

MARY: *Nearly choking with nervousness.* Yes. I got it.

EDWARD: Ah. Well. Would two weeks be satisfactory then?

MARY: Yes. That would be just fine. I wouldn't want to put you to any trouble.

EDWARD: No. It's no trouble. *They sit in awful silence. He leans over and away from her, to spit. He notices her watching him and swallows it instead.*

MARY: Oh feel free.

EDWARD: Ah, no. I didn't really feel like it.

MARY: It's quite hot, is it not?

EDWARD: Yes. It's usually quite hot here in August. It's going to get a lot colder though.

MARY: What kind of farm do you have Mr. Peters?

EDWARD: It's a *good* farm. I raise wheat, built most of a barn, got a good frame house. I think you'll be very comfortable there. Nice furniture. Rough, but it's usable. I built it myself. I'm good with my hands.

MARY: *Trying hopelessly to relax him and herself.* Yes —

EDWARD: And I don't drink.

MARY: *Not really happy about it.* Oh.

EDWARD: I bought a cow.

MARY: You did —

EDWARD: Yes. I thought you'd be used to fresh milk so I went and bought a cow.

MARY: *Pleased.* And what's her name?

EDWARD: *Embarassed again.* Cow.

MARY: Cow?

EDWARD: Well when you only have one, you just . . . call it . . . cow . . .

MARY: *Feeling their lack of success in communicating.* Oh —

EDWARD: But you could go ahead and give her a nice name.

MARY: I could?

EDWARD: Sure. You'll be milking her and looking after her. You could go ahead and name her.

MARY: Thank you.

EDWARD: You're welcome. *With great relief he spots someone coming up the street.* That's George. See that big fellow on the wagon there? That's my brother George. He's come down to take us back to the farm.

MARY: Now?

EDWARD: Yes.

They start across the stage, Mary in front of Edward. Mary stumbles and almost falls. Edward catches her by the arm. It is the first time they've touched. They smile.

EDWARD: You've got to watch where you're walking, Mary. There's ruts.

MARY: Yes.

They go off together.

THE LADY IN THE COACH

Enter Lady Backwash, an English gentlewoman of the memoir-writing ilk. (Note: This role has been played by both male and female actors.)

LADY B.: Ladies, I should like to talk to you this evening about my adventures in Upper Canada. I call this lecture — Roughing It In The Bush. The Bush is a term which these quaint Canadians use when describing the vast trackless forests which cover nine-tenths of the colony; dark impenetrable woods much like a jungle, complete with insects, but not the heat. I was on my way to visit a very old and dear friend Colonel Stockton, in Niagara-on-the-Lake.

As she speaks, the coach driver appears, brings in and harnesses his horse to the coach and settles in for the ride.

LADY B.: We were to have a sumptuous meal and then witness the spectacular beauty of Niagara Falls by moonlight, which I shall describe later in this evening's talk. Our transportation from Toronto to Niagara was to be accomplished by coach. Now I use this word in the broadest sense of the term, for the vehicle which was produced for our conveyance, if 'twere in England, would not be called a coach. It would be called a great many other things, but certainly not a coach. However, despite this hardship, it was with the greatest of anticipation, that I set out, with my man Johnson *(Enter Johnson, with a discreet bow toward the audience. Johnson is a young lad, notably Cockney)* to travel from Toronto to Niagara.

They enter and are seated in the coach. The driver lets out a "hyaaah" to his horse and they are off with much bumping.

DRIVER: Giddup Winnifred — whoa — hyaah — giddup . . .

LADY B.: Johnson, have they never heard of springs in this country?

JOHNSON: I don't believe so madam —

They hit an enormous bump, then bounce, stop and the coach rocks from side to side. The Lady and her man are discomfitted. The driver has leapt from his seat down to the side of the coach and is straining to push it out of the hole in which it is stuck.

LADY B.: Johnson — the driver has jumped off!

JOHNSON: I don't blame him. I'd get off too if I could.

LADY B.: Driver. *The driver does not respond.* Driver! We've stopped.

DRIVER: *Hoping she'll go away.* That's right, ma'am.

LADY B.: Why have we stopped?

DRIVER: Well ma'am — it's the mud.

LADY B.: Mud? You hear that Johnson — mud! My dear man, I have a very important dinner engagement in Niagara-on-the-Lake this evening, and with some candor I might tell you that if I am forced to go without my dinner tonight, you shall be obliged to do without your job tomorrow. Mud or no mud!

DRIVER: Ma'am — if you think this is bad, why we've got bogs up the way ahead of us that'll make this look like a puddle. Now we'll be able to get on our way in a minute if you'll just step out of the coach.

LADY B.: Out? Get out? My dear man, your impertinence is only matched by your incompetence as a driver. It is my duty to ride in this coach from Toronto to Niagara. It is yours to get me there. Now I am doing my duty. Kindly do yours.

DRIVER: *Patience, patience.* Ma'am — if you won't get out of the coach, to lighten the load, so that I can push her out of this hole, we'll never get to Niagara.

JOHNSON: *Aping his mistress' tone.* Absolutely not. We paid good money to ride in this coach and we're not getting out of it. *Turning to Lady B., pleased with himself.* Got to be firm with his type.

LADY B.: *Interrupting Johnson.* Johnson, you and I shall get out of the coach.

JOHNSON: *Stung.* Wot —

LADY B.: *Firmly.* — thereby lightening the load, thereby facilitating this nincompoop in getting us out of here.

DRIVER: Thank you ma'am. There's a dry spot here —

JOHNSON: I don't see no dry spot —

The driver tries to help Johnson down. Johnson tries to avoid being dropped in the mud. The upshot is, the driver is holding Johnson aloft. Lady B. stands up grandly and strides out of the other door of the coach onto the side of the road. She notices the confusion with Johnson and upbraids him.

LADY B.: Johnson, come over here. Don't worry about a little mud. Where

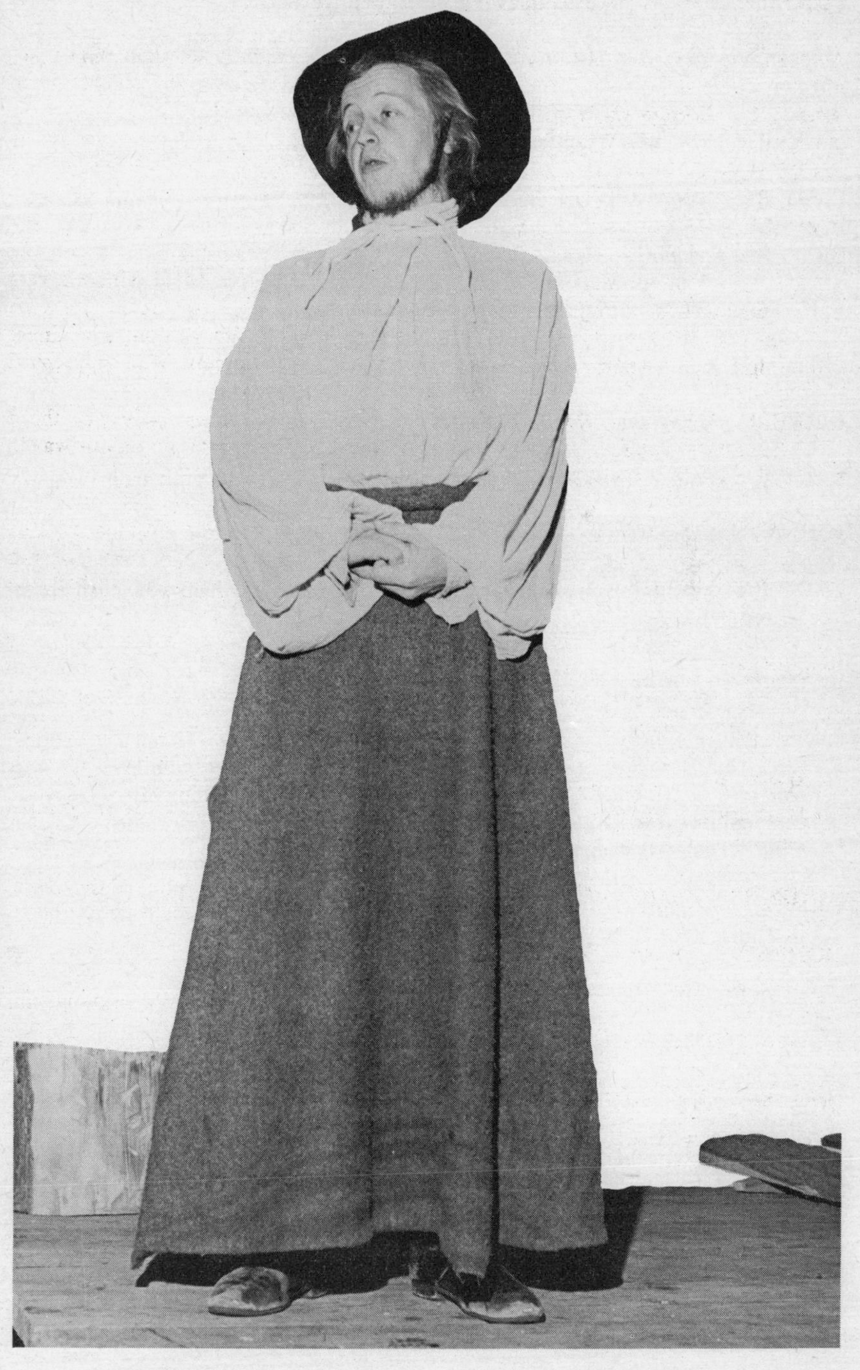

would the glorious Empire be today if it weren't above mud?

Johnson crosses to her and stands beside her. The driver puts his shoulder to the wheel.

DRIVER: Now pull Winnifred. Pull girl —

LADY B.: *To driver.* Oh you'll not do it that way. You're not strong enough.

DRIVER: *Straining.* Hyaah, hyaah —

JOHNSON: He's not smart enough either.

LADY B.: He's not smart enough to know he's not strong enough.

DRIVER: *Giving up.* Whoa Winnifred —

LADY B.: Told you so. No, Johnson shall have to help you push from behind.

JOHNSON: *Stung.* Wot?

LADY B.: Yes, Johnson shall have to get in the mud and help you push from behind.

JOHNSON: Wot — me get in the mud and push that thing. Not likely —

LADY B.: *Cutting him off with great master-servant authority.* Johnson! *Johnson breaks off his tirade and assumes instant humility. He has remembered his place.* This colony is having a most disturbing effect on your personality. Now into the mud and push! *Johnson jumps obediently into the mud.* That's British pluck.

DRIVER: Alright Mr. Johnson. You just put your back into it, right about there, and give it what you've got —

Johnson wrinkles his nose at the driver.

LADY B.: Johnson, push with a will — the eyes of England are upon you.

DRIVER: Alright Winnifred, pull girl, hyaah —

They strain away. Enter, rear of Lady Backwash, an Indian carrying an axe. He is amused by the sight and wanders up. Lady B. hears his laughs, turns to see him and emits a shriek.

LADY B.: Eeek. Johnson, I'm being attacked by a savage!

JOHNSON: *Springing to the rescue.* Savage is it? That's my job. *Runs up to confront the savage.* Alright Savage — put 'em up. I studied with the Marquess of Queensbury, I did — Omygawd, he's got an axe! *Flees to the other side of the stage and climbs a tree.*

DRIVER: *To Indian.* Hello Bart. How are you today?

INDIAN: *Moving over to Lady B.* Fine. Hello Ma'am, Wells is the name.

He offers his hand which she shakes, her mind already grinding away about how she can use this new arrival.

INDIAN: *Moving on to driver.* Where did you find that one?

LADY B.: Johnson, come down from that tree. You're not a monkey. *Johnson obeys.* Johnson, it *(Referring to the Indian)* speaks English. And if it speaks English, it can take orders. Johnson, you shall take the savage in hand and push from behind. Driver — Johnson and the savage shall push from behind. While they push, you shall lift from the middle, and I myself shall take Winnifred by the head, and encourage her to greater effort. Right Winnifred?

WINNIFRED: *Whinnies.*

They assume their appointed positions.

LADY B.: Altogether now — push, pull, come on Winnifred, it's coming —

They are straining, pushing, lifting. Suddenly with a lurch, the coach comes free. They are all — except for Lady B. — panting from the effort. She is babbling more than ever.

LADY B.: *Elated.* There! We did it! What did I tell you? Just needed a little leadership. Johnson — you were superb. Driver — you were tremendous. Savage — you were alright. And Winnifred — you pulled with a will.

INDIAN: *To driver.* You sure it's safe for me to leave you alone with her?

LADY B.: Johnson, I haven't felt so good since I arrived in this wretched colony. *A sudden inspiration.* Johnson — quickly, my diary. *Johnson fetches it and takes down her dictation. She addresses posterity.* We had fought the good fight and won. We had been faced with insurmountable obstacles and we had overcome them. And now we took the rest of the victorious, and what better place than here, in Nature's Cathedral.

JOHNSON: *Copying.* Oh, I like that.

LADY B.: I looked up at the tall trees, like giant columns supporting the vast infinite blue of the sky above. The birds sang, the bees — um, the bees — *she searches.*

JOHNSON: Might I suggest "buzzed"?

LADY B.: *Accepts with alacrity.* Buzzed. Of course — buzzed. Very good, Johnson. And everywhere was peace, tranquillity and beauty.

WINNIFRED: *An impatient whinny.*

DRIVER: Ma'am can I suggest you get back into the coach. Once Winnifred gets us out of one bog, she just can't wait to get us into the next one.

JOHNSON: Huh?

LADY B.: An example of Canadian humour, I believe, Johnson. *They chuckle.* That's enough Johnson.

They get back into the coach. The driver is about to crack the whip. Lady Backwash takes one final look at the site of this enchanted event.

LADY B.: Farewell, brave bush!

DRIVER: Hyaah!

The coach bounces into motion. They are bouncing with it.

BLACK.

THE HEAD

Note: Sir Francis Bond Head was Lieutenant-Governor of Upper Canada in 1837. Mackenzie could rarely resist punning on his name. In this scene four actors comprise themselves as Head's head. Two of their heads are his eyes, two arms his arching eyebrows, two other arms his nose. So on for his mouth, dimple etc. The scene begins with the narrated, piece by piece construction of the head, after which the "head" talks.

VOICE: Two piercing blue eyes, *Enter the eyes.* arching eyebrows, a long aristocratic nose, a firm mouth — and a dimple on the chin. Sir Francis Bond Head, Lieutenant-Governor of Upper Canada, addresses an assembly of voters before the election of 1836.

HEAD: *Sniffing, scowling, smiling etc. as the speech proceeds.* Gentlemen, as your district now has the important duty to perform of electing representatives for the new Parliament, I think it might practically assist if I clearly lay before you the conduct I intend inflexibly to pursue. If you choose to dispute with me and live on bad terms with the Mother Country, you will — to use a homely phrase — only quarrel with your own bread and butter. If you choose to try this experiment by again electing members who will oppose me, do so. On the other hand, if you choose to embark your interests with my character, I will take paternal care of them both. Men — women and money are what you want. And if you send to Parliament members who will assist me, you can depend upon it, you will gain far more than you possibly can by trying to insult me. But — let your conduct be what it may — I am quite determined, so long as I occupy this station, neither to give offense, nor to take it. Gentlemen, you may now cast your ballots.

BLACK.

Further Note: The above is a quotation from an actual speech by Sir Francis at the time.

THE ELECTION OF '36

A Tory and a Reformer.

TORY: Hey!

REFORMER: Yeah?

TORY: How're you voting?

REFORMER: Me? Reform.

TORY: Oh yeah? *Ploughs him one.*

ANOTHER REFORMER: Well — you're obviously voting Tory.

TORY: That's right.

REFORMER: Uh-huh. *Ploughs the Tory. Then loudly proclaims:* Reform!

ANOTHER TORY: Didn't hear that. All votes have to be heard to be recorded.

REFORMER: I said — Reform!

TORY: That's what I thought you said. *Wham.*

ROBERT DAVIS: *This character has, for some reason, been played by a woman in all productions of 1837 so far.* Hey, don't hit him like that. This is no way to carry on an election —

All then turn on this poor peacemaker and attack him, screaming their political slogans as they flail away at each other and particularly at Robert Davis. The cry of "Tory" rings above the others. The Tories are obviously most proficient at this political bullying. The mayhem concludes with the brutal cry, "God — Save — The Queen!" Freeze.

THE CANADIAN FARMER'S TRAVELS IN THE U.S.A.

Robert Davis, Upper Canadian farmer, drags himself out from the bottom of the brawl during the election of 1836.

DAVIS: Would you believe that was an election? I would! Lost two teeth in it — and that proves it's an election around here. My name's Robert Davis. I have a small town here in Nissouri Township. Lived here all my life. Got two fine kids. Taught myself to read and write. But this election was just about the end for me. Why we've been working for reform for fifteen years — and now things in Upper Canada are worse than ever. I'd about lost hope. And I needed to get my hope back somehow. So I decided I'd take a trip to the United States. I'd heard things were different down there, and I thought — if I can see that someone else has succeeded, maybe I can keep on trying myself. So I started out. *Walks.* Now the first place I came to on my way to the border was the little town of Chatham. Beautiful little place for a town, but very sleepy . . .

The Town Council of Chatham comes to order.

MAYOR: My friends, as members of the Town Council of Chatham I think we should establish what is going to be happening here for the next twenty years.

DAVIS: Good. I'd like to see that. What have you got in mind?

The members of the Council yawn, fall flat on their backs, and snore.

DAVIS: See that! That's despair — I'm not going to stay around here. *Walks.* So I kept on, till I came to the town of Sandwich, that's right across the river from Detroit. Look around. There's nothing happening here.

BOATMAN: All aboard for Detroit.

DAVIS: Can you take me to Detroit?

BOATMAN: Yup. Get aboard fast. Miss this boat and there isn't another one for a week.

DAVIS: That's ridiculous — one boat a week!

They start across the river.

DAVIS: And as we left Sandwich snoozing in the sunshine, I could see a kind of stir on the other side of the river. And sounds — sounds like I'd never heard before —

The bustling sounds of Detroit begin to come up.

DAVIS: And suddenly we were surrounded by boats, big and little, carrying grain, and goods, and *people* —

BOATMAN: *Yelling.* Detroit! Gateway to the American Dream —

The sounds of industry and trade explode around poor Davis. People rush back and forth past him, happy, productive —

AMERICAN: Howdy stranger, I'd like to stay and shoot the breeze, but I'm too busy getting rich.

DAVIS: Look at all these people — and this *industry*, and — and — two thousand immigrants a day — most of them from Upper Canada!

IMMIGRANT: *Kissing the ground.* America! America!

RUNAWAY SLAVE: *To Davis.* Excuse me sir, I'm a runaway slave. Which way is Canada?

DAVIS: No, no. Don't go there. It's terrible. Stay here. I'm sure things will get better for you. *Turning.* Oh — look. A four-storey brick building! *Someone plays it.* Isn't it wonderful?

WRECKER: 'Scuse me fella. Gotta tear down this four-storey building.

DAVIS: *Horrified.* Why?

WRECKER: *Knocking it down.* 'Cause we're gonna put up a *six*-storey one in its place! There — *Whoosht — up it goes.*

DAVIS: Oh — and look at what it says on it — Museum!

MUSEUM: Sure. Come on in —

Davis enters, sees statues of American heroes — "We got more than we know what to do with" — Whistler's Mother, or some such nonsense. By the way, this scene has never been "set". Davis has seen different things nearly every time he has taken his trip.

DAVIS: This is all fine, but you know I'm a farmer, and I'll really know what to make of your country when I see what's happening outside the cities. So can you tell me how I get to the country?

AMERICAN: Sure. How'd you like to go?

DAVIS: How? I thought I'd walk —

AMERICAN: Pshaw — nobody walks down here. Now you can go by coach, or canal —

DAVIS: Don't talk to me about canals! Did you ever hear of the Welland Canal? They've been building it for twelve years. It's only twelve miles long. It's cost us millions of dollars and you *still* have to dig your way through!

AMERICAN: No kidding. Well we've got the Erie Canal. Five hundred miles and clear straight through —

DAVIS: *Stunned.* Five hundred miles . . .

AMERICAN: But if you don't like that, you can always take the train.

DAVIS: Train? What was that word you just said?

Zip. He is suddenly in the country.

DAVIS: So I went to the country. Acre after acre of cleared, fertile land —

FARMER: Excuse me friend, would you mind moving your foot?

DAVIS: My foot? Why?

FARMER: Well, do you feel something moving under it?

DAVIS: Moving? Why yes — I do!

FARMER: Just move it aside — there.

They both watch as a crop of wheat grows from the floor to the ceiling.

FARMER: Crop of wheat I planted this morning. A little small this year. Well, watch yourself while I harvest it. *With his axe.* Timber!

DAVIS: Wheat — and apple orchards — and thousands of head of cattle — and sixty pound cheeses!

These appear — or fail to do so — at the whim of the other actors onstage. The most fun occurs when someone introduces into the scene something Davis and the others have not expected.

DAVIS: And then I went to one of the hundreds of thriving country towns —

SCHOOLHOUSE: Bong! Bong! Come on kiddies — everybody into school for your free universal education.

DAVIS: Free? Universal? You mean your schools aren't just for your aristocracy?

SCHOOLHOUSE: You watch your language down here. We don't use words like that!

DAVIS: Everyone can go to school? Does it work?

SCHOOLHOUSE: Hah! Where's that dumb kid. C'mere kid, get inside.

The dumb kid walks through one door of the schoolhouse and emerges from the other.

FORMERLY DUMB KID: $E=MC^2$.

CHURCH: Ding Dong — Methodist.

ANOTHER: Ding Dong — Lutheran.

ANOTHER: Ding Dong — Quaker.

Somebody has not declared himself.

DAVIS: What are you?

TOWNSMAN: I'm an atheist.

DAVIS: You allow atheists down here too?

CHURCH: We don't like them but we allow them.

DAVIS: But which one is your established church, you know, the official church?

They all laugh.

TOWNSMAN: Say — you must be a Canadian.

DAVIS: *Delighted.* I am. How'd you know?

TOWNSMAN: Say house.

DAVIS: House.

TOWNSMAN: Say about.

DAVIS: About.

TOWNSMAN: I knew it. Now excuse us, we're going to have an election.

DAVIS: *Panicking.* An election? Let me out of here — I'm going to hide — I've lost enough teeth.

He watches from a distance.

FIRST VOTER: Having searched my conscience, I have decided to cast my vote as a Democrat.

The next voter steps up. Davis winces in expectation of the clash.

SECOND VOTER: Well, in that case, I'm going to vote Republican.

THIRD VOTER: Then I vote Democrat.

FOURTH VOTER: Let's see — the Republicans won last time, so I'll vote Democrat too.

ALL: Hurray!

They all commiserate with the lone Republican.

DAVIS: Hey — wait a minute. When does the fight start?

VOTER: Fight? What do you mean? This is an election. Now come here, uh, what's your name?

DAVIS: Davis.

VOTER: No, I mean your first name. We all use first names here.

DAVIS: Bob.

VOTER: Well, Bob, I'd like you to meet the new governor of our state. This is Ole. Ole, this is Bob, from Canada —

OLE: *A very slow-speaking farmer.* Well, how do you do. You wouldn't like to buy a pig would you?

DAVIS: Pig? You mean you're the governor of this state and you still work as a farmer.

OLE: Well, gotta make some money somehow—

DAVIS: You know, you've all given me new hope. You've proven to me it can be done. This is what we've been working for for years, and I can go home now and —

VOTER: Home? Wait a minute Bob. Why don't you stay right here with us and make this your new home?

DAVIS: Here? But why should I?

ANOTHER VOTER: Because it's the best darned country in the world. That's why.

DAVIS: But — but I've got my family back there.

ANOTHER: Bring 'em down here. Bring your whole country.

DAVIS: But — but there's my farm.

ANOTHER: Tell you what we'll do Bob. We'll give you a four hundred acre cleared farm right here. Just for you.

DAVIS: *Getting excited.* Cleared? *Suspicious.* How much?

ANOTHER: Nothing. Just take good care of it.

DAVIS: I can have that farm?

ANOTHER: Sure. We'll just sweep those Indians off of it and —

DAVIS: Why that's wonderful! You're all so generous! This must be the finest —

ANOTHER: See. He's starting to act like an American already. Being happy and talking loud —

DAVIS: No. No, I can't do it.

ANOTHER: Those words don't exist in America.

DAVIS: I can't stay. You see — its not my home. I can't just leave Canada. It's up to us to do there what you've done here. But you've given me hope. Now I know it can be done — *He is leaving.* So I went home.

Lethargic, snoring, apathetic Canadians surround him.

DAVIS: And I said — Don't lie around. Get up. Help each other. You can do it. *He drags them to their feet. They are rubbery-legged. They cling to each other and anything they can find.* I've seen it now. I know it can be done. We can do it too, if we stay together. Now is not the time for Reformers to fawn and crouch. Now is the time to unite and fight!

BLACK.

THE DUMMY

A political rally in rural upper Canada. Attended by angry Reform farmers.

FARMER: He's here, he's here alright. The great man is here. I saw him just out back.

They cheer.

FARMER: He's come down here to talk to all of us — now you put that jug away, this is a dry meeting — but before the great man talks to us, a couple of the folks have worked up one of their little skits to do for us. So come on up here and get it over with, so we can all get on with hearing the great man's speech. *Two farmers come up front.* And don't forget your lines this time.

The two stand in front of the rally. One assumes the role of the ventriloquist. The other plays his dummy.

VENTRILOQUIST: Ladies and gentlemen. Presenting for your enjoyment, straight from England, John Bull — your Imperial ventriloquist, and his companion, Peter Stump — the Canadian axeman. Say hello to the people, Peter.

PETER: *The Ventriloquist is throwing his voice.* Hello.

JOHN: Aren't you forgetting to add something, Peter?

PETER: God Save The Queen.

JOHN: Good, Peter. Very loyal. I say — what is that in your hand?

PETER: My axe.

JOHN: What do you do with your axe, Peter?

PETER: Chop down trees. *He chops.* Timber!

JOHN: And what do you do with the wood you cut?

PETER: Send it to you in England, John.

JOHN: Very fine Peter. Say what else do you have there?

PETER: My rifle.

JOHN: Aha — and who are you going to shoot?

PETER: Yankees.

JOHN: Good. And quickly too — *Hides behind Peter.*

PETER: Bang, bang, bang, bang —

JOHN: *Emerging.* Whew! Well done, lad. Now could you loan me twenty of your dollars?

PETER: *Protesting.* John, I'm short myself —

JOHN: *Picking his pocket.* There. I knew you wouldn't mind. Now is there anything else I can do for you?

PETER: Yes.

JOHN: What's that?

PETER: Please take your hand away from my neck.

JOHN: *Surprised.* I beg your pardon?

PETER: Take your hand away from me.

JOHN: If I do that, you will be helpless. Do you understand?

PETER: I want to try.

CROWD: Let him go. Give him a chance.

JOHN: Very well, Peter — *Yanks his hand out. Peter stands stock still. John moves away from him.* Now Peter, now let's hear you speak. Ha! Chop down trees Peter! Shoot Yankees! Can't do a thing can you?

CROWD: Come on, Peter. You can do it.

JOHN: Without me, John Bull, you are nothing. Pathetic isn't he, ladies and gentlemen? A pitiable, colonial —

PETER: *With his own voice, for the first time.* Mm —

JOHN: *Stunned.* What? What was that?

PETER: *Louder.* Mm — mm — I — I —

JOHN: Peter, Peter — what are you up to?

PETER: *Slowly finding his voice.* I want to say: (More confidently) Thank God for the man who is giving me a voice — *Shouting, no longer a dummy at all.* William Lyon Mackenzie!

The crowd cheers. Enter Mackenzie and bounds onto the rostrum.

THE SPEECH

MACKENZIE: Thank you, ladies and gentlemen, thank you. Now let's start off this meeting by giving three cheers for the men who made it possible, or rather I should say necessary. Let's have three cheers for Archdeacon John Strachan. Hip hip hurray! Hip hip, hurray! —

CROWD: Booo —

MACKENZIE: Come now my friends, you won't cheer John Strachan? I didn't realize feelings ran that high. Now I was talking to someone the other day who said about Strachan — if that man's godliness were gunpowder, he couldn't blow his own nose. Alright then, if you won't cheer Strachan, let's have three cheers for Christopher Alexander Hagerman. Hip hip hurray —

CROWD: Booo —

MACKENZIE: My friends, these people tell us over and over that they are the nobility of this colony so we should cheer them. Come on now —

CROWD: No!

MACKENZIE: Alright then, let's give three cheers for the real nobility of Upper Canada. Three cheers for the farmers!

CROWD: Hip hip hurray! Hip hip hurray! Hip hip hurray!

MACKENZIE: Alright now, I'm going to tell you a story. It's an old story, but there's no stories like the old stories. It concerns a little Reformer who goes to the Assembly to see what he can do to rectify the wrongs in this colony. So he puts forward all those bills he feels are for the general good and he opposes all those bills he feels are against the general good, please or offend whom it might. And it seemed to offend some people. For Bolton called him a reptile and Hagerman called him a spaniel dog. Now that shows you one thing about Hagerman, and that is — that his knowledge of dogs is only equalled by his knowledge of decent government. For anybody who knew anything about dogs could tell you that this Reformer was not a spaniel dog — but a Scots terrier hot on the tail of a rat!

CROWD: *Cheers.*

MACKENZIE: But these men didn't stop at calling him names. They thought that more forceful action was necessary. So they grabbed him by the seat of the pants and the collar of the coat, and they threw him out of the Assembly! *Mackenzie leaps into the crowd.* But what did the people do?

CROWD: We put you back. *Hoisting him back onto the platform.*

MACKENZIE: And they threw him out again! *Leaping out.*

CROWD: And we put you back —

MACKENZIE: And out again —

CROWD: And back again —

MACKENZIE: And a fourth time —

CROWD: And back a fourth time —

MACKENZIE: Yes, four times they threw him out, and four times the people sent him back. And that's round one for the people. For try as they might, these men cannot oppose the will of the people to send to the Assembly who they want. So the little Reformer finds himself securely in the Assembly. But what can he do? His hands are tied. So he says to himself, I've got to go above the heads of these people, above Strachan and Bolton, and Hagerman. I've got to go to the top — to the King of England! So the little Reformer goes to England, and he's armed with a petition of grievances that's half a mile long. And the signatures on that petition aren't one, two, three, or four names. Oh no no no — there's twenty-five thousand names on that petition. And the King of England looks at it, and he goes — Oh my my my my! And he calls for the Colonial Secretary, and the Colonial Secretary gets the Colonial Office moving, and the Colonial Office gets our government over here moving, so everybody's moving hither-thither, helter-skelter, but out of all this government activity what real good comes? What happens here in this colony?

CROWD: Nothing!

MACKENZIE: Nothing? Not quite. For the Pharaoh of England in his wisdom sends us a saviour — a new Lieutenant-Governor, Sir Francis *Bone* Head. Now what are Sir Francis' credentials for holding this very important office?

CROWD: None! He hasn't got any!

MACKENZIE: Oh yes he does. It's a long and impressive list and I'm going to tell you what they are. Number one. He's a damn fool. Number two. He's English. Number three. He's arrogant. And number four. He's very good with a lasso.

CROWD: What?

MACKENZIE: The lasso. Sir Francis' speciality is the lasso — a skill he picked up in Argentina, used there for herding cattle. So the first thing Sir Francis does when he gets to our colony is he gets out his lasso, and he circles it above his head once, twice, three times — and he lets it go! And who does he catch? You! He catches the people of Upper Canada, and there we all are in Sir Francis' lasso. And he pulls it a little tighter and he says — alright, now it's time for an election; all those in favour of Reform, stand up! And he pulls very hard and he pulls all of us off our feet. Now how did one man pull all of us off our feet? I'll tell you how he did it. We're all in that lasso and we're pushing this way and pulling that way in our frustration and despair. But I tell you that, if as one man we took hold of that rope and turned to Sir Francis, then with one mighty tug, we could pull him off his high horse and send him back to England on his ass!

CROWD: *Cheers.*

MACKENZIE: And that's what I want to talk to you about today. Pulling as one man — Union! For the power of the people is as nothing without union and union is nothing without confidence and discipline. Now the Tories have been following me around to these various meetings, taking what I say back to Toronto, and I'm flattered by the attention. But I don't want to get in trouble with the authorities — treason or anything of that sort, so I'm going to talk to you now in a roundabout manner. Now first of all I think we have to form ourselves into small groups — say fourteen to forty people — just to talk. There's no law against talking. And each of those groups is in contact with other such groups around the province, so we know who our friends are in case of an emergency. But I think the time for talking is past. It's gone by. And I think now it's time for us to work on our muscle power, develop our strength — and I think the best way to do that is through turkey shoots.

CROWD: Turkey shoots?

MACKENZIE: Yes —

CROWD: We know how to shoot turkeys!

MACKENZIE: But don't you think a turkey shoot would be more fun if there was a little drilling beforehand? And don't you think you could shoot turkeys a bit better if everyone shot at once — bang bang bang bang. Because you see, the thing about a Tory — I mean a turkey — the thing about a turkey is you can shoot it with a rifle, you can cut its head off with an axe, a pike is an excellent tool for getting turkeys out of high places — and if worst comes to worst, you can always grab a turkey in your own bare hands and wring its bloody neck!

CROWD: *Cheers.*

MACKENZIE: Now once we get very good at killing turkeys, we go down to that turkey parliament, and we say — this is what we want! And this is what we intend to get! And if they refuse —

CROWD: Yes! What then?

MACKENZIE: We declare open season on turkeys and you'll all have one on your plate this year for Christmas!

CROWD: *Cheers.*

MACKENZIE: Now who's going to be the first to come up here and sign this paper and pledge themselves to shooting turkeys?

CROWD: Me! I will!

MACKENZIE: That's the spirit!

Freeze.

BLACK.

LOUNT'S FORGE

Samuel Lount's blacksmith shop at Holland Landing. Lount is at stage centre, hammer in hand, standing over his anvil. Around him are various voices of discontent. All lines are spoken to the audience.

LOUNT: Oh yes! I'm back — doing what I know how to do. I've been a farmer, a surveyor, mostly a blacksmith — but the most useless job I ever tried was politics!

MAN: It took me twelve years to drain the swamp off my land. Then, last summer, the Canada Company dams up the river and floods all the low lands. You look now — you've never seen such bog!

LOUNT: Samuel Lount for the Assembly! Sam — You've got to run. Sam — we need you.

WOMAN: I can work in her kitchen, but she doesn't want me in the rest of her house. Well I know all about it anyway — because my husband built it!

LOUNT: So off I go to the Assembly. Every man's vote behind me. And went to sleep for two years.

WOMAN: Sure it's a nice farm. And the town's over there, two miles. But there's no road between our farm and the town — because all the land in between belongs to John Strachan and his accursed Church of England!

LOUNT: I'd no sooner stand up to propose a bill, than some Tory would call for a recess.

MAN: Here's a road. Fine road too. Except for the river that runs across it. Now they won't build the bridge. Now what the hell good is a road without a bridge?

LOUNT: Tories got you scared Sam? That why you're not going back? Yes I'm scared. Scared if we waste two more years with this government, there won't be anything left in this country worth saving!

MAN: Now I don't know anything about politics. But there must be **something** wrong in this province. Because there ain't no women!

LOUNT: So Mackenzie comes to me. "Sam, it's time. We need you." I've heard that one before.

MAN: See this cabinet? Took me four months to make. Know why I can't sell it? Because it was made in Toronto!

WOMAN: Yes, I took in travellers for the night. And maybe I did a few favours for men in return for money. But what else can a woman alone with six children do? So they put me in jail and took away my children. Well watch out Mister — because your turn is coming and it's coming soon!

LOUNT: Mac — I said — I'm a blacksmith, not a politician. "Fine, Sam — that's just what we need. A blacksmith."

MAN: I voted Reform in the last election so the Colonel foreclosed on my mortgage. Now that's four years work all gone. But that's all right. Because now I've got nothing to lose!

LOUNT: So I'm back. But I'm not making horseshoes. And I'm not making laws. I'm making pikes —

He raises the redhot pike he has had on the anvil and lowers it into a bucket of water.

ALL: Sssssssss —

BLACK.

ACT II

DOEL'S BREWERY

Mackenzie sets the scene. Onstage with him are three of his Reform associates, and a brewery worker.

MACKENZIE: November 11, 1837. Doel's Brewery, at the corner of Bay and Adelaide Streets, in Toronto. I've called an emergency meeting of the leading Reformers of this city: John Doel — he owns this brewery; lawyer Parsons; Dr. Rolph. These gentlemen are all leading and respected citizens. And this man over here — he's one of Doel's workers — and a good man he is too. We don't seem to have any influence with the government of this country. We have none at all with the King of England. But to my surprise and delight, I find we have some influence with someone up there *(skyward)* for the opportunity which has been presented to us can only be described as heaven-sent. The brave French patriots under Papineau in Lower Canada have struck for their own freedom. Now that means two things to us. First — it indicates to us in Upper Canada the route we too must take to achieve our ends. Second — and even more important — it means there isn't one English soldier left here in Toronto tonight. They've all marched off to Lower Canada. But our blessings don't stop there. No no no no — for in City Hall are four thousand muskets, still in their crates, not even unpacked yet. Guarded by only two men! Now anyone who would leave four thousand muskets guarded by only two men cannot be averse to them being used. At Government House, Sir Francis Bond Head has just come in from his ride; he sits before his fire, feet up on the fender, sipping a glass of expensive French brandy, and imagines he presides over the most contented colony in the entire Empire. He is guarded by only one sentry. At Kingston, Fort Henry lies open and deserted. A steamer only has to sail up to the wharf and it's ours *Turning to his colleagues.* Now here's the plan — we seize Sir Francis, we take him to City Hall and seize the arms, which we distribute to our friends here and in the country. We then declare a Provisional Government and demand of Sir Francis a Legislative Council responsible to a new and fairly elected Assembly. If he refuses —

DOEL: Yes? If he refuses?

MACKENZIE: We go at once for Independence and take whatever steps are necessary to secure it! *Grabs Doel and pilots him across the stage.* Doel, it's so easy, all you have to do is come along here, pick up those muskets, and we've won!

DOEL: *Pulling away.* Shhhh. Now we all want the same things Mac — but we *don't* want to cause trouble.

MACKENZIE: Right! And if we do it this way it'll be no trouble at all —

PARSONS: *Trying to settle him down.* Now Mackenzie — you're our leader, we all agree to that. But why don't you just sit down for a moment and —

MACKENZIE: *Springing back up.* This is no time to sit down! It's time to rise up and act!

ROLPH: *Authoritatively.* Mackenzie! What if we fail?

MACKENZIE: Rolph, with this much nerve — this much courage — we cannot fail.

DOEL: Now Mac — don't rush like this. We've put four months of careful organization and preparation into this.

MACKENZIE: Doel, what in God's name have we been organizing *for?*

PARSONS: Mac, I want to go with you, but I just don't know how to make the jump — *Miming it.*

MACKENZIE: If you want to jump — you jump. *Leaps across stage.*

ROLPH: We don't have the men.

MACKENZIE: We do! We've got Doel's own workers. We've got Armstrong's axemakers, Dutcher's foundrymen — they're strong, dependable, and they're ready to *act* —

The worker starts moving determinedly toward the stand of muskets (indicated by one or two guns). The three reformers scurry to interpose themselves before the weapons actually are seized. They head off the worker by a whisker.

ROLPH: Mackenzie — we have pledged ourselves to Reform — not Revolution.

MACKENZIE: It doesn't matter what you call it Rolph. The question is, what are you going to do about it?

DOEL: Well, if it's force we want, I move we bring down our friends from the country.

MACKENZIE: That's the way is it, Doel? Bring down the farmers to do your dirty work? Besides — it will take four weeks to get the farmers down here.

PARSONS: Well alright then — four weeks. That makes it what? — December seventh.

DOEL: Yes. Agreed. December seventh.

ROLPH: December seventh.

DOEL: Mackenzie?

MACKENZIE: *With a helpless look at the worker, and a gesture of disgust toward his colleagues.* Alright — December seventh!

BLACK.

DRILLING

A farmer is alone onstage, with a pitchfork, drilling with it as one would with a rifle.

FARMER: Present . . . Attack! Present . . . Attack! Present . . . Attack!

Enter another farmer, sees the drill and starts to chuckle about it. First continues drilling, but is irked by the derision.

SECOND: Come on. Come on now.

FIRST: Present . . . Attack! . . .

SECOND: You're not going to march to Toronto with that?

FIRST: Present . . .

SECOND: What are you going to do with it? Feed hay to the British?

First wheels on second and presses the very menacing point of the pitchfork against his throat. (In fact, this scene has always been played by two women.)

SECOND: Wait — what're you doing?

FIRST: Go on. Laugh some more.

SECOND: Alright. Stop.

First continues pressing. It is quite ominous. That is a real pitchfork up there onstage.

FIRST: Say it —

SECOND: Alright, alright —

FIRST: *Say* it!

SECOND: Say what?

FIRST: Present —

SECOND: *Practically a whimper.* Present —

FIRST: *Whirling and stabbing the fork directly out toward the audience.* Attack!

TIGER DUNLOP

DUNLOP: The date is November 19. The place — Gairbraid, near Goderich, home of William "Tiger" Dunlop — raconteur, wit, doctor of medicine, and arch-Tory.

Enter Mackenzie and Colonel Anthony Van Egmond, an older man. They join Dunlop and all three participate in a hearty after-dinner laugh.

DUNLOP: Yes — I believe that was the same evening we were dining at your home, Van Egmond, and your housekeeper said to me — *Imitating the housekeeper.* Doctor, why is it sir, we never see you in church? And I said, Because, Madam, I have an abiding distrust of any place where one man does all the talking, you're liable to meet your wife, and people sing without drinking! *They all laugh.*

VAN EGMOND: An amazing likeness, Tiger, and I must tell you that she still anxiously awaits your return. Tiger here is one of the most eligible bachelors in the tract.

DUNLOP: And intending to remain so. But — that was a long time ago. Strange, isn't it, what time does — to men like Van Egmond and myself, who spent so much time in the same camp in the bush — yet now find ourselves in such separate camps.

VAN EGMOND: Perhaps.

DUNLOP: But, times being what they are, I'm sure you gentlemen haven't come here to hear my old stories. Not with having brought this screaming Reformer with you. I imagine you've come for something — so tell me — What can Tiger Dunlop do for you?

MACKENZIE: Tiger Dunlop can let us help him.

DUNLOP: I beg your pardon.

MACKENZIE: Let us help you.

DUNLOP: What could you possibly do to help me?

MACKENZIE: What do you think of John Strachan?

DUNLOP: I hate the bastard.

MACKENZIE: And Thomas Mercer Jones?

DUNLOP: Jones. Well, anyone who would marry Strachan's daughter can't be all good.

MACKENZIE: Dunlop, you and I seem to concur in our opinions of these people.

DUNLOP: Yes. I believe we do.

MACKENZIE: Everytime we turn around in this colony, we see its wealth being carted off someplace else. And what about the honest, hardworking people — the farmers and the labourers? The fruits of their effort are being scooped up to support the idle dandies in Toronto or London —

DUNLOP: Just a moment, Mr. Mackenzie. When you start in about the honest, hardworking people, it's obvious you're about to launch one of your famous political speeches. Now don't let my reputation fool you. I'm still a man who likes plain speaking. I beg you — speak to me plainly.

MACKENZIE: Alright, I'll speak to you plainly. There's going to be some changes in this colony, Dunlop. Big changes. It's going to be out with the old and in with the new. Now the question is, Tiger — are you going to be part of the new or are you going out with the old?

DUNLOP: You talk about changes. Now I have always stood for change in this colony. Isn't that true, Colonel?

VAN EGMOND: Yes. Yes, Tiger — that's the man I remember. Long ago, before this part of the country was even opened up, Tiger here, John Galt — remember him, Tiger? — and myself, we used to go up on a rise by the lake, look about us and talk of the tremendous potential of the country. And Tiger had the most vivid dreams of all. Eighty thousand families, I believe you said, could be supported by the Huron Tract alone. And we set about to make that a reality. We built roads — remember Tiger? — pushing the roads through the bush to bring in the settlers — built mills, provided for schools, and churches, shipped in supplies — anything that would bring in the settlers. And the towns. That you founded. But look about you, Tiger. Where are the eighty thousand? For every one settler there should be a hundred more. The roads that were built to bring people in are leading them out. By the thousands. Land value is where it was five, ten years ago. Why? What has happened? I think you have let go of your dream, Tiger. Given it up to men like Jones, Strachan, Hagerman. Fops and dandies. Mushroom aristocrats. Bladders of pride and arrogance — who care not a damn for the country — but only for their own fiefdoms — filling their pockets. I don't think you are the kind of man to let this abuse continue. John Galt could not tolerate such leadership and he resigned his post with the Canada

Company. I rather think you are cast in the same mould as Galt.

DUNLOP: Time brings changes, Colonel, and might I say — compromise?

MACKENZIE: Compromise! Dunlop, I've been from one end of this colony to the other. Now there is discontent, vengeance, rage — in men's minds. But not compromise! I've seen it at over two hundred public meetings. Thousands of signatures, names of men pledging themselves to use force of arms if necessary to alleviate their suffering. This colony wants cheap, efficient responsible government, and it's going to have it, and there's nothing that the Lieutenant-Governor, or the King of England, or the whole British army can do to stop it.

VAN EGMOND: Tiger, you know what the people want, what they think. You talk to them, high and low alike. They admire you. You are a brilliant man — I don't flatter — you have ideas, and you have the energy to put those ideas into effect.

MACKENZIE: An independent country. A new nation. Think of it, Tiger. Think what this country could be with its natural bounty, under the leadership which men like yourself could provide — it could be one of the greatest in the world. It's a tremendous responsibility staring you right in the face. Now are you man enough to meet that responsibility, Dunlop?

DUNLOP: *Deliberates a long while then chuckles.* Excuse me, gentlemen, but you remind me of a couple of Yankee schoolboys who just read the Declaration of Independence. Now I'm a political realist. Change is one thing, but I call what you're talking about rebellion.

MACKENZIE: Call it revolution if you want, Tiger.

DUNLOP: Well, I don't think you're the man to lead it. My God, man, you can't even buy a cow without offending the herdsman. Colonel, you're a dear and old friend, but it is the truth sir — you are old. Waterloo was long ago. Now if you gentlemen will permit me, I believe I have a responsibility to history. Dr. William Dunlop does not join in insurrection against the rightful government of —

MACKENZIE: I take it all this pomposity is leading up to a "no".

DUNLOP: Yes — I mean, no.

MACKENZIE: Well, it's a long ride back to Toronto, Dunlop. Goodbye. *Exit.*

VAN EGMOND: Tiger, do you know that you are twice as old as I am?

Van Egmond starts out. Dunlop calls to him as he is almost out the door.

DUNLOP: Van Egmond —

VAN EGMOND: Goodnight. *Exit.*

Light on Tiger alone.

Fade to black.

LEAVING

The following six scenes concern people leaving for the battle. Each is introduced by a verse from the song, **Across Toronto Bay.**

ALL: Up now and shoulder arms, and join this free men's march boys,
It's time to show the Tories that this country's no man's toy.
So it's march, march, march to Toronto town today
And we'll use that fork to pitch Bond Head — across Toronto Bay.

A merchant and the man who does his chores. The employee is carrying an armful of wood. He drops it with a crash.

MERCHANT: Rather sloppy of you Thomas.

THOMAS: That's just my way of saying goodbye sir.

MERCHANT: Goodbye?

THOMAS: Yes sir. I'm going to be leaving your employ.

MERCHANT: You've never mentioned anything of this before.

THOMAS: Well, you see the way I figure it sir, I think there's going to be a fight and I have just the merest suspicion that you and me are going to be on different sides.

MERCHANT: Thomas, I would not become embroiled in this if I were you.

THOMAS: I just don't think it would be fair, sir, for me to keep taking your wages, in case we met on the battlefield — and I had to shoot you dead. *He is chortling.* So I'll just be off now sir. Goodbye — and good luck. *A hearty laugh as he goes out.*

ALL: It's time to do a different job and take a different stand,
They said we're good for chopping wood and clearing off the land.
So it's march, march, march to Toronto town today,
And we'll use that fork to pitch Bond Head — across Toronto Bay.

Harold, a farmer, holding a pistol.

HAROLD: I just can't do it. I can't. I never thought I'd have to really shoot somebody when we were drilling. I — I'll tell them I can't go. No that's no good. I know — I'll say I can't go tonight, I'll meet them tomorrow.

Enter his friend Tom.

TOM: Ready Harold?

HAROLD: Tom — uh, yeah, I'm ready.

TOM: Good!

HAROLD: Uh, look — I even stole a pistol.

TOM: A pistol! Well then — you're in charge!

They exit together.

ALL: So let those Tories have their fun and slop up all that tea,
I'd just as soon I killed myself a Tory as a tree.
So it's march, march, march to Toronto town today,
And we'll use that fork to pitch Bond Head — across Toronto Bay.

Fred Bench and his new wife Ruth, both of whom we met in the tavern scene in Act I. They are in bed.

RUTH: Fred — I heard awful stories in town today. People were talking about the Rebels. They say that they're going to burn Toronto.

FRED: Some people have just cause Ruth.

RUTH: Fred Bench, don't you talk that way. Oh Fred! You wouldn't yourself — don't tell me that you'd —

FRED: Now Ruth — I'll do what I think is best for you.

RUTH: Well that's better. Don't let me even think that you'd . . . oh well, I'm sure the governor will soon put a stop to all this.

FRED: Uh — huh.

RUTH: Goodnight.

FRED: Goodnight Ruth.

She falls asleep. He feigns sleep, then rolls out of bed, grabs his boots and rifle, and steals toward the door.

ALL: A war will bring some death, boys, it's sure to bring you sorrow,
But if we stand back to back today, we'll own this land tomorrow.
So it's march, march, march to Toronto town today,
And we'll use that fork to pitch Bond Head — across Toronto Bay.

A boy sneaking through the woods. His younger brother and sister intercept him.

BOY: How'd you two get in front of me?

SISTER: We followed you.

BOY: Well, you're not supposed to. Go home.

BROTHER: You're supposed to be looking after us.

BOY: I can't for now. So get on home.

SISTER: We know where you're going.

BOY: I don't care if you know. You're not coming with me.

BROTHER: We'll tell.

BOY: Don't you dare tell! Just take your sister and get on home.

They whine.

BOY: Get going. I'll be back.

He exits. His brother darts after him. The sister looks around, lost, and cries.

ALL: Now Old Mac says we've got a cause to load our rifles for,
So leave that stove and woman home and march right out the door.
For it's march, march, march to Toronto town today,
And we'll use that fork to pitch Bond Head — across Toronto Bay.

Isaac Casselman's Tavern, as in Act I. Emma and Jamey are cleaning around. Enter Isaac, carrying his rifle and pistol.

ISAAC: Emma, put out the fire. Jamey, you lock the tavern. This tavern is closed.

EMMA: What's going on?

ISAAC: There's a war on, by God, and Isaac Casselman is going off to fight.

JAMEY: Isaac — gimme your pistol. *Grabs it and points it into his mouth.*

ISAAC: Jamey — what're you doing?

JAMEY: I'm going to kill myself.

ISAAC: *Grabbing the pistol back.* Why?

JAMEY: Well if you're closing the tavern, I've got no reason to go on living.

ISAAC: Jamey — why don't you come along?

JAMEY: *Scornful.* Naaa —

ISAAC: Maybe there'll be a rum ration.

JAMEY: Rum? *Grabs the pistol and leads the way.* Forward —

ALL: Now all across this country, you can hear the Rebel yell,
We'll follow you Mackenzie, to Toronto or to hell.
So it's march, march, march to Toronto town today,
And we'll use that fork to pitch Bond Head — across Toronto Bay.

Mary Macdonald, whom we met in Act I, fresh from Scotland, is sitting in her farmhouse doing some chore. She is singing to herself.

MARY: Speed, bonnie boat, like a bird on the wing, Onward the sailors cry —

Enter her husband Edward.

MARY: Edward, you're home early.

EDWARD: *Kissing her.* Mary —

MARY: Is anything wrong? *Edward sits down uncomfortably.* What is it, Edward?

EDWARD: You remember when we first met — and we didn't know each other at all — and we were afraid things wouldn't work out —

MARY: Yes. I remember —

EDWARD: I know I've never said very much. That's just my way. But I want you to know that it's been . . . Hell — I've got to go fight.

MARY: *Accepting it with difficulty.* Yes. Of course.

EDWARD: *Relieved.* Of course? Do you think it's wrong — us being married such a short time?

MARY: No. I don't. Of course you must go. *Edward is immensely grateful that she accepts it.* When do you have to go?

EDWARD: They said they'd come by about daybreak.

MARY: Oh. We have some time then.

EDWARD: Yes. *Getting her drift.* Oh. You mean . . . *He takes her hand and leads her upstairs. There is a knock at the door.* Who's there?

FLETCHER: *Outside.* It's Fletcher, Edward. There's been a change in plans. We have to go meet Lount at the crossroads right now.

EDWARD: But they said tomorrow —

FLETCHER: I don't care what they said. We have to leave right away.

EDWARD: I'll be right out.

FLETCHER: Right now!

EDWARD: *Angrily.* I *said* I was coming!

MARY: I'll get your things.

She hands him his coat and his rifle. They embrace. He starts toward the door, stops, returns to her.

EDWARD: I love you. By God I do. I love you. *He rushes out.*

MARY: *Sobbing.* Oh no. No. He never said that to me before. No. No —

Fade to black.

VAN EGMOND'S MARCH

During this scene the focus is on Colonel Anthony Van Egmond as he travels toward Toronto. But around him many things take place: the daily work of the people he passes; events occurring in Toronto; encounters with people on the road. A small table serves as Van Egmond's horse.

VAN EGMOND: Colonel Anthony Van Egmond — age sixty-seven, veteran of the Napoleonic Wars, owner of a parcel of fourteen thousand acres in the

Huron Tract near Goderich — is appointed commander-in-chief of the Patriot forces. December 3, 1837, he sets out from his farm on horseback, to meet with his troops at Montgomery's Tavern, north of Toronto, on December 7 — the date set for the advance on the city. *He mounts his horse and begins his march.* Day one. There is a light snow falling, muffling the sound. I shall travel alone to avoid suspicion. If we are to get the advantage of the enemy, we must take them by surprise. *Notes as he goes:* St. Columban —

MESSENGER: *Rushing from the opposite direction.* Colonel! Colonel — I'm glad I caught you sir. There's been a change —

VAN EGMOND: Change?

MESSENGER: Yes sir — they've changed the date. From the seventh to the fourth.

VAN EGMOND: Who issued this change?

MESSENGER: It's a message, sir — from that Dr. Rolph.

VAN EGMOND: Dr. Rolph does not have the power to make such changes. Only Mackenzie does.

MESSENGER: Yes he does, sir. He said —

VAN EGMOND: There has been no change! December 7 is the date for the advance on the city!

MESSENGER: Yes, sir. No change. *Exits.*

VAN EGMOND: *Continuing his march.* We could not possibly muster enough men before December 7. *Noting his progress:* Mitchell. Ah — another homesteader. He shall see such changes made!

A TORY PICKET IN TORONTO: Anderson! *He fires a shot. Anthony Anderson, a rebel is hit, lurches across the stage, and falls dead at the feet of Van Egmond.*

A FARMER: *To Van Egmond.* You — you hear the news?

VAN EGMOND: News?

A FARMER: Yup. Seems a man named Anderson — Anthony Anderson — and another fellow named Moodie — both shot outside of Toronto. Don't know any more about it.

VAN EGMOND: *Dismounting for the night.* Seebach's Inn. Sebringville. *To the Innkeeper.* What do you know of events in Toronto?

INNKEEPER: I heard that a government man named Moodie'd been shot. And a Rebel name of Anderson.

VAN EGMOND: Confirmed.

INNKEEPER: No, no — that's just talk as far as I know.

VAN EGMOND: Anthony Anderson was the only other Rebel leader with military experience.

Freeze.

VAN EGMOND: Day two. *Remounts his horse.* Stratford. There's much more activity on the roads today.

A TRAVELLER: Where are you going, sir?

VAN EGMOND: Toronto.

A TRAVELLER: You can't go there. The Americans have attacked. They're going to burn the city —

VAN EGMOND: The Americans have not attacked.

A TRAVELLER: Yes they have. I heard it from somebody who heard it from someone who was there —

VAN EGMOND: Nonsense.

A TRAVELLER: I'm warning you. I wouldn't go on — *Exits, blathering.*

VAN EGMOND: Mackenzie, you must hold fast for more forces!

A mounted horseman enters, dismounts and posts a handbill advertising a reward for Mackenzie. (This was done using the character who played Mackenzie and, as it were, nailing him to the wall as though he were the poster.)

HORSEMAN: By authority of the Lieutenant-Governor, a reward of one thousand pounds is hereby offered to anyone who will apprehend and deliver up to justice William Lyon Mackenzie. God Save the Queen.

VAN EGMOND: *Dismounting.* Helmer's Inn. Waterloo. *He approaches the "handbill" and addresses it, with Mackenzie's own call to arms.* Canadians, do you love freedom?

MACKENZIE: *i.e. the Mackenzie in the handbill.* I know you do. Do you hate oppression? Who would deny it. Then buckle on your armour and drive out these villains who enslave and oppress our country.

VAN EGMOND: *Responding.* Long after we are dead, free men shall salute us. *They embrace. Freeze. Van Egmond remounts.* Day three. Breslau.

OLD MAN: Sir — have you heard the news from Toronto? *As he tells this news to Van Egmond, someone else recounts it directly to the audience.*

A REBEL: Well I can tell you exactly how it happened because I was there. It was a hell of a battle and it was right there at the corner of Yonge and College. You see, Sheriff Jarvis stationed his men behind a fence, just waiting for the Rebels to come marching down. Well, we came alright — in the dead of night. We moved out of the tavern, formed up at the tollgate at Bloor Street and then marched down Yonge, proud as peacocks, five abreast. They waited till we got really close, and then they let loose. Well they cut some of us down, but we fired back. And then we dropped down to let the men behind us fire. But the men behind — they were green — they thought we'd dropped because we were all dead. So they turned around and ran back to the tavern. Sheriff Jarvis' men — they were even greener than that — they threw away their guns and ran back to Toronto.

Great confusion onstage. People milling and fleeing. Van Egmond tries to stem the tide.

VAN EGMOND: Wait! If you want something you stay and fight for it!

But they push past him, leaving him alone and dejected. He dismounts and sits down despairingly.

VAN EGMOND: What is happening in Toronto? Why didn't they wait? Fools — so much at stake — if only I *knew*! I am an old man; there is still honour in retreat. I shall return home —

Enter a Rebel, overhears Van Egmond.

REBEL: Yah, you go home, go back to your farm. Whatever you do, don't go to Toronto.

VAN EGMOND: Have you come from Toronto?

REBEL: I *ran* from Toronto. I'm going home.

VAN EGMOND: What is happening there?

REBEL: Macnab's in the city. He's brought four hundred armed militiamen. They're barricading the city. They're going to shoot us like rats —

VAN EGMOND: Macnab? I'd like to fight Macnab.

REBEL: You're welcome to him.

VAN EGMOND: What is the condition of the patriot forces?

REBEL: Bad.

VAN EGMOND: Are they still coming in?

REBEL: Yah, they're coming in —

VAN EGMOND: They are —

REBEL: But they're leaving just as fast as they come in.

VAN EGMOND: Why?

REBEL: Because there's no leadership there. Nobody knows what they're doing. Someone orders this. Another one orders that —

VAN EGMOND: If there had been a leader there — whom you trusted — would you have fled?

REBEL: I'm no coward. I'd have stayed.

VAN EGMOND: *Extending his hand.* Colonel Anthony Van Egmond, son —

REBEL: Colonel —

VAN EGMOND: Will you march back to Toronto with me?

REBEL: Yes sir.

A chorus of "yes sir" begins to build in the background.

VAN EGMOND: You see Macnab is no soldier. He is a bully but he has no strategy. Help me up. *He mounts.* Have you ever been in a real battle, boy?

REBEL: Only on Yonge St., sir.

VAN EGMOND: That was no battle. It was a skirmish. Do you know — I was fifteen years in the Napoleonic Wars. Wounded fourteen times and never once in the back.

The chorus of "yes sir" builds and transforms into the Marseillaise.

A REBEL: Remember Moscow!

VAN EGMOND: Macnab, you'll rue the day —

REBEL: Remember Waterloo!

VAN EGMOND: Mackenzie, hold fast now —

REBEL: Think of Montgomery's Tavern!

VAN EGMOND: Lancers ho —

A SENTRY: Halt!

Silence.

SENTRY: Who goes there?

VAN EGMOND: Colonel Van Egmond.

SENTRY: Hot damn general — are we glad to see you!

VAN EGMOND: Where is Mackenzie?

SENTRY: He's inside, sir. I'll show you. We didn't know if you were coming at all. Some said you were. Some said you weren't.

VAN EGMOND: Well I'm here aren't I?

SENTRY: Yes sir. You are. He's right in there. Don't tell him I forgot to salute —

VAN EGMOND: Mackenzie — *He storms in.*

THE BATTLE

This scene continues directly from the previous scene.

VAN EGMOND: Mackenzie, what in hell is going on here?

MACKENZIE: Colonel, thank God you're here. Rolph changed the date. Everything's in a mess. Macnab's in the city with four hundred men.

VAN EGMOND: How many do we have?

MACKENZIE: Two hundred and fifty.

VAN EGMOND: Not enough. When do we expect more?

MACKENZIE: Tonight. December 7. They'll be down tonight.

VAN EGMOND: Then we wait till they arrive.

MACKENZIE: Colonel, we can't wait to be attacked.

VAN EGMOND: You cannot go against Macnab with a handful of men.

MACKENZIE: We've got to do something —

REBEL SOLDIER: *To audience.* It is finally decided to send a diversionary force under Peter Matthews to the east to burn the Don Valley Bridge and draw off the main Loyalist force. The rest wait at Montgomery's for reinforcements. Meanwhile, back in Toronto, the Loyalist army is drawn up in front of Archdeacon Strachan's residence — known as The Palace — on Front Street.

The Loyalist army forms up.

BOND HEAD: I am Sir Frances Bond Head. I have a double-barrelled pistol in my bandolier, a rifle leaning against my thigh, and a brace of pistols in my belt. So good to see so many respected citizens standing in the ranks today.

THE RANKS: Pip pip —
Hear hear —

BOND HEAD: We march at noon. Forward — march!

They set out.

REBEL SOLDIER: Meanwhile to the east, Matthews and his men have crossed the bridge and moved west on King Street. They meet a contingent of militia and retreat back across the bridge, attempting to burn it as they go. In the exchange of fire, one man is fatally shot through the throat. *This all is acted out.* The bridge itself is saved.

A LOYALIST: But the main Loyalist force is already moving north toward Montgomery's. *Shouts.* Bugler — strike up a tune!

The Loyalist army marches to **Yankee Doodle** *— an old British parody of Americans and Americanizers.*

A LOYALIST: Six hundred men remain in the centre with Bond Head. One hundred fifty off to the right flank. Two hundred on the left.

A REBEL SENTRY: Hey wake up —

HIS FRIEND: What? *Looking out at the approaching army.* Good God!

SENTRY: There must be thousands of them —

FRIEND: I'll stay and watch them. You go tell Mackenzie —

SENTRY: *Riding off.* Mackenzie! They're coming this way — you'd better go see —

MACKENZIE: Form up the men! *The Rebels form up.* There is the enemy! They outnumber us. They are better armed. And they have artillery — but they are the men we came to fight. Will you fight them?

A hearty Rebel cheer.

MACKENZIE: Forward —

A REBEL: A force of two hundred and fifty under Van Egmond and Samuel Lount advance into the woods to the south of the tavern. Another sixty position themselves behind rail fences on the other side of the road. Two hundred yet unarmed men remain in the tavern.

The battle is staged. The Rebel soldiers talk frantically among themselves as they watch the overwhelming force of the Loyalists moving toward them. The battle itself is bitter and very brief. The two nine-pound cannons of the Loyalists decimate the Rebel formations. The Rebels are crushed. In the end the Loyalists are totally triumphant. The bodies and weapons of the Rebels litter the field. The Loyalists clean up. All of this with much screaming, swearing and writhing.

MACKENZIE: *As he escapes.* Mackenzie is the last man to leave the field. Together with Van Egmond he goes to a nearby farmhouse. The farmer's wife diverts soldiers while Mackenzie escapes, but Van Egmond, exhausted, is captured. Mackenzie heads west toward the Niagara border. Rewards are offered for him everywhere, but not a soul who sees him reports him. Within days he has established the provisional government of the State of Upper Canada on Navy Island in the Niagara River. He arrives with twenty-six men but soon has hundreds more. Macnab encamps on the opposite shore with a government force of five thousand. Mackenzie gathers the arms and provisions which will enable him to return and join Dr. Charles Duncombe, who has raised a Rebel army near London. He waits for his chance to move. *Stepping into character.* And while I wait, I fire my four cannons here at Macnab across the river — just to let him know I'm still here!

Boom. Boom. Boom. Boom.

BLACK.

KNOCKS ON THE DOOR

An old Canadian tradition. The following three scenes depict break-ins by government forces at the homes of suspected Rebels.

Knock, knock, knock in the dark. Lights up as a soldier breaks through the door and in on a woman alone.

SOLDIER: Get the hell out of here. We're burning this house down!

She screams. He shoves her out. Black.

Knock, knock, knock in the dark.

SOLDIER: Open up in the name of the Queen!

Lights up. A woman opens. He barges in.

SOLDIER: Where's your husband, Mrs. Polk?

WOMAN: I have no husband.

SOLDIER: No? Then who's that ugly man you've been living with for the last seven years.

WOMAN: Go away —

SOLDIER: *Searching.* Where is he?

WOMAN: He's dead. There's nothing here for you, so please leave my house —

SOLDIER: He's been seen Mrs. Polk. He's gone too far this time —

He is bashing away at her belongings with his rifle butt. She leaps on him furiously from behind. He wrestles her to the ground, pins her there. She struggles futily.

SOLDIER: We're going to get him, and we're going to hang him, but before we do, I'm going to punch his face off. And then, Mrs. Polk, what're you going to do for a man —

She spits in his face. He raises his fist.

ANOTHER SOLDIER: *From outside.* Come on George. There's no one here.

SOLDIER: I'll be back. *Exits.*

Black.

Knock, knock, knock in the dark.

Lights up. Enter Harold, the fellow from the earlier scene who was afraid to go off to fight. He rushes in and hides under a stair, floorboard or the like. Enter Tom, the friend with whom he'd left to fight the rebellion. Tom is carrying a rifle and clearly

searching for Rebels. (Because of all the doubling by actors in this play, it is not immediately evident to the audience, that these are Harold and Tom from an earlier scene. This works to the advantage of this brief scene as it develops.)

TOM: *Nervously.* Now I seen you come in here. So come on out.

HAROLD: *Coughs.*

TOM: If you don't come out by the time I count three, I'll shoot — *Aims at the place Harold is hiding.* One, two, three — *Shoots, but his gun misfires.* Goldarn gun —

Harold leaps out of his hiding place, jumps on Tom, the two struggle for several seconds before they recognize each other.

TOM: Harold!

HAROLD: Tom!

TOM: What're you doing here?

HAROLD: I'm hiding! What're you doing? You were with me at Montgomery's Tavern!

TOM: I doubled back through the woods and joined up. Otherwise they'd have arrested me. They're making everyone search. Harold, they know who you are —

HAROLD: I know. They nearly got me twice today. Tom, you gotta help me. I haven't even got a — gimme your gun.

TOM: I can't do that. They'll ask me where it went.

HAROLD: *Grabbing it.* Tell them — tell them you were searching down a well and it fell in. Thanks Tom — *Rushes off.*

TOM: *Calling after.* You hide good next time, Harold — *Looks down at his hands, realizes he's stuck without a gun.* What in hell am I —

BLACK.

THE ROPE

Captured Rebels being led to jail in Toronto. A rope is looped over each of their necks. Their hands are tied behind their backs. They march single file. They state their names in turn. When they have gone round once, they go round again.

REBELS: Jacob Beemer, farmer. Taken January 3, 1838, near Stratford.
Richard Thorpe, labourer. Taken December 7, at Montgomery's Tavern.
Caleb Kipp, yeoman. Taken on the road to Buffalo.
John Bradley, teacher. I'm no Rebel. I voted Reform but I'm not Rebel.
Absalom Slade, farmer.
Elijah Rowe, tinker. Taken December 7, at Montgomery's. But it took six of them.
They're burning. Look at that smoke —

I can't feel my toes.
William Stockdale, farmer.
Jonathan Grimes, ropemaker.
Damn the Tories! What're you looking at, lady?

They reach their destination.

Hey, lookit who's here!
There's thousands of us!
Hey, anybody here from Newmarket?
Hell, the whole country's in here —
Newmarket? —

A rising babble of greetings etc.

BLACK.

EMIGRATING

A Rebel woman. She is packing, and talking to a neighbour.

REBEL WOMAN: Now the coach is coming at four, got to be ready. And my brother is picking that up, and this is for you. You always admired it and I want you to have it now. We won't need no winter coats where we're going. Yes, I finally convinced my Dan, I just sat down the other day, had the kids all around — they've been getting an awful time from the other kids — and I said, Now Dan, we've tried. We voted Reform, we did what we thought was best, we lost, it's time to face facts. And I just got this letter from my sister. She's got a farm and a fine husband and she said we could go down and stay with them as long as we want, and oh the kids were yelling and screaming and — well what can he say? So we're going. You know, this place, it's my home, the kids were both born here, but times have changed and we're going to change with them. I wouldn't stay in Stouffville one more day, I'll tell you. But I want you to know you're welcome to come down and visit us any time you want. Oh, it's going to be so fine down there, we'll have a big house, and the kids will go to school — *Calling out window.* Hey, Mrs. Phipps, you know those two plates you borrowed from me two years ago? You can keep them. She never did like me. What are you people staring at? Anything else in here you can come and take when we're gone. We're leaving it behind. We're going to have five times better. You know why? Because we're going to the Yew-Nited States!

BLACK.

THE HANGINGS

Toronto City Jail.

VAN EGMOND: April 12, 1838. Government forces have scattered Dr. Duncombe's army in the west. Mackenzie himself has fled Navy Island for the United States. Toronto City Jail. Near King and Church Streets. The cells are cold, dark, wet, filled for the most part with patriots awaiting trial and sentencing on charges of high treason. Today they press against the bars of their cells to witness the executions of two of the patriot leaders, Peter Matthews and Samuel Lount. It is the laws, and not their crimes, that condemn them. Anthony Van Egmond might also have been witness to this spectacle but he died, untried, in his cell, December 30, 1837.

Matthews and Lount advance to the gallows.

LOUNT: My friends. I address as friends all those in the jail behind me, in all the jails across this province, in the ships bound for Van Diemen's Land, in exile in the United States — there are over eight hundred of us. I am proud to be one of you. John Beverly Robinson — Chief Justice Robinson — you seem to fear we will become martyrs to our countrymen. Well still your fears. This country will not have time to mourn a farmer and a blacksmith. It will be free, I am certain, long before our deaths have time to become symbols. It cannot remain long under the hell of such merciless wretches that they murder its inhabitants for their love of liberty. As for us, I do not know exactly how we came to this. Except by a series of steps, each of which seemed to require the next. But if I were to leave my home in Holland Landing again, and march down Yonge Street, I would go by the same route, only hoping that the journey's end would differ. And there will be others coming down that road you know, and others after them, until it does end differently. But for us, the only way on now is by the rope.

MATTHEWS: *A bitter laugh.*

LOUNT: What Peter? What?

MATTHEWS: Sam, we lost —

LOUNT: No! We haven't won yet.

The trap falls. They dangle by the ropes.

BLACK.